# I'd rather you call me Charlie

**Reminiscences filled with twists of devilment,
devotion and a little danger here and there**

Reminiscences

## Charlie Sewell

ISBN: 1532876114
ISBN 13: 9781532876110

# Disclaimer

I apologize up front for any grammatical errors that you find. I am not an English major, and I lack the knowledge to correctly identify them. I also lack the funds to hire an editor to find and correct them on my behalf. I am excited to share my memories with you, and I hope you enjoy them as much as I enjoyed writing them.

# Preface

Like most people, I always enjoyed telling anecdotes about my involvement in events and things I observed. Throughout the years, many people listened to my stories and several said, "Charlie, you should write a book." I wasn't a writer and never gave it much thought. By chance, I started writing a newspaper column about nine years ago, and during that time I was able to hone my writing skills a morsel and a crumb. About a year after retirement, I reflected on a message that I shared throughout my law enforcement career with anyone who had been willing to listen. I had some time on my hands, and I started jotting some notes about how police officers should treat people. Before I knew it, I was reminiscing and taking notes about all aspects of my life. As I continued to write, the notes started reading more like short stories. One short story reminded me of another, then another, and I pretty quickly found myself writing a manuscript. I found it exhilarating, and you are reading the results. Many names have been changed or eliminated to protect privacy, to prevent embarrassment, and because my memory has left the building.

Could a redhead with low self-esteem actually amount to anything? I had no goals and no plans for the future. I just wanted to be "good-time Charlie." I was different from other kids because I had bright red hair, blue eyes and I wore eyeglasses starting at age three. I simply wanted to be nice to people, but to some kids that didn't matter. They called me Strawberry, Opie, Rooster, Woody Woodpecker, Red Skelton, and Clarabell the Clown. They also said phrases like, "I'd rather be dead than red on the head," and a couple of vulgar ones that I won't repeat. If I heard "Howdy Doody" once, well, I heard it a lot and I would always tell people, "I'd rather you call me Charlie."

Over the years it never ceased to amaze me that when I introduced myself to other folks as Charlie, many people said, "Good to meet you, Charles," or "Chuck, or Chaz." I would usually respond by saying, "I'd rather you call me Charlie."

This book is filled with the dreams of a five-year-old that came to life with humor, mischief and some degree of peril as I grew into my teen-age years. The collection of stories, based on real life events, also includes my surprising and poignant forty-two year law enforcement career. While writing, I came face to face with suppressed memories, some of which hurt me deeply. I also recognized the many challenges that I faced in my life of trying my best to help whomever was in need.

Memories ebb and flow and tales sink and grow as we age, so I turned to my sister Gail and brother Jim to make sure I had the facts right. I extend a heart-felt thanks to Brenda Adams, Robyn Cobb, Jane Daniel, Jean Gaissert, Judy Hall, Cynthia Lanning, Brenda Stubblefield and Endora Feick for their valuable feedback. And of course, a special thanks to my wife who endured a bazillion questions and the retelling of some of the stories she heard me tell many times before.

# Introduction

The county police radio operator cracked the calm and quiet night with a broadcast of a shooting that had just occurred in the county south of me. The radio operator's voice thickened as she gave a description of two white male suspects in a large blue pickup truck last seen heading southbound. Two o'clock in the morning in my small town was about as exciting as getting a root canal, so even though I didn't expect to be involved in the tragedy, I drove my police car toward the south end of town.

A man named Chris was driving his girlfriend Kelly southbound on a dark county road and didn't pay attention to the headlights behind them. A truck started to pass, and Chris naturally looked over his left shoulder. When he did, he saw a shotgun leveled outside the truck's passenger window. Tucking his head into the steering wheel as the shotgun was fired, he felt twelve-gauge pellets rip the back of his head. Kelly also turned to look, but she saw a ball of fire and caught the blast of twelve-gauge pellets directly in her face.

The driver of the truck accelerated southbound at a high rate of speed leaving Chris and Kelly to die. Even though he was seriously injured, Chris drove another mile looking for help until he found a county police officer parked on the side of the road.

My adrenaline was already pumping as I listened to one chilling radio transmission after the other. Unexpectedly, a small green pickup truck with two men drove past me headed northbound. It was obvious that both occupants had an eagle eye on me as they passed, but I was accustomed to people staring at my highly marked police car. The size and color of the truck didn't fit the lookout, and I am not certain if it was a gut feeling or wishful thinking that made me pull onto the road and start following the truck.

My police car was equipped with a Motorola mobile radio with the city police frequency and another with the county police frequency. Our department was small back then, and I was the only police officer on duty. Picking up the microphone on the county radio frequency, I advised the radio operator what I had observed. The truck slowed, turned into a gas station, and stopped beside a full service pump. The operator responded to my transmission by asking if I had a back-up. I had no sooner replied to the operator with "no" than I began to hear sirens approaching. I was a rookie police officer, but I knew I needed to keep my distance from the truck and wait for help. I parked my police car in the gas station driveway as far from the gas pumps as possible.

The gas station attendant removed the gas nozzle from the pump and the gas cap from the truck and began to "fill `er up." The next thirty seconds seemed like the time between birthdays. The approaching sirens were now screaming, and a county police car with screeching tires suddenly slid sideways into the gas station. I jumped from my police car with my bull barrel Colt Trooper Mark III 357-cal. revolver drawn just as the county police officer slapped a patrol rifle across the roof of his car. The attendant was directly in my line of fire, and he didn't seem to understand my scream for him to get out of the way. He may have been startled and distracted by the commotion as a second county police car skidded to a stop on the opposite side of the pumps.

The second officer vaulted from his car like a cat jumps out of water. When the attendant looked back at me, he noticed my nickel-plated revolver pointed in his general direction. He dropped the gas cap and nozzle and rolled backward away from the truck. The gas cap rolled with the attendant and the nozzle spewed gasoline on the side of the truck. With three guns now pointed at the occupants of the truck, it was anyone's guess if it would be fight or flight. I presume it was forethought to obey our loud verbal police commands to exit the truck because they were out gunned. As the two men exited, hands on the top of their heads, the parking lot began filling up with county police cars. One by one they entered the lot until there were no remaining places to park.

The hubbub of police officers reminded me of shoppers scrambling and scurrying for last-minute Christmas gifts. Blue lights lit up surrounding buildings in holiday style, and 1955 had suddenly come to life in beautiful Technicolor. I remember, as a five-year-old, noticing my first police car with a single red light flashing and siren blaring. Dad pulled his car to the side of the road, and I locked my eyes on the police car and didn't release my gaze until it was long out of sight. I believe it was that very moment I first imagined being a police officer.

After the occupants of the truck were searched, cuffed, and then placed into separate police cars, the county police officers began a search and inventory of the truck. By this time I was nothing more than a by-stander watching an army of ants carting items out of the truck.

One of the county police officers called me over to the truck and pointed out the shotgun in the floor board and a revolver on the seat. The officer said, "They were just about to kill you." Those words resonated and made a mess of my head, my adrenaline vanished, my legs trembled, and I suddenly realized the danger I had faced. It was certainly not the delight felt by the five-year-old noticing his first police car twenty years earlier.

Later, I went to the hospital to check on Chris and Kelly. What I saw when I got inside the emergency room took my breath. Doctors were treating Kelly's face, but the only thing that looked human was her deep blue eyes. I had never before seen a person's head that mangled, or had I?

Kelly had been abducted and raped by the brother of the shooter a couple of months earlier. Quick police work nabbed the rapist and tucked him away in the county jail. Most police officers assumed the truck driver and shooter believed there would be no need for a rape trial if they killed the rape victim.

Months later I testified in the attempted murder trial of the shotgun wielding passenger of the truck. After leaving the witness stand, I glanced in his direction; the shooter slowly turned his head toward me and mouthed the words, "We'll get you."

He might as well have shouted the words because his lips pierced my soul, mind, and spirit, and I felt everyone in the room was frozen in time except the two of us. I continued to walk, but I wanted to address the judge with what I had observed. The more I thought about it, the more I realized that I was likely the only witness to the threat, and I couldn't prove my claim. I returned quietly to my seat.

The shooter, the get-a-way driver, and the rapist were all convicted of their crimes and went to prison. Kelly and Chris recovered, but both would bear the memory of that horrible night forever. The wound on the back of Chris's head is no longer visible, but Kelly will always have visible scars on her face and many emotional scars in her mind.

I was not on trial, but I received a sentence just the same. Constant concern about retaliation limited my freedom. I lived with the threat for months. Each day I used a different route to work. On my way home, I often doubled back to see if anyone was following, and sometimes I would stop in a parking lot for a few minutes to look for anything suspicious. When I came home, I always jumped to peek over the solid wooden fence that surrounded my rear patio. I started answering my door bell with my service revolver in hand, and I closely inspected any car before I entered. The threat of retaliation may not have been serious, but I was serious that I didn't want to bring suffering home to my young bride.

Time passed and my spirit healed, but the shooting of Chris and Kelly helped me learn safety habits that I would exercise for the remainder of my career. It has taken an eternity to get where I am today, but it seems like yesterday that I started. When I went to bed the other night I was five, but when I woke up I was sixty-five. Life just has a way of happening.

## Chapter 1

## Along Came A Whirlwind

On a Saturday in 1950, Hurricane Able produced 140 mile per hour winds, but it did not make landfall. Able was the first hurricane named under the U.S. Weather Bureau's new system of naming hurricanes. Two days later, another hurricane did make landfall in Huntsville, Alabama. I was the first child born to Forrest Vernon and Jo Doris Foutch Sewell. They named me William Charles and nicknamed me Charlie. I never thought much about it back in the day, but looking back, perhaps I was a little whirlwind.

My dad was a high school football and basketball coach in a town called Vina, Alabama. Two years later, he accepted his first job as a principal at a seven-teacher elementary school in Goodwater, Alabama, a small town between Birmingham and Montgomery. Life was good in Goodwater. It was a wonderful way of life that many people have never experienced. For me, it was a life that enabled me to engage in antics and adventures that would prepare me for an amazing journey into adulthood. But as good as life was, nothing could prepare me for the traumatic events of my 'tween and teen years, and beyond.

During the end of her last trimester carrying my sister, my mom, my dad, and I were staying with Mom's parents on Butter and Egg Road in New Sharon (Lick Skillet), Alabama. My grandfather, William Repsie (Pa) Foutch, was an elementary school principal, and Martha Keith (Grannie) Foutch was a first grade teacher. When

SCHOOL DAYS 1951-52

Mom went into labor on August 7, 1952, Dad was at work, so Pa and Grannie started driving her to the hospital in Huntsville. Against Grannie's objections, Pa loaned his car to a neighbor the night before after the neighbor promised to fill the gas tank. Promises were made to be broken, and, of course, as fate would have it, they ran out of gas. They were a long way from the hospital, and the baby didn't seem to understand the need to wait.

Good Samaritans in the form of a young couple with children stopped to see if they could help the stranded motorists. They had no way of knowing that they were soon going to be pseudo-godparents. They took Pa, Grannie, and the ready-to-deliver Jo Doris into their car and rushed toward Huntsville. Somewhere near Meridianville, Alabama, on U.S. Highway 431, Wanda Gail got tired of waiting and was born in the back seat of the total strangers' car.

When I started writing this story, I called Gail to make sure I had the details correct. She told me she didn't remember anything about that day. She did, however, tell me that Grannie ribbed Pa about it for years.

My memory here is only from photographs and stories, but my folks operated a small gas station just outside of town sometime around 1952-1953. It was a cinderblock building on the right side of Alabama Highway 9 at Coosa County 52. A few years later my paternal grandfather built "Lynda's Dairy Bar," directly across the street. Both buildings remain to this day. Our first house in Goodwater was a small four-room house behind the Baptist parsonage on Weogufka Street. For reasons unbeknownst to me, about the time I turned three, we swapped homes with the family that lived in a bigger house next to the parsonage. Sometime around 1954 we moved to yet another rental house on Harris Street directly across the street from the home of the high school principal.

The house had white slate-shingle siding, and we could see the high school football field from the rear windows. We were so close that we could easily hear the John Phillip Sousa marches being played on the public address system during football games. The back of the house sat on cinder block stilts, and it was high enough in places that I could walk upright. The dirt underneath the back of the house was gray, dry, and powdery, and I could usually find several doodlebug holes. The holes were perfectly tapering pits about one to two inches in width. I may have misunderstood when I heard older kids reciting their little ditty to the doodlebugs, but I often sat next to one of the pits and chanted, "Doodlebug, doodlebug, come out of your hole; If you don't, I'll smash you black as a mole." I seriously doubt that my chant had anything to do with the little bugs coming out of their hole, but at the time I was sure-fire convinced that it did. A doodlebug, also known as a roly-poly and pill bug, was frightened of people, so when I found one and picked it up, it would roll itself into a tight little ball shape for protection. Sometimes I would get two or three and use them like tiny marbles on the porch.

## Curls

Even today I think I still have a good lawsuit. Mom's hair dresser, Italine Byrd, was also her good friend. My hair was a little long for a little boy, and I am not exactly certain if I should blame my mom or Italine, but one of them came up with the notion that my curly red hair needed a permanent. After the curlers came out, I walked out of the beauty parlor feeling as smug as a preschooler could be until I ran into another kid. I am not certain if I was four or five, but the kid was just a little older. He told me I looked like a girl, and, of course, that wiped the grin right off my face. My emotions were crossed between crying and wanting my head shaved. I felt so ashamed and foolish that I ran into the woods to hide. Before I came out, I distinctly remember scooping up a handful of dirt and rubbing it through my hair.

The following day, Dad took me to his barber who cut hair in the living room of his home. Up to that point, Mrs. Byrd had always cut my hair, but this day I was going to be a big boy. After Mr. Williams, the barber, called my name, he placed a plank across the arms of his barber chair and lifted me onto the plank. He reached for his manual hair clippers, and it was over in just over a minute. On the floor, my beautiful bright red curls looked like someone had sheered an Irish Setter. He spun me around to look in the mirror, and I was stunned. I had never had a crew cut, and I didn't like it one bit. My head was so white that it would have lit up a dark room as well as a 100 watt light bulb. I was about to cry when Mr. Williams pulled out his strop and started smoothing the rough edges on his straight razor. I froze and my eyes got wide. I had no idea what he was about to do. Dad said, "Mr. Williams, I think you can dispense with that, there's not enough hair on his neck that we can't wash it off with a wash cloth.

## My Buddy The Milkman

On Saturday mornings I was always excited when I saw the milk truck coming. I was intrigued by the milkman; he was a nice man, and he was my buddy. In the summer when he saw me out playing, he usually gave me a small chunk of ice, gave me a big smile, and patted me on the head.

As he neared my house one morning, I lay down in the middle of Harris Street directly in his path. I have no idea why; I just did. He saw me and blew his horn. When I didn't move, he stopped the truck and blew his horn again. He tried shouting to get my attention, but I already knew he was there. What I didn't know was his horn blowing and shouting got the attention of my mother. When I saw her moving swiftly in my direction, I moved alright.......right into the kitchen where my backside was introduced to the palm of her hand three times. That was the only time Mom ever hit me, but it wasn't the last time I ever got in trouble. The lesson I learned was not to do stupid stuff near Mom.

# The Tale of My Eyeglasses

My mother knew I was a rough and tumble going on six-year-old boy, and she accepted that I was hard on my clothes. Mom and Dad both knew that I needed a subscription rather than a prescription for eyeglasses because from the time I got my first pair at age three, I broke or lost a pair on a regular basis. My folks gave me the freedom to run all over the neighborhood, but freedom didn't come without consequences.

At the high school football field one day, several kids were sliding on a red clay embankment down a groove carved by rain. When I got to the top of the groove, one of the other kids started to slide down. I spotted a horse shoe post on the ground, and I thought it would be funny to put it in the groove. Releasing the pole seemed like a good idea at the time, but when it hit the kid's tailbone I instantly felt remorse.

After sliding down the groove myself, I checked to make sure the kid was OKAY, and then I ran away. A short distance away I tried jumping over a small stream, but when I hit the bank on the other side, it gave way, and I fell in the water. When I surfaced, my eyeglasses were gone. I had only had this pair for about a month because I lost my last pair jumping around bleachers at a football game. I frantically searched the creek, but my eyeglasses were gone. I figured I was really up a creek with my parents now.

When I got home, Mom asked me about my eyeglasses, my wet clothes, and red stained jeans, so I told her exactly what happened: "As I was walking home some older boys started chasing me. I had to slide down a bank and jump over a creek to get away." When she asked, I told her I didn't know who the boys were, but I knew they were going to beat me up. Mom gave me a little sympathy then put my jeans in the wash. I'm not sure what she told Dad, but I kept wondering what he would say to me. Would he be angry, or would he understand? When Dad was angry, he did a great job of holding his temper, but regardless of his emotion, his eyes always had a message. I am not sure Mom believed my tall tale, but I got another pair of eyeglasses, and the subject never came back up, not even from Dad.

## God is Great

Our preacher from the Goodwater Baptist Church came to dinner one night, and Dad asked me to say the blessing. I recited *God is great, God is good*. The following week we had a covered dish dinner in the fellowship hall at church and before we ate, the preacher surprised me when he told everyone he was going to ask little Charlie Sewell to say the blessing. I am sure I stammered out something totally goofy, but I got through it. When we got in the car to go home, Dad said, "Charlie, the preacher wanted you to say the blessing like you did when he ate dinner with us last week." I said, "I sure wish he would've told me."

## Goats Hill

My paternal grandparents had a farm and farm house in Titus, Alabama, that they called Goats Hill. It was perhaps a quarter mile from Sewell Road down a winding dirt road. The house was built on a concrete slab, and it had a living room, two bedrooms, and a kitchen. The family pumped spring water uphill into three barrels using a Ram pump that didn't need electricity. When they needed water in the kitchen sink or outdoor shower, they turned on a spigot, and the water gravity fed from the barrels. There wasn't an indoor bathroom, and the house was heated by some type of wood-burning stove. As a little kid I was comfortable anywhere except the doctor's office, and as far as I was concerned, they lived in luxury.

I don't remember ever seeing any goats on the farm, but there were lots of cows. Grandmother, Janie Lois Snider Sewell, would call the cows in from the field each evening with a loud "soo wee," which was a traditional pig call. Depending on where the cows were in the field, they were as regular as clockwork coming across a rise after she belted out her call.

During one visit my granddaddy, Isaac Moody Sewell, said it was just the right time of year to slaughter a cow, so he picked one that he said was just right. I don't recall how he killed the cow, but I do remember the cow being hoisted up on some type of cross member. When Granddaddy brought out his knife and started cutting, I decided to turn away. When I finally got the nerve to look again, I turned around just in time to see him accidentally cut open one of the cow's stomachs. The stomach contents, which had been brewing in slimy stomach goo to break down the cow's food, gushed onto the ground. It was quickly followed by a horrible smell and flies. By the time Granddaddy finished carving the cow, I thought this was going to be one of the most upsetting bloody messes I would see in my lifetime. That was my first experience with what I would one day learn was my aversion to seeing flesh being cut, and it was something I never wanted to see or smell again.

There was a creek about a quarter to a half mile down the hill from the farm house. Many times a bunch of relatives would walk down to the creek to swim and pick blackberries along the way. The area of the creek where we swam was called Sandy Bottom because of a very large area that looked like a beach. One irritating and startling thing about swimming in the creek was the occasional fish or turtle that would nip us somewhere below the waist.

There were about a half dozen family members swimming at Sandy Bottom one day when Granddaddy went completely under the water and stayed submerged for what seemed like a very long time. When he did come out of the water, he was bottom up exposing his lily white posterior. Grandmother said, "There goes your Granddaddy shooting the moon again."

# The Revival

Grandmother worked as a cashier and a cook a couple of times, but she was mostly a homemaker. Granddaddy was a farmer, grocery store operator, dairy bar owner, garage and café operator and an ordained Methodist minister. During one visit I went with him to a revival where he was preaching. I regularly attended the Baptist Church, but I had never seen anything like what I saw that night. I didn't know what to think when he started washing people's feet. I couldn't believe he could stand to touch the wrinkled and smelly feet of those old folks. Leaving ticklish aside, the thought of having someone wash my feet in public was highly embarrassing. Not understanding why and not wanting to be involved, I slowly worked my way back to the vestibule and hid out until the revival was over.

## Chapter 2

## Living in A Mansion with Siblings

When I was about ready to start school, Dad bought a fixer-upper off of Queen Street. It had a shed, chicken house, rabbit pen, outhouse and a big old fig tree. The back yard was huge, and beyond the fenced yard was a pasture on one side, a lumber mill quite a ways down on the other side, and a pasture in the back. The pine thicket out front on the far side of our driveway provided me with many hours of sweat, plenty of ticks, and sap stained jeans. The thick trees cut out most of the sun, and the snakes and other small creatures provided lots of interesting excitement.

Between the house and the lumber mill I had my own personal field of dreams. I would lie hidden in the tall grass under the warm rays of the sun watching as the clouds moved by. The cumulus clouds were my favorite. They often made me think of an explosion as plumes of clouds rolled upward like billowing smoke. Sometimes I could pick out different faces or images. The light cirrus clouds were vaporous thin, and I always imagined they would one day grow up to be cumulus clouds. The most fun was when the sky was like a canvass for a soft painting in silky blue. But when the gray stratus clouds rolled in, they were thick and seemed like they took over the sky. They weren't the fun clouds, but rather a signal for me to go indoors. I rarely sat still, but this was a place of solace, a place to relax, and a place to stop and think. No one could see me, and I felt like I could lie and watch the fun clouds forever. It was hypnotic.

A little creek with minnows, frogs, crawdads, and enough aquatic life to keep me entertained all day ran through the back side of the rear pasture. On hot summer days, I often ditched my shoes and waded in the cool water. If it was really hot, I would sit to cool off. There was something magical about the running water and smooth rocks that made hours easily zoom by. It often inspired me to pretend that I couldn't hear my mother calling me to come home.

The house had red asphalt siding, a large screened porch on the back, and a porch on the front that was large enough for a glider rocker. Our new two-bedroom house didn't have a bathroom, central heat or cooling, and it sat on stilts made out of stone. I could see daylight underneath the house from one end to the other. The living room was large enough to lay out the entire track for my Lionel train set, and the kitchen had a large pantry. I thought we had a mansion.

Dad started converting the master bedroom closet into a tiny bathroom. He dug the hole for the septic tank and a ditch for the field line by hand, and that gave me a place to play army in the trenches. I'm sure that wasn't a safe place to play, but a cave-in was nowhere on my radar. I was quite disappointed when he messed up my military stronghold by soldering, sealing, and placing cast-iron pipes in the ditch.

For several weeks while Dad finished building our indoor bathroom, we used the outhouse that was about twenty yards behind our house. By that time I already had experience using an outhouse because both sets of grandparents and my Dad's oldest sister had one. But "day in, day out," using the outhouse proved to be foul.

Ours had a one-hole seat that was so large I was always afraid of falling in. It didn't have any lights, and it had a stench that would rival a pile of rotten eggs and a million smelly farts. It smelled so bad that even if it was frozen over, the gaseous odor would have burned your nose like sniffing a blow torch. We usually kept the door ajar to get a little daylight, or to see if there was anything noteworthy in the yard. Actually, the most likely reason was to get fresh air. The best part about using the outhouse was closing the door on the way out.

At bedtime, Mom, Dad, Gail and I went to the outhouse together. Dad always carried a flashlight, but that did little good for the person inside. When the night was cold, the wait to go inside seemed to be a lot shorter. Even if our outhouse had been filled with pictures, fresh paint, a high-fidelity radio, lights, grandmother's doilies and fancy quilted toilet paper, it still would have been nothing more than a creepy reeking crevasse for excrement.

Dad kept a broom just inside the door, and if it wasn't covered in spider webs, we used it to clean out any other spider webs in the outhouse. There wasn't any way to eliminate the flies, but we did keep a fly swatter hanging on a nail. We were also fortunate because we could afford real toilet paper. That wasn't always the case when we visited relatives. People joke about having Sears and Roebuck catalogs in an outhouse, but one of my relatives actually stocked their outhouse with various old magazines. There were usually a few red and white corn cobs in a bucket hanging overhead, but I only heard people talk about how they were used.

The first morning when our new indoor bathroom was ready for use, my four-year-old sister Gail christened the bathtub by dumping in a bottle of liquid white shoe polish and some talcum powder. That first afternoon, I stopped up the toilet with a half roll of toilet paper. The first night, we celebrated because we didn't have to be herded to the bathroom at bedtime. And from that time forward, the trips to the outhouse were just a memory.

Dad enclosed the large screen porch on the back of the house to make a bedroom for me and one for my sister. I guess we were too poor for him to add any type of heat. It was so cold sometimes in the winter that getting ready for bed felt like I was playing in the snow in my birthday suit. Trying to move under two or three of Grandmother's heavy crazy quilts was difficult, but they were so warm that I never wanted to leave my bed on cold mornings.

Saturday was often the day that I got to have quality one-on-one time with Dad. If we weren't out fishing, we were working on a project around the house. By age six, I was already an accomplished "fetcher." I knew the name of every tool in the shed, I could run fast, and I could ask an endless array of childish questions.

One Saturday we were outside using Red Devil Lye for some type project, and Dad told me the container had a warning that it could cause serious burns. I am not exactly sure how it happened, but the lye splashed, and I got a single shot of lye directly on my lips. Before I could say ouch, Dad started torturing me. He invented waterboarding that very second, except he forgot to use a cloth over my face. With a gushing water hose in my mouth, and water squirting out of my nose, I experienced the sensation of drowning. The shot of lye must have been small because I came out wet but no worse for wear.

I got my first bicycle and learned to ride rather quickly. Lumber trucks were frequent on Queen Street where we lived, so Mom made me ride in the yard. A lot of my time at home was spent irritating Gail. It wasn't uncommon for me to do something goofy or *semi-sorta* mean to her and then flee on my bicycle.

One Saturday afternoon Gail was in the front yard making designs in the dirt, and I pretended to stumble through her design which of course messed it up. Immediately seeking an escape, I jumped on my bicycle and headed around the side of the house. Gail was only four and she couldn't have caught me on foot anyway, but it seemed a lot more theatrical to have a bicycle as a get-a-way vehicle. As I rounded the corner into my back yard, I was feeling pretty smug for just a second. I never saw it coming, but I had a losing battle with Mom's clothes line. The wire caught me square in the throat, stopped me in mid-air, and then slammed me to the ground. It knocked the wind out of me, and I lay flat on the ground for several minutes. When I got up, I went into the house looking for Mom to tell her what happened and get her sympathy. The next day my neck looked like I had been shaving with a chain saw. That was my first lesson in karma.

To me, one of the best things about our mansion was our dirt driveway. When it rained, I had really nice mud puddles in the ruts of the driveway that I could sit in, play in with toy boats and make mud pies. Anytime there was a puddle and it was warm and not lightning, that's where I would be. Like pretty much everything else I did, Mom took it in stride. She didn't seem to mind and dutifully scrubbed the mud from my nasty clothes.

Mom had been getting fat in a family way, and on Sunday, July 8, 1956, she and Dad went away for a few days. Gail and I stayed with Grannie and Pa. When Mom and Dad came home, they brought a scrawny little baby boy with almost no hair. I thought to myself, *wow, what in goodness sakes are we going to do with that?* They named him James Richard and nicknamed him Jimmy. When Jimmy got old enough to talk and anyone asked his name, he would say Jimmy Baby Sewell. When he was three, an uncle explained to him that Jim was his nickname for James and Dick is a nickname for Richard, so the rest of the year Jimmy called himself Jim Dick James Richard Jimmy Baby Sewell.

## Estelle

Before Gail and Jimmy started school, Mom hired Estelle as a babysitter and housekeeper. Estelle was a black woman about Mom's age, and she was as sweet as she could be. She was like a second mother, and I often spent the night at her house and enjoyed playing with her son. I wasn't a deep thinker, and I never thought about the enforced separation between blacks and whites in our town. I knew there was a separate school for black students, and black patrons were relegated to the small balcony at the Iris Theater. When my grandfather opened Lynda's Dairy Bar, he had a sign on the front window that said "Whites Only." There was a smaller window on the side that said "Colored." Regardless of these obvious wrongs, I loved Estelle and her family and always thought us equal.

## Chapter 3

## Double Trouble

Sometime after school started that year, a first grade girl stood directly in front of me at the water fountain about to take a drink. I thought it would be rather funny to tip her nose in the water. I put my hand on the back of her head and pushed it down, but I accidentally pushed down too hard and she bumped her nose on the spigot. I certainly didn't mean to hurt her, but no sooner had she risen up crying, I felt a large hand grab my shoulder. The school principal was right there in real life, up close and personal, and with a hitch and a step, he hauled me off to the boy's bathroom. He wasted no time in removing his belt, and I wasted no time in trying to run. He won, I got a lashing; it hurt and I cried.

At home that evening I was still a little tender on my back side and Dad walked up to me and told me to come with him. He took me into his bedroom and said, "I gave you a whipping today because I was your principal, now I am going to give you another one because I am your father." He said he was disappointed that I hurt the little girl, and he hoped I was learning a lesson. I could see something in his eyes that I had never seen before, but I wasn't sure exactly what it was. Indeed I learned a very valuable lesson that day…look for Dad *before* I pulled practical jokes.

## Behind The Cafeteria

It was an exciting day in the third grade when my entire elementary school walked to the Iris Theater to see the movie Bambi. I am not exactly certain how the curriculum was worded to justify taking two hundred elementary school students to a Disney movie, but as an eight–year-old that didn't make no never mind to me.

A classmate named Mary walked directly in front of me. She had a perky stride and golden curly ringlets that bounced with every step. I wasn't interested in girls because they had cootie bugs, but something was different about Mary. Her smile was infectious, and it only took me one glance in her direction to feel like I just inherited an entire case of chocolate candy bars.

Dad had given me a dollar bill and I was supposed to purchase a movie ticket, popcorn, and a drink for me, and the same for my first-grade sister Gail. When Mary stepped up to the cashier, I am not exactly sure what happened, but I found myself reaching around her to hand the cashier my dollar, and I told her it was for two. In return, she gave me two movie tickets and 50¢ in change. When I turned around, I handed Mary one of the movie tickets and she beamed. There must have been a subliminal message attached to her smile because I instantly knew that she needed popcorn and a Coke. She followed me into the theater and sat right next to me. I don't recall watching a lot of the movie. I guess I was afraid Mary would disappear if I didn't keep my eyes on her. I don't know what happened to Gail, but I guess she fared okay because Mom or Dad never said a word.

A few days later our class was at recess on the playground, and Mary walked over to me with one of her captivating smiles. She told me she had something for me and started walking to the rear of our wooden cafeteria building. Being my usual impetuous self, I loyally followed. Once out of sight of the teachers and classmates, Mary walked up real close to me. I am pretty certain I had never been that close to a girl other than Mom, Gail, Grannie, or Grandmother, and I was surprised that she smelled good. I saw it coming and I couldn't get away in time, but she leaned over and kissed me square on the lips. Like it was no big deal, she stepped back, smiled, and skipped away. Her kiss tasted sweet and I liked it, but I was slow to go back to the playground for fear my classmates could see on my face that I had just kissed a girl.

## Sly Fox

One of my elementary school buddies told me one day he thought I was always sneaking around and getting into trouble, and then out of trouble before anyone would find out. He told me that I was sly like a fox. A week or so later we were playing in his dad's junk yard, and we spotted a red fox running across the back of a field. He hollered, "There goes Charlie." For the next three years, until I moved away, he always referred to me as Fox. In one form or another, the nickname Fox would follow me through life.

## Hypersensitive to Hypodermic

When a new girl in a wheelchair joined our class everyone asked her why she used a wheelchair, and she said bluntly that she had polio. That evening I told Dad about the new girl with polio, and I said I didn't know what polio was. He told me it was a disease that causes muscle weakness and paralysis. He said it was an awful disease, and any prudent person would be thankful for the opportunity to receive the Salk vaccine. "As a matter of fact," he said, "all students in your school will be vaccinated next month."

Every day in class I saw the girl in the wheelchair, and it made me think about my upcoming vaccination. A shot in the arm had to be 100,000 times better than being confined to a wheelchair, but I was terrified of needles, and I could hardly think of anything else.

The dreaded day finally came, and our teacher told us it was time for our class to go to the school gymnasium to be vaccinated. When we got to the gym, we lined up single file behind another class. After each student in the other class got their vaccination, they walked past us on their way back to class. A few were smiling, a few had tears in their eyes, and a few were bawling. I was terrorized at the thought of getting a huge needle shoved in my arm, but I didn't want to cry because Mary was in line somewhere behind me. I saw Jack in line in front of me, and that gave me hope. Jack cried easily, and I thought if he walked away from the foot long needle without crying, I had a chance of living through the day.

Jack received his vaccination then started walking back down the line past me, but he wasn't the ray of sunshine that I was hoping to see. My place in line was getting shorter by the minute, and my fear was getting bigger by the second. Now second in line, I made the mistake of watching the nurse stick the hypodermic needle in a boy's arm. When he turned away and I stepped up, I could barely walk, and I felt like I couldn't breathe. I turned my head so that I couldn't see what was coming, and it was over in a flash. It turned out to be my shining moment when I smiled as I walked past Mary. My grin may have changed to a groan and a frown or a pout and a snort when I left the gym, but at the moment I passed Mary a short smile was good for the while.

## Trips to The Store

My parents bought a grocery store in downtown Goodwater. It was in a two story brick building at the corner of Railroad Place and N. Main Street. The only bathroom was upstairs in an abandoned area that was previously an attorney's office. The only access was a metal staircase on the outside of the building. There wasn't much light, it was normally spider infested, and it was a little creepy when I went there. Mom was a teacher, and Dad was still the elementary school principal, so they hired relatives to run the store during school hours.

I was always jealous when they went to work at the store on Saturday and left me and my siblings with Estelle. I had already thought of myself as a strategist, so I didn't think it would be hard for me to invent the perfect solution to keep them home.

Mom was a talker, and it took her forever to tell a story. If we asked her what she had for supper, she started with breakfast and worked her way through the day until she finally told us what she had for supper. It also took Mom forever to get ready to go anywhere, so one Saturday while she and Dad were dressing to go to work, I slipped out to Dad's car and carefully placed a nail under one of the tires. When Mom and Dad got in the car, Dad started backing down the driveway, the nail punctured the tire, and it naturally went flat.

I truly don't know what I was expecting, but when Dad opened the door to inspect the flat tire, I could see a strange look in his eyes that I remembered seeing once before. I thought his eyes were piercing, and I ran away wondering what my funeral might be like. He changed the tire then drove off leaving me quite mortified and afraid. As the day wore on, my fear started to dwindle, and by late afternoon, it had completely gone. I even started to feel a little arrogant because I had gotten away with sabotage, or so I thought. When Dad came home he asked me about the nail, and I confessed. My day of play became an evening of pain. Much to my sorrow, I was the lone prized recipient of the very uncomfortable portion of his belt. I learned a very valuable lesson that day which was never to mess with Dad's tires.

I really liked hanging out at the store. Taking a tube of bologna out of the cooler and using the electric slicer to cut a thick slice was a regular highlight on the rare occasions that I was allowed to visit. When I folded a slice of bologna between a slice of white bread, I thought it was about as good as it gets.

A week went by, and it was again time for the folks to go to the store. Mom was almost ready to go, so I had to come up with another plan quickly. I knew dang well not to mess with the car tires. It hit me like a bird hits a windshield. If they won't stay with me, I will just have to go to the store with them.

Because I was a little kid, it was easy to hide in the rear floorboard of our big ole Oldsmobile 98. I thought it was going to be so funny when we arrived at the store, and I would jump up and yell "surprise." Mom and Dad loved me unconditionally, and they were going to be so excited to see me. When the car stopped, I jumped up and yelled surprise and learned at that very moment that unconditional love didn't disqualify me from unconditional anger. My grand scheme turned into a grand misfortune. For me, the good news came in my only form of punishment was having to walk the one mile back home.

## Vacations with Sister

Our family rarely took a vacation because the store was open six days each week, but when we did go out of town, it was always to visit friends or family. Our Oldsmobile didn't have air conditioning, so Dad usually woke us up for trips before dawn in order for us to travel when the temperature was cooler. He would lay a suitcase in each of the rear floorboards and fill up the remaining portion with blankets to make the entire backseat area level like a large bed.

That worked so well that Gail, Jimmy, and I could go back to sleep until sunrise. When we woke up, Mom would put Jimmy in a car seat that hung over the front seat. Seatbelts were an optional purchase in those days, so the huge backseat became a place to wiggle and wag in order to work out nervous energy. Gail wasn't the best rear-seat partner because she often got queasy. I am not sure why my folks didn't learn from past experience with Gail and give her some pink stuff then let her ride up front. I for one wanted very much to avoid her projectile vomiting. When she hurled to-matoes, it was like a long-tongued Gecko reaching the entire width of the back seat. When I got spattered, I reciprocated, and when I uploaded so did Jimmy. It didn't take but a time or two wearing foul-smelling splatter matter to realize the best place for me to ride was under the window on the rear deck. When I did, that gave Gail the entire back seat as her barf bag.

## Chapter 4

## Loose in Goodwater

I guess it was his consideration for the small town charm and the lack of crime that Dad finally allowed me to ride my bicycle to the store every Saturday. I sure had plenty of things to keep me occupied at home, but for some reason our little town offered excitement. The railroad track that ran right behind our grocery store was a great playground to keep a mischievous little boy out of trouble. Well, let me suffice it to say I never got caught, and it was the beginning of a grand affection toward trains. The Iris movie theater was directly across the street from our grocery store, and the Western Auto was just down the street. On the opposite side of the street, there was a drug store that served Coke floats and a five-and-dime store that sold toys, so what more could a kid want? Incidentally, in those days, we used the word "coke" as a generic term for all soft drinks.

In Goodwater in the 1950s, it was common for parents to look out for each other's children. Being a little redhead freckled faced boy, I had no chance of going unnoticed, and everyone knew I was the elementary school principal's son. I knew that if I was naughty, there was a good chance of being spanked by most any adult in town.

## The Spoon

Dad was a heavy man, and sometimes his mannerism matched his weight. One morning before school Jimmy threw his spoon on the floor. Dad told Jimmy to get out of his highchair and pick it up, and Jimmy said, "No. you pick it up."

Dad never was a cajoler, and Jimmy's refusal made Dad angry, so he popped Jimmy on the hand. Jimmy just glared at Dad, and when he told Jimmy again to get down and pick up the spoon, Jimmy again said, "No." Another pop on the hand, another glare, and another demand followed by another no. This scene repeated itself several times until Dad gave up and left for school. For one, I sure was glad it was over, because watching this battle for dominance made me wonder if Dad might give up on Jimmy and start in on me.

## I Was A Fighter Pilot

I had a vivid imagination and I could enjoy playing with just about anything. A large cardboard box could be my train, biplane, my truck, or my store. It could be my dance floor, a hideaway or just about anything I could imagine. Our fig tree was my fort, our shed was my dungeon, and our silver 325 gallon propane gas tank was my horse.

We had a rabbit pen with a flap door on the top, and I was the perfect size to slide inside. This made a very great fighter airplane cockpit, and when I strapped myself in the pilot's seat and took to the air, I shot down many enemy aircraft. When I got tired of flying my fighter, I converted the rabbit pen to an M4 Sherman Tank.

I quickly became a crack shot with the tank and was credited with destroying many enemy targets. One day I was in the tank making loud kaboom sounds when my dad walked directly in front of my gun barrel as I fired. It really startled me when he grabbed his chest and fell to the ground. I flipped open the flap door and ran like mad to check on him. When I got to him, his eyes glittered when he got up, grinned and said, "You got me." I knew better than to mess with Dad, but it did cross my mind.

## The Guard

Dad always told me that he lied about his age so that he could join the Navy during WWII. Over the years I heard stories about people doing that, but I always wondered if he actually had. Many years later I would know the truth. A few years after he was discharged, he was commissioned as a Second Lieutenant in the National Guard. He became the commander of the newly formed Goodwater National Guard Armory.

Dad must have bent the rules because one summer he let me ride all the way to camp in the convoy with the guard. Riding in an open-air jeep was exhilarating for me, but probably a drudgery for Dad. The guard was scheduled to train for two weeks, but I was on top of the world when he let me stay two days and a night. Sleeping on a military cot today would be one step up from sleeping on a rock, but as a kid, it was like sleeping on Grandmother's feather bed with a mint on my pillow.

A few of the soldiers either considered me a novelty, or they were trying to win favor with the company commander because they treated me royally. They bought me a uniform and told me I was their company mascot. I ate with them in the mess hall, helped them with KP, and they got a kick out of it when I pretended to be a superior officer inspecting their barracks.

## It Was A Piece of Cake

My elementary school, called Hill Top, had an annual festival with food and fun activities. Since Dad was the commander of the National Guard and the elementary school principal, one year he arranged for the festival to be held at the Armory. I remember kids playing Go Fish, tossing basketballs into hoops, throwing darts at balloons, and lots of other fun activities. Bobby Livingston, a well-known and defiled teenage prankster, took his turn bobbing for apples. I watched him thrashing around in the tub of water while blowing bubbles. I wondered if he was actually trying to bite an apple, or if he was putting on a show. When he finally lifted his head, he didn't have an apple. He did, however, have streams of water mixed with nasal mucus running down his face and into the tub of water. It was interesting that the line of kids waiting to bob for apples swiftly disappeared.

It was a cheerful evening of music, hotdogs, chips, drinks and sweets. Another thing I particularly remember is a large circle with numbers drawn in chalk on the concrete floor for the purpose of having a cake walk. When Dad announced the cake walk, I was one of the first people to stand on a number. The music started and people started walking around the circle stepping from one number to the next. When the music stopped, everyone stopped on a number. Dad pulled a small piece of paper with a number from a box and called out my number.

I looked down at my number on the concrete to make sure I heard what I heard, but it didn't register with me that I won a cake. An older lady behind me said, "Charlie, that's your number." When I didn't move, the lady called out to Dad and told him that was my number. The lady gently pushed me forward and told me to go get my cake at the same time Dad told everyone we would have to play the game again.

It simultaneously sunk in that I won a cake, yet I wasn't getting a cake. It was robbery because I won fair and square. Perhaps I should say I won fair and circle. It hurt to think my own father did this to me. It was a case of reverse favoritism, and I didn't understand. At home later that evening I asked him why he didn't let me have the cake that I won. His eyes were watery and not smiling. He said, "Because I am your father." I thought his answer was rather odd and certainly incomplete. Heck, I knew he was my father, but I let it go.

# The Gunslinger

Mom and Dad earned just under $3,000 per year working at the elementary school. We were well fed, had comfortable clothes, and a comfortable home. I received one dollar each week as an allowance, and I was supposed to use it to purchase school supplies and sundries. The dime store and Western Auto were just down the street from the drug store, and after school each day, I was a regular visitor at all three. Ten cents for a Coke float was a bargain but my daily dose of Coke and vanilla ice cream took a financial toll on the money I could spend on toys. Mom was an easy touch, and when I blew my allowance, she always made sure I had school supplies.

Allowance was doled out on Sundays. After school one Monday, I went to the Western Auto store just to look around. As soon as I opened the door, my eyes were drawn to a counter full of bright yellow and red boxes. There was a brand new shiny Mattel Fanner-50 Smoking Cap Pistol in each box. I had been seeing the Fanner-50 advertised on television, and I knew it was something I was destined to have, but I knew it would cost just a little more than the dollar in my pocket. I noticed a sale sign on top of the boxes, and I knew it had to be incorrect. The more I looked at the sign, the more I thought I was seeing a plain ole miracle. The guns were on sale for ninety-seven cents each.

I would be the envy of all my friends, and I would even be able to out draw Wild Bill Hickok. Without a second thought, I proudly selected my Fanner-50 box and walked over to the cashier. Just about everybody in town knew everybody along with everybody's business, and the cashier was no different. She asked me if I was sure I wanted to spend all of my allowance money. Thinking about my easy touch Mom, I told her it would be OKAY with my mom.

After school hours, Dad always went to help close up the grocery store for the day. During my walk to the store for a ride home with him, I guess I killed a couple of dozen gunslingers. On our ride home, Dad's mind must have been preoccupied because he didn't ask me about my six-shooter, and I didn't mention it.

After school the following day, I stopped by my mother's classroom and asked if I could have some money. She asked me why I wanted money because she knew I got my weekly allowance two days earlier. I went into a dissertation about seeing the ads for the Fanner-50 on television, how long I had wanted one, the great sale at the Western Auto and how glad I was to be at the right place at the right time to buy one. I told her it was just my good luck. Well, Mom wasn't as easy as I thought and neither was my luck. She didn't tell Dad I squandered my allowance, but neither did she offer to help me with my bankruptcy. It was a very long week.

## Here Comes The Train

Playing on the railroad track behind my dad's grocery store was always one of the highlights of hanging out at the store. As a matter of fact, playing on any railroad track was thrilling. Like so many kids before and since, I often put a penny or two on the rail when I knew a train was approaching. This didn't hurt the train, but it did help my pocketbook. A flattened penny would bring a nickel when I sold it at school, and that was the equivalent of one half of my daily Coke float fix.

If a flattened penny had a value, I thought perhaps a flattened railroad spike would have value, too. I placed several railroad spikes on the track, and I guess it was a good thing I forgot to tape them down because they all vibrated off before the train arrived. Now I can't actually say that the train would have derailed, but I suspect ten spikes would have come closer to making that happen than ten pennies. As for the tape, I will just have to take the Fifth Amendment about the day I remembered it. Trains, airplanes, and cars were always of great interest to me. Many years later all three would play a large part in dark events that would help fashion who I would become.

## Peanut Butter Breath

One day before school, a friend of my dad's gave me a package containing two Reese's Peanut Butter Cups. She was a visiting teacher and a big muckety muck in the county school system. My third grade teacher, Mrs.

Rogers, didn't allow eating in the classroom, so I placed the candy with my books under my desk. In the middle of the day, our class went outside for recess, and when we returned I found my pack of peanut butter cups opened and one of the cups missing.

That was the first time I had ever been the victim of a theft, and I was determined to find the culprit. When I visually browsed the room looking for an empty cup, it was to no avail. The bell hadn't rung for class to start, and Mrs. Rogers was standing in the doorway talking to another teacher, so this was my opportune time to investigate.

There were eight boys and six girls in the class, and I calculated the thief had to be one of the boys. There was no way of knowing if the theft happened as we left the room for recess or when we were returning, but if it was the latter, I theorized the thief would have peanut butter breath. I was trying to figure out how to smell the breath of another boy without looking creepy, and then I had an idea. If I could get a boy to wrestle me, I could smell his breath without anyone knowing what I was doing.

I had two suspects in mind, so I got out of my desk and walked toward the back of the room to the nearest one. Common sense might have triggered me to look toward the classroom door before I initiated my plan, but all I could think about was my missing candy. I grabbed suspect number one by his arm and gave him a strong jerk. Instead of starting a wrestling bout, the boy yelled "Ouch," followed immediately by Mrs. Rogers bellowing, "Charlie Sewell, come here."

I loved Mrs. Rogers, but I didn't love the whacking on my hand that she gave me with her long wooden ruler. I wasn't able to flush out the thief, but I did put the remaining peanut butter cup in my shirt pocket for safe keeping. By the time I got home from school that afternoon, the candy had melted. As usual, when I caused her extra work, Mom gave me an annoyed glare, shook her head, and then put my shirt in the washing machine.

# 4-H

I started raising chickens for my 4-H project, and I gave each little chick tender loving care. But caring for chickens wasn't as much fun as playing in the creek, the big fig tree, in the mud puddles or riding my bike. One by one the chickens died, and with each one, Dad told me to bury it in the back yard.

I enjoyed digging as long as I was digging a hole to play in, but burying chickens wasn't fun, so I found the old outhouse to be a much easier method to dispose of the departed. Each time I put one through the hole in the outhouse seat, I would think, *drop 'til you stop with a belly flop*. I did everything the 4-H teacher told me to do, and I even followed the written instructions on how to care for the chicks. I had very good intentions, and it was always my goal to be a good kid and be as helpful to others as possible. I came to the conclusion that if I had devoted much more time caring for them, the end result would have been the same. As far as I know, until right now, no one ever knew I pitched the chicks.

# Down By The River

Pa and Grannie had moved south-west to Owens Cross Roads, Alabama, and Pa was a deacon in the Baptist Church. When the doors of the church were open, he was there. Of course if we were visiting, we were there too. On one visit the local river had recently flooded, but most of the water had receded. A baptism was planned for a church member after church on Sunday, and the church didn't have a baptismal, so we all gathered on the banks of the Flint River.

After the preacher and a teenager walked into the muddy river, the preacher said some words before taking out his handkerchief and placing it on the teenager's nose. He slowly immersed the teen backwards into the water and emerged a second later empty handed. The congregation gasped and one woman screamed. The water was still moving rather quickly because of the recent floods, and the teen was nowhere to be seen. The preacher dove under the water, came up quickly then dove under again. When the preacher popped up again, the teen popped up ten or fifteen feet down the river. He was gasping for breath, but he was okay. I overheard an older man behind me mumble, "Was the kid fishing or looking for Jesus." A lady standing next to him said, "He should have been standing on the promises."

## Chapter 5

# The Twister

In 1959 Dad's National Guard Unit was transitioning from an engineering company to an artillery company. During this time, he was assigned to Fort Sill, Oklahoma, for four months of training. We moved into a rental duplex in nearby Lawton.

During a routine day, I was visiting Fort Sill, and I thought it looked like fun when I saw three soldiers raising the barrel on a 105 Howitzer and taking turns polishing it by sliding from the top to the bottom. I asked if I could slide, and I was a little miffed when I was told no. One of the soldiers told me it was dangerous, and he didn't want me to get hurt. It was probably a good thing.

Back at the duplex the next day, Gail and I were playing in the front yard, being careful not to get the painful sandburs stuck in our feet. Mom came outside and told us she saw a report on television that a tornado was spotted nearby. We continued to play, but pretty soon the sky started turning dark. Mom and baby brother were sitting on the porch watching us play when Mom shouted for us to look. She pointed way off in the distance and we could see what looked like a funnel that didn't really appear to be moving. We watched for the longest time until Mom said it was time for us to go in. There wasn't a safe place to go in our tiny duplex, but Mom made us all get in a hall closet. She told us to lie down, and she removed all the clothes from hangers and covered us.

The wind picked up quite a bit. Soon we could hear things hitting the outside of the duplex. The wind grew louder and louder, then roared, and suddenly we heard a huge bang. I knew a tornado had come inside the living room, and we were all going to die. My poor brother Jimmy was just a baby, and it was sad thinking I would never be able to teach him how to throw a baseball. Gail whimpered, and Mom held us tight.

The noise slowly started to dwindle, and Mom opened the closet door. The huge bang was caused by the front door being blown opened. There was a large hole in the sheetrock behind the door, a couple of windows were shattered, and the venetian blinds were broken. It was wet and messy, and there were sticks and sticks covering the living room floor. It looked like a garden full of sticks, leaves and trash. All the pictures had been knocked off the walls, and it was a "mell of a hess" for sure. Our nerves were a little frazzled, but thankfully, we were unhurt.

## I Drove The Olds

We moved back to Goodwater, and Dad bought a new linear look body style, 1959 Oldsmobile 98. It had a "Rocket" V-8 engine, it was two-tone brown, and it had white wall tires. I was always an inquisitive kid, and I enjoyed emptying a cabinet just to see what treasure I could find. If I couldn't find anything else, I drug out all the pots and pans to make a drum set. My family was preparing to take the 98 for a drive, and I got tired of waiting, so I headed for the car early. I was nine and almost grown, and I felt I could conquer anything. In a brief moment of regular curiosity, I climbed into the driver's seat instead of my usual back seat spot. With no malice aforethought, I put my left hand on the steering wheel and pulled the gear shifter down with my right.

It wasn't exactly what I was expecting, but the car started slowly rolling backward down our dirt driveway; then it started rolling faster. I knew about the brake pedal, but in my disbelief that the car was actually moving, and in my excitement, I didn't think about using it. I became concerned that it would roll into the deep ditch on the side of the driveway, so I reacted by jerking the steering wheel. Thankfully, I somehow managed to miss the ditch. Unfortunately, I didn't miss the 100-year-old oak tree. Three hundred dollars in damage in 1959 was a sizable amount of money, and I guess Dad was so happy that I didn't get hurt that he didn't have the heart to hurt me. I waited for a couple of days for the whipping that never came.

## First Payback

My first payback for wrecking Dad's car came on my next birthday when he bought me a control line gas airplane. My next payback wouldn't come for twenty years. The airplane was a pretty dark blue wingover with a small yellow stripe down the side. Dad started the little motor on my airplane, and Dad's brother Julian manned the controls while I watched. The airplane took off, but instead of flying around in circles it went straight up then flopped over and landed in the grass on its back. Second verse, same as the first, Uncle Julian flipped my airplane again. Switching roles, it was Dad's time to fly my airplane. The airplane took off and flew as high as the two control lines would allow before it took a nose dive directly into the ground. The impact broke the motor out of its plastic housing rendering the airplane useless. Well, not totally, my imagination found me whizzing and whooshing through the yard with the busted airplane in my hand while making buzz-buzz airplane noises. I think it was probably more fun than turning in circles until the airplane ran out of fuel.

## Chapter 6

# Moving On Up

Affter my fourth grade year in 1960, Dad sold the store and decided to move the family further north to Hokes Bluff. I don't specifically recall saying goodbye to Mary, but neither do I have many memories of her much past the kiss.

Hokes Bluff was Dad's first job as a high school principal. When the school year started, I was assigned to Mrs. Riley's class. She seemed really sweet. It wasn't long, however, that my sweet teacher started acting strangely. Walking back to meet my fifth grade class didn't turn out to be the happy reunion I expected. Mrs. Riley sent me on an errand to the front office and told me to join my class on the playground when I finished. Ricky Walton ran up to me sweating profusely and tried to get real close to whisper in my ear. He smelled, I didn't want him that close, so I pushed him back. It was real clear that he had something to tell me, so I kept my distance and asked him what he wanted. Ricky said Mrs. Riley told the class that I thought I was special because my dad was the school principal.

I was pretty sure I hadn't pretended to be better than anyone else because I was a very bashful kid who tried hard to make friends. If I ever had a goal up to that point, it was simply to be nice and helpful to everyone. At home that evening I repeated to Mom what Ricky told me. She said something to the effect that perhaps Ricky misunderstood Mrs. Riley. Then she told me she knew I wasn't like that and perhaps I should just forget about it, so I did.

I didn't put two and two together, even when Mrs. Riley only picked me to run errands. Later, I heard from several different classmates who told me that every time I left the room she had something disparaging to say about me. It turned out that Mrs. Riley disliked me because my dad was the school principal. Before we moved there, Mrs. Riley's daughter, a cheerleader, came to school when she wanted to and basically did as she pleased. I learned that Dad had a conference with Mrs. Riley and her daughter and told them both that everyone had to follow the same rules.

It seemingly bothered my dad that I was treated so poorly, but I wondered why he didn't treat me special because I was his son. I cried at home a few times, and I always got good sympathy from Mom.

About three months into the school year, when we thought we were getting settled in at school and at home, Dad was called to active military duty again, this time because of the Berlin Crisis. On October 15, 1961, he was sent to Fort Polk, Louisiana, where he stayed for the next eleven months. Our family moved into a single family rental house in nearby Leesville. It was not easy to move again so quickly, but thankfully, I did not have to deal with Mrs. Riley again.

Dad's youngest sister learned she had multiple sclerosis. She and Uncle Joe lived in Chattanooga, Tennessee, and we didn't get to see them very often. Everyone loved my Aunt Martha Jean, but on August 1, 1962, she committed suicide with a small derringer. She was pretty, very talented, so sweet, and she was certainly going to be missed. We drove from Louisiana to Tennessee for the funeral, and that was the first personal loss I had experienced. On our way home to pack up and prepare to move again, I asked Dad what was going to become of the derringer. He was driving and didn't look at me, but he said, "Not sure, we'll see."

After our eleven months in Louisiana we returned to Hokes Bluff. That would have been around September of 1962 right after the start of my sixth grade year. During that school year, Mrs. Riley was killed in a car accident. I guess it was some more of that karma stuff; my folks sent flowers.

## Leaving Goats Hill

Grandmother and Granddaddy owned a rental house on Sewell Road in Titus, Alabama, about a quarter-mile in front of Goats Hill. The house was a dog trot style, and by today's standards it was extremely primitive because it didn't have electricity or indoor plumbing. Their tenant, a widow with six children, moved out after disassembling the back half of the house and burning it in a potbelly stove for heating and cooking. The only parts of the house that remained were two bedrooms, a living room, and a portion of the kitchen.

They started remodeling what was left of the house and had plans to rebuild the part that had been dissembled. As the house on Goats Hill started to age and give them problems, they abandoned it and moved into the partially restored dog trot.

When school was out, I went to stay with Grandmother and Granddaddy for a week-long visit. The house now had electricity, but the wiring was visible running up the walls and across the ceilings. The bathroom, back porch, and master bedroom were under construction, but they had not been finished.

The first evening, we were sitting on the front porch trying to stay cool while popping and stringing beans. As the sun started setting, and the temperature started to fall, Grandmother walked out to the yard and picked up a crude straw broom and started sweeping the yard. Grass hadn't grown in the yard for probably 100 years, or certainly not since the two huge old trees started producing shade. She had pots of begonias and petunias that needed tending, just like the rusted plow out front that Granddaddy needed to haul off to the junk yard.

The sweat was beginning to dry on my back as I saw the first lightning bug for the night. Jumping up to a dash, I ran into the kitchen to find a jar to catch the little intermittent flashers. I threw open the screen door and started out across the concrete porch. I heard crickets chirping in rhythm with my footsteps and in the distance I heard a bullfrog croaking. The spring on the screen door pulled it swiftly backward, and the door slammed closed with a loud whack. The night became silent as the crickets stopped chirping, but a brief moment later they resumed their musical chorus. I ran and I jumped, I grabbed and I snatched lightning bugs one by one until my jar was one big shimmering light.

With my full jar, I walked onto the porch and caught the reflection of my red hair in the front window being illuminated by the porch light, and the glow made me think of the glow in the jar of lightning bugs I held captive. I had no use for them, and I had had my fun. I walked back to the yard, took the top off the jar, and the sprinkle of lights slowly scattered into the trees, the pasture beside the house, and across Sewell Road.

Grandmother and Granddaddy were about finished with the beans when I got back to the porch, and Grandmother was humming a whispered tune. The moon was visible over the distant trees, and the night started to cool down as the stars started to shine. When they snapped the last bean, Granddaddy said it was time to go in for the night. Once inside, he turned on the television and said he wanted to watch the news. Titus is about thirty-five miles from the television stations in Montgomery, Alabama, and the old black and white television with rabbit ears as the antenna wouldn't receive more than three channels. There wasn't any news on the television, so about ten minutes later, Granddaddy said it was getting late and time for us to go to bed. It was nine o'clock. I was directed to sleep in the right front bedroom. As I got ready to get into bed, looking down through the cracks in the floor, I could see the ground.

As I lay in bed, my thoughts turned to the children who previously lived in the house. I knew they were poor, I wondered if they had shoes, and I wondered if the cracks in the floor kept them cold in winter. What had become of them, where did they go? Were their hearts a bastion of good deeds, and were their minds sharp to do useful things? If they could be good, then I knew that I could. The night was quiet and as I drifted to sleep, I knew I could help people, and I knew that I would.

The next day Grandmother spent most the afternoon in the back yard washing clothes with Duz Detergent and her electric Maytag wringer washer. It was a little labor-intensive, but even when it started to sprinkle, she washed clothes and hung them on the clothesline.

They finished building the back part of the house within the next two months. Even when the renovations were complete, including an indoor bathroom, Grandmother and Granddaddy still kept a slop bucket under their bed to use at night. To this day, I can't fathom how they did it, and more importantly, why they did. They lived in this house until my grand-daddy died in 1973 at age seventy-three. Grandmother lived with family until she died in 1990 at age ninety.

## The Bayonet

Digging around in an old shed at Granddaddy's home one Sunday afternoon I found a bayonet and sheath. I took it to Granddaddy and asked him about it. He told me I would have to ask my dad because it was his. I went to Dad and asked him about it, and the only thing he would tell me was that he brought it home from the war.

I asked Dad if I could keep the bayonet, and he told me that I could. I was tickled to have a fifteen inch treasure in a twenty inch treasure chest of a sheath. Back in those days it was common for boys to carry pocket knives everywhere they went, even to school. As a matter of fact, since I was eleven I had already been hunting by myself with a .22 rifle, so it wasn't a big deal for me to have the bayonet at age twelve. Over the years, I would put my hands on it from time to time, and I always felt that if it could talk, it could tell a story. In the early years, the only story I learned about the bayonet was that it was made at the Nagoya Arsenal in Japan sometime between 1923 and 1945. Five decades after I first found it, I would learn the chronicle of my treasure.

# The Traffic Jam

After a nice weekend visiting Granddaddy and Grandmother, and me in possession of my mysterious and prized bayonet, we left about 3:00 p.m. that day for a two hour drive back to Hokes Bluff. After school the following day, I was riding with Dad and a buddy of his on the way to go fishing, when we drove up on stopped traffic. We lived in a very rural community, and traffic jams almost never happened. With my touch of ADHD, sitting still for me was very difficult. Time started to drag and I needed to move, so Dad let me get out of the car to move around. My curiosity got the best of me, so I wandered in the direction of the stopped traffic.

When I walked past the forth car, which was at the crest of a small hill, I could see several more cars, a police car, and a hearse at the bottom of the hill. There was a small crowd of people gathered that made it hard to see what was going on. This fueled my interest, so I kept walking. It looked like a traffic accident between a convertible and a log truck. When I got closer, I could see the car wasn't a convertible, but rather a car with its top sheared off. There was something in the back seat that I couldn't make out. When I saw the hearse driver bring a stretcher to the car, I assumed someone had died, but I was apparently too far away to see clearly what had happened. I started walking past a man to go to the other side of the car to get a better look, but the man grabbed my arm, jerked me back, and yelled, "Get out of here."

As I started walking back past the line of cars with my head hung low, I recognized the sound of Dad's footsteps on the pavement, and then I looked up to see him coming to get me. We got back in the car, turned it around and left for home without going fishing.

Later that day Dad got a telephone call, and when he hung up, I overheard him tell Mom that a little girl from his school had been decapitated in a traffic accident. I didn't know what decapitated meant. I also didn't know who he was talking about until I got to school the next day. As soon as I walked into school the following morning, I learned that one of my classmates, Carolyn Massey, had died in a traffic accident. We didn't get a crisis intervention team, but one of the room mothers did bring cupcakes to our classroom. It was a solemn day, but the fascinating thing was the way we just got over it. We were curious, and it was hard to lose a classmate, but we just kept marching. I thought it was coincidental that I saw the aftermath of an accident on the same day Carolyn died, but I didn't know if the two were related. Dad never said, and I never asked.

## Going Up But Not Down

My buddy Steve and I zipped up the first three levels of stairs on a fire lookout tower like speeding bullets when my twelve-year-old adrenaline started to kick in, or so I thought. The further up the stairs I went the slower I got and the harder I clinched the rail. Steve reached the trap door in the floor long before I did, and he was having a nice conversation with the fire lookout when I finally reached the top. We really weren't supposed to be up there, so the fire lookout had to give us a little scolding, then he proceeded to explain his job and show us his tools. The scolding was worth it. The view was remarkable and I thought I could see Nevada.

Time to go and the fire lookout opened the little door in the floor, and I looked down. Perhaps if I had not looked down but had gone feet first and kept my eyes on the horizon, I might have been okay. But I couldn't bring myself to get near the door. I realized at that moment what I thought was adrenaline was nothing but pure unadulterated fear. Steve easily made it to the ground, but I theorized someday a fire lookout would find my skeletal remains right there. After unsuccessfully trying to coach me down, the fire lookout climbed down through the trap door and held me like we were a tandem parachute couple. I didn't open my eyes until we reached the ground. I never had the inkling to climb a fire lookout tower again, but I never got over my love for them.

## It Was Nothing to Cheer About

We finished that school year and went on our usual vacation to visit family. When we came home, we found a super-special surprise in our yard. Because Dad was a school principal, it was not uncommon for us to get our yard rolled with toilet paper. But this wasn't like anything we had ever seen. We later learned that the local high school cheerleaders spent days shredding newspapers into very tiny pieces before showering our yard with homemade confetti. Rolling a yard was supposed to be done to poke fun at people you liked, so the cheerleaders must have really adored my dad because our yard was deep in admiration. I took it personally.

It became even more personal when Mom, Gail, and I had to clean up the mess. For several days after school the following week, we raked and bagged minute pieces of newspaper. My personal insecurity grew faster than my anger about my yard being trashed. I never did know why Dad and Jimmy were exempt from the cleanup. I guess Dad was busy, and Jimmy was just little.

## Chapter 7

## Was it Haunted?

*I* n 1963 Dad accepted a different high school principal's job. After my seventh grade year, we moved west and settled in another little small town named Hanceville. We moved into a house that was owned by the school system. It was kind of like a parsonage, but for a principal. It was close enough to walk to town, to school, and to church, so it suited me just fine. Except for a latch on the rear screen door, the house didn't have door locks.

It was getting harder to change schools and change friends, but in a strange way I believe it gave me strength. Now don't get me wrong, in the seventh grade during sock hops I was always the one sitting in the corner. It was not a good idea to ask me to speak up in class or say the prayer in Sunday school. But in little increments, my greater sense of confidence was beginning to form by the time I started in the eighth grade.

My bedroom was in the right rear corner of the house, and with old wooden floors it was easy to hear when anyone was walking about. I was home alone after school one day when I heard the front door open and close. Dad had come home earlier than usual, and I could hear him walk step-by-step down the hall toward my bedroom. He was a very big man, and the sound of his footsteps were unmistakable. I was putting a model car together, and I stopped to look up so I could greet Dad when he entered my room. The sound of the footsteps stopped just outside my doorway, but Dad didn't come in. I called out to him, but he didn't answer. I called out to him again, and again he didn't answer. My dad wasn't a joker, so I became alarmed.

I picked up my baseball bat for security, and I eased over to the doorway. I didn't think Dad would jump out and scare me, but I slowly peeked around the corner, and he wasn't there. I called out to him once again, and when he didn't answer, I dropped the bat, jettisoned the house and ran all the way to his office. When I found him sitting at his desk I was relieved at first, then more frightened. Knowing what he would say, I asked him if he had just been home. He looked up from his desk and peered over his reading glasses with a curious look in his eye. He said "No, why?" When I told him what happened, he smiled, and told me I was imagining things. A vivid imagination had followed me for years, but this was different, it was haunting. It wasn't ghostly, it wasn't monstrous, but it was a lingering memory. It was a shadow.

On my way back home I tried to rationalize that Dad had not been home that afternoon, but in my mind it remained undeniable that he had. I tried not to think about it too much, but from that point forward I tried not to be home alone. When that couldn't be avoided, I always dragged a large piece of furniture in front of each door.

## Hobo Woes

My thirteen-year-old buddy, Billy Peoples, shared my mad passion for trains. His Dad worked at the local production company which was right alongside the railroad tracks. Once in a while Billy and I would walk to see his Dad at work, and when we did, we often saw the train pass by. The train slowed down when it came into town and didn't speed up until it passed the production company which was on the outskirts of town. We weren't sure if he was an employee of the railroad or local post office, but one day we saw a man attach a mail bag to a crane alongside the tracks. When the train passed by, an iron rod hanging from the side of one of the railroad cars snatched the mail bag. We thought that was the coolest thing.

The next Saturday Billy suggested we go down to the production company to watch the train snatch the mail bag. I was perfectly fine with this idea because I had several years of experience playing around railroad tracks. What I didn't know was my experience was about to dramatically change.

As we walked near the production company, Billy said "Do you see how slow the train is going?" He started running at full speed, and of course I followed suit. Before I knew what was happening, Billy grabbed hold of a handle on the front of a boxcar and pulled himself onto the moving train. His stunt was pretty impressive, so of course I needed to prove that he wasn't any better than me. Still running, I instinctively reached up and grabbed a handle on the back of the box car, and I was surprised that it was going a little faster than it looked. It took precise timing, but with a hard push of my feet, I pulled myself onto the boxcar. I was very proud of myself for a moment, and then I started to think, *now what Einstein?* Riding on the outside of the train was fun and exciting, but neither of us were prepared for the consequence or the immense danger of what we had accomplished.

It was only five miles to the next town so it wasn't long before I saw a sign announcing Garden City, and as we approached a very sharp curve, the train started to slow down. Billy had worked his way across the top of the boxcar and climbed the ladder down to just above where I was standing. As the train rounded the sharp curve, I noticed a grass covered hill that sloped down to a small pond. Just as Billy had hopped on the train without sharing his intentions, he jumped off. He flew over my head and down toward the grassy slope. I was in full-scale panic, and I couldn't think straight. I didn't look back, and I had no idea what became of Billy.

There was a line of trees ahead, and I knew if I was going to jump it was now or never. Fearing the train might not stop until it got to California, I jumped. The grass was slicker than I thought, and the ground was harder. I flipped twice, rolled once, and thought I was going to slide into the pond. I reached my hands out, dug my fingers and heels into the ground and stopped just as my tennis shoes hit the water. A plain ole miracle had occurred once again because I still had on my eyeglasses. It was an exhilarating experience, but it was also painful.

Even though neither one of would admit that we would never try that again, Billy and I climbed back up to the track and had fun bragging to each other about our daring feat. We walked the remaining quarter mile to Garden City and found a gas station that had a couple of vending machines. We bought two packs of crackers, a six-ounce Coke for me, and a six-ounce RC Cola for him.

Walking part of the way back on an old dirt road eating our crackers, we located treasures along the way. We found trash piles that included things like hypodermic needles, empty bottles, broken small appliances, and other things only a thirteen-year-old might find interesting. The most fascinating find was a quarter-mile paved road with center line markings that abruptly stopped at each end. The entire section of pavement was completely surrounded on all four sides with fifteen-year-old loblolly pine trees. It was like a section of road was dropped into the woods by a helicopter.

We kicked rocks, broke tree limbs, tossed our drink bottles in a pond, and had fun on our way back to town. The dirt road eventually crossed the railroad track, so we followed it on the final leg of our exciting journey. When we neared the production company, we were surprised to see a large group of people, and two deputy sheriff's cars.

As we got closer and started talking to people, we learned that a young boy had been hurt trying to jump on a train. It didn't take us long to find out the young boy was Billy's little brother Wally. Apparently, Wally followed us and tried to mimic our stupid stunt of hopping the train. Unfortunately, Wally didn't have the speed or strength to keep a hold on the handle of the moving boxcar. He held on and was dragged for a few seconds, then lost his grip, and was slammed into a pole beside the track. He had a broken back, a broken leg and a serious chest wound.

Wally didn't tell anyone that Billy and I hopped on the train, and we never mentioned it. We both, however, felt like we had still gotten into serious trouble. Wally was hurt because of my irrational and reckless act, and I felt profound remorse. I told myself there would be no more injuries, and no more death. I was thankful that I was not there to see Wally get hurt. My mind wandered, and I got lost thinking about my future and my past. I was grateful that I wasn't around when Aunt Martha Jean and Carolyn Massey died. At age thirteen, I had had enough.

Wally would recovered, but he had a small limp. He would weigh on my mind for years to come. That was the last time I tried jumping on a moving train, but my love of trains is still strong.

## Skateboarding

One Saturday, Billy and I were bored and trying to find something fun to do without getting into more trouble. Trouble had a way of following me even though I was considered a good kid. Rumbling through Dad's spider-infested storage shed, we found an old pair of Speed King roller skates. They were dirty, and the leather was cracked, but a vision of possibilities popped in my head before I could even reach to pick them up. Even though skateboards were already commercially made, I had never seen or heard of one, but I envisioned a sidewalk surfing scooter.

Tools were scarce in my family back then, but with my vivid imagination, the lack of tools wasn't a barrier to my inventive mastermind. A rough piece of plywood, a hand saw, a hack saw, a hammer, some nails and a pair of pliers, and we were on our way to a community first. We removed the plate from one skate and cut it into two sections. We nailed each piece to one side of the plywood about two feet apart, then hammered down the exposed nails on the other side. The bent nails proved to be a little uncomfortable to sit on, so we headed back to the shed to discover a solution. We found a large and worn out alpaca blanket that we figured would add just the softness we needed. After we wrapped the top of our creation with the blanket and trimmed and tacked the excess flaps under the plywood, we produced a mighty fine looking sidewalk surfing scooter.

There was a steep sidewalk near our school where we often enjoyed rolling model cars, rocks, balls, and hula hoops down the slope. Bicycling down the sidewalk had become old hat, and the new sidewalk surfing scooter seemed like a rational sequence of fun. This sidewalk wasn't simply steep, it was so steep that people who walked down the hill used ski poles with rubber tips to keep from falling over. Being the aforementioned adrenaline junkie that I really wasn't, I proudly sat on the sidewalk surfing scooter and began the maiden voyage down the hill. Even with wooden wheels, the noise was very loud as each sidewalk crack came faster and faster as my speed was getting out of control. There was a curb and roadway at the bottom of the sidewalk that I was approaching with rocket speed. In my rush to test drive our brilliant invention, I hadn't given any thought about not having brakes. Gently at first, then harder and harder, I pushed the heels of my tennis shoes onto the sidewalk. The scooter stopped just before hitting the curb. Since I had been traveling at Mach speed, the sidewalk wore the heels of my tennis shoes down like an eraser on sandpaper.

I know Billy and I didn't create the first skateboard, but I do know our creation was the first one ever seen at our local indoor skating rink. The owners of the rink were delighted for us to bring our skateboard because it garnered so much attention. There were lots of kids that wanted to ride it, and we accommodated a few, but it was so much fun, we were probably a little stingy. As a result, we started seeing other similar homemade skateboards at the rink and soon our prized party plank invention was no longer a novelty. Just over a month after we became a skateboard sensation, all skateboards were banned from the rink because the owners felt the number of skateboards had gotten out of hand.

## A Stitch in Time

By the time I turned fourteen, playing tricks and hiding from my younger siblings was more fun than swimming, eating watermelon, and shooting off firecrackers. We were fooling around in the kitchen one day, and I took an ice cube out of the freezer and put it down the back of Gail's blouse. She screamed and I started running. With her in pursuit, I bolted outside and jumped on my bicycle. Both pedals had long since fallen off the stem, and when I stood on the stem to gain pedal thrust, my foot slid off. Wearing short pants didn't help as the end of the stem ripped the inside of my right leg. I could see the muscles through the heavily bleeding wound. Gail ran to get help while I lay on the sidewalk freaked out, in shock, and holding my leg.

Mom drove me to the local clinic which was about ten minutes away. A nurse saw me limp in holding direct pressure on my wound, so she escorted me straight back to a treatment room. The doctor wasted no time with triage and told me he was going to sew my leg up. Never having had stitches, I didn't know what to expect. When I saw him preparing a hypodermic needle, I squirmed because I thought I knew what was coming.

He inserted the needle through the open cut and into my leg muscle. The pain wasn't what I expected, but rather so intense I thought I was going to pass out. The initial pain from the needle was worse than the actual cut, but as the anesthesia started to work, the pain started to ease. The stitching didn't take long, and it didn't hurt, but the tugging of the thread through my skin was an awful feeling. After the fourteen stitches were removed, and my leg healed, I was left with a huge scars.

## There is Pressure in The Cooker?

Blue Laws in Alabama required stores and most places of work to close on Sundays so people could attend church. There were only a few restaurants open on Sunday in our area, and Dad wasn't fond of eating out, so our ritual on our day of worship was having a big meal at home after church. We only lived a few blocks from church, so I always walked to Sunday school and then home after the preacher's sermon.

One Sunday, Mom and Dad were dawdling after the church service so they could mingle with the preacher and friends. Knowing I would get home first, Mom had asked me to take the potatoes out of the pressure cooker when I arrived. I was very familiar with baseball cards, model cars, bicycles, and skateboards, but I didn't know anything about pressure cookers. Gail probably watched Mom take the little "jiggling" weight valve off the top to release the pressure inside the cooker, but that was just another doohickey to me.

When I got home I moved the cooker from the stove to the sink and slid the two handles sideways to pull it open. There was a thunderous pop that hurled the lid backward at lightning speed barely missing my face. Boiling water, steam and scalding hot potatoes shot upward. We had a scalloped potato ceiling, gratin potato floors, mashed potato appliances, and potato salad windows, but we didn't have potatoes for dinner.

I was still digging potato out of crevices with a kitchen knife when Mom got home from church. When I told her I thought it was caused by the ghost that sounded like Dad walking in the house after school, she explained how a pressure cooker worked. She wasn't angry, just relieved that a miracle happened that day. With an incident that could have been a very serious, if not fatal accident, I came out unscathed.

# The Bug

Mom was enrolled in a graduate program one summer and used the only family car to drive to class. Dad borrowed Pa's 1949 Volkswagen Beetle (Bug) to have transportation when Mom was gone. The Bug was faded coral red, had a six-volt electrical system, a twenty-five horse power engine, and most of the summer it just stayed parked. I was fascinated with cars, and since the bug was never locked, I took every opportunity I could to sit behind the steering wheel and shift gears.

One day I decided since Dad had often allowed me to crank his new Buick before he drove it, cranking the Bug shouldn't be a problem. Dad was sitting in his easy chair near his new window air conditioner watching baseball on television when I approached him. I told him I needed to move the Bug because it was blocking an area where we were playing. I don't know if he was just too comfortable watching the tube or if he wasn't thinking, but he handed me the keys.

I cranked the Bug, and for the next ten minutes I practiced with the clutch moving the car back and forth about half a car length. Over the next three weeks, I borrowed the keys time and again and got pretty comfortable using the clutch in first gear and reverse. Dad often asked me to go outside and turn the television antenna so he could get a better reception. One particular day, when I was handling that request, I spotted the Bug, and it told me to come drive it. When I went back inside, I told Dad I wanted to drive the Bug. I don't know if he was just too comfortable watching the tube or if he wasn't thinking, but he handed me the keys.

Driving in first gear out the back side of the carport wasn't a problem. Driving in circles in second gear in the back yard wasn't a problem. In third gear I took to a field behind the house, and it wasn't a problem. Other than many years earlier steering Dad's car into the 100-year-old oak tree, this was my first time to drive. It was a lot more exciting than riding a bicycle, but I figured I had enough fun for one day and headed back to the house.

I stopped beside the house to determine exactly where to park. The most logical place was back under the carport, but I knew Mom would be coming home soon, and she would be grateful if I left her the choice parking spot. Back in first gear, I eased the clutch out and slowly started moving forward to park beside the carport, but this was a problem.

As I tried to squeeze the Bug between the brick pillar of the carport and a telephone pole, the pole jumped over and smashed the Bug on its right rear fender. Upon inspecting the fender, I saw a dent the size of a dinner plate covered in creosote. I had less than a year to go before I would be eligible for my driving permit, and now I calculated I had ruined that eligibility for life.

With my spirit lower than the Titanic, and my apprehension higher than the clouds, I went inside and told Dad. He got up from his easy chair and put his arm around my shoulder and said, "Well son, let's go take a look." Within a minute he had the dent pushed out, and other than the creosote, we could hardly tell there had been a problem. Dad gave me two dollars and told me to ride my bicycle to the store and pick up some polishing compound. When I got back and using Dad's instructions, I was able to remove all the creosote from the fender, but this caused another problem. That part of the fender was now so shiny it didn't match the faded red paint on the rest of the car. It took me the rest of the day and part of the next day to polish the entire Bug. When I finished, both arms were pretty tired, but I was proud of my accomplishment just the same. I rushed in the house to get Dad to show him what I had done. He looked at me and I thought I saw a glimmer in his eyes. He said, "I will be right there." When he came outside, he looked at the car and said, "That looks good, son," then he gave me two dollars and told me to ride my bicycle to the store and pick up some car wax. Back to the Bug; it was rub it, rub it, toil and scrub it. I learned that taking care of a car was a lot harder than wrecking one.

## The Hardware Store

Going to the hardware store to look at pocket knives and BB guns was becoming just about as much fun as going to the toy store to buy model cars. One Saturday while perusing knives at the hardware store I spotted a Barlow-style pocket knife that I knew I couldn't live without. The only problem, however, was I didn't have enough money to buy it.

A model car cost as much as my weekly allowance, and I wasn't quite ready to give up models. That put me in a quandary. I walked up to the owner of the store, Mr. Westbrook, and told him my situation not expecting anything except sympathy. It was with surprise and disbelief when he told me I could have the knife on credit. I don't recall the exact price, but it was probably around five or six dollars. Coughing up a one dollar bill from my wallet and a few coins from my pocket, I gave him a down payment and proudly walked out with my pocket knife.

Just as promised, the next two Saturdays I went back to the hardware store and gave Mr. Westbrook my weekly installment of one dollar. The following Sunday, Dad threw a monkey wrench into our world when he announced that we would be moving. The following Saturday we were loading our belongings on a truck, and I missed my trip to pay Mr. Westbrook. The hardware store was closed on Sunday, and we moved on Monday. I didn't pay off my debt, and that weighed heavily on my mind for the next six years.

## Chapter 8

## Moving North

In the summer of 1965 we moved to Decatur, Alabama, and this new town was our first town that I would describe as a city. We had a neat home with a large screened porch over a carport and a barbecue grill built into the brick next to the fireplace in the den. There was a tiny duck pond out back, lots of woods, and a great guy named Gary who lived next door. On weekends we often had six or eight guys over for flag football in the small track of land between our houses. Gary and I were in the same grade at Austin High School. I attended there my sophomore and junior year. Life was grand.

## Driving with Dad

After I got my learner's license, I begged Dad to let me drive every time I was in the car. His car was huge which made it a little difficult when negotiating right turns on narrow downtown streets. Without a lot of experience I always slowed way down to make those type of turns so I wouldn't hit anything. Dad would fuss saying I was going too slow, and we would get hit in the rear.

Dad was usually pretty patient with my driving, but in retrospect I don't know if he was really all that patient or if I was a naturally good driver. A one-way street was something I hadn't experienced other than reading about it in the driver's manual. Once when I was driving in a larger town,

I stopped at a stop sign at a one-way street and looked in both directions before I proceeded. Dad let out a noise that sounded like a cross between a chuckle and a grunt then said, "You only need to look in the direction of the traffic flow on a one way street." I told him my Driver's Ed teacher taught me to look both ways when the traffic light turned green because some people run red lights. When I told him I figured some people don't pay attention to the one-way directional arrows, he said, "Well……. okay."

The car had an adjustable needle that Dad could set to any speed. When the speedometer needle reached the position of the adjustable needle, a disturbing buzzer would sound to let him know he had reached his desired speed. At first, Dad always set the adjustable needle at the speed limit. But after we had the car for a couple of weeks, he got tired of frequently hearing the buzzer, and he started setting the adjusting needle about fifteen mph higher than the speed limit.

When we got out of the city limits and into the countryside, I reached up and adjusted the needle ten miles per hour over the speed limit. Dad's voice sounded concerned and perturbed when he asked me what I was doing. I told him I was doing what he always did because I didn't want to hear the annoying buzzer. He reached over and turned the needle back near the posted speed limit. I never asked him, but I suspected that when we got home he had a mechanic disable the buzzer. He always kept the adjustable needle set at the speed limit, but I never heard it buzz again.

## Etch-A-Sketch

It was the Saturday after Thanksgiving, and the family was out for a drive in Dad's new Buick. Mom announced that she wanted a new dress for Christmas, so Dad stopped at the local department store. Whenever Mom went shopping, Dad and I knew it wasn't going to be a quick stop, so he always went toward the barbecue grills or fishing equipment, and I usually spent time looking at baseball equipment or toys. After trying on a few baseball gloves I wandered over to the toy aisle and saw a younger boy sitting on the floor with a red slate-type toy in his lap. He seemed to be having fun making vertical and horizontal lines by turning the two white knobs on the front. Intrigued, I took another one from the shelf and read the word Etch-A-Sketch on the top. This was the first one I had seen, but within a few minutes I could write in cursive. I was utterly fascinated with the toy, and I lost all track of time.

Dad came to get me and said Mom, Gail and Jimmy were heading toward the cash register and we would be leaving in a couple of minutes. Before I put the Etch-A-Sketch back, I wrote my name and telephone number on the toy thinking if anyone who knew me saw it, they would brag about my new skill.

About fifteen minutes after we got home, the telephone rang and I beat Gail to it. A man on the telephone said he was Bret Williams, the manager of the department store, and wanted to talk to Charlie Sewell. I couldn't imagine what I had done wrong. I knew I returned the Etch-A-Sketch to the correct shelf, I hadn't poured out any bottles of liquid, and I certainly hadn't stolen anything. I reluctantly told him I was Charlie Sewell, and he said, "I found the Etch-A-Sketch with your name and telephone number on it." By this time I was shaking to the point I didn't think I would be able to talk. He continued, "I wanted to know if you would be willing to demonstrate the Etch-A-Sketch to our customers during the upcoming Christmas Holiday?" My trembles started dwindling, my voice smoothed, and I could feel my red face return to white as I told him it sounded like fun.

Except Sundays and Christmas day, Mom drove me to the store every day at 10:00 a.m. and picked me up at 4:00 p.m. during the entire two-week holiday. Before long I was able to turn the Etch-A-Sketch topside down making the writing to me reversed, as in a mirror. With the toy facing the customer, they could easily see what I had written. It was my very first job, and according to Mr. Williams, I was a hit because his store sold more Etch-A-Sketches that season than any other department store in their chain.

## Cliff Diving

My new friend Gary's older brother, Harry, was old enough to drive. Sunday afternoon was always fun to get away from the restrictions of home and hang out at the river, a basketball court, or any place we could find to hang. Gary told me about a great swimming hole nearby, so he convinced his brother to take us for a swim after church one Sunday. We found about a dozen teens already swimming and a lone fisherman in a small John boat fishing a short distance away.

We saw the other kids jumping off a rock, and it looked like fun, so we followed suit. A short time later Gary asked me if I had seen his brother, and I replied that I hadn't seen him recently. It never occurred to us that Harry might have drowned. We just figured he had gone off to answer the call of Mother Nature. About that time we heard what could have been the Ape Man yelling, followed by a huge splash about fifteen feet from the jumping rock. Harry had jumped from an outcropping of rock about twenty feet up a cliff.

The climb to the top was not particularly easy, but Gary, Harry, and I, along with three other knuckleheaded swimmers made several jumps that day. As the summer progressed, it got to be a tradition to go to the swimming hole every Sunday afternoon, and by summer's end, we had a regular armada of boats and spectators watching us make the jump. We had taken a leap of faith, not because hitting the water was dangerous, but because no one had bothered to make sure there wasn't any type impediment under the water.

# Spelunking San Souci

Not far from the swimming hole we found another new playground. Harry had been telling me and Gary about how much fun and excitement we could have at San Souci Cave, so one Saturday we all decided it was time for a little spelunking adventure. The entrance to the cave looked a little like an orchestra shell, except instead of seeing chairs and music stands, we saw beer cans and cold fire pits. It was the obvious scene of previous teenage parties.

In the very back of the shell was a small opening that led into a small tunnel. We crawled in on our stomachs and went about forty feet with the ceiling scraping our buns. It didn't take long before we came to a room that measured about ten feet wide, twenty feet long and twelve feet tall. There were no cave paintings, no bones, and no signs of ancient life, just a single tennis shoe. It wasn't the treasure trove I pictured, but for fun, we would later speculate if the shoe was brought in by an animal, washed in with a flood or left by a panicking teenager.

Cave crawling was indeed turning out to be fun and exciting. There were two additional tunnels that led out of the room; one was about two feet off the floor. We crawled into this new tunnel which was slightly larger than the first one, and after we crawled about ten or fifteen feet in it abruptly turned upward. We climbed about twenty feet up the shaft before we reached an opening in the ground. The opening was barely large enough for us to climb out, but we squeezed out and looked down at the hole. Because of plant life, the hole was barely recognizable as a hole, and we were quite surprised that we hadn't seen bones of animals that died after falling in.

Being experienced cave crawlers by now, we walked down a hill and back around to the orchestra shell and crawled back to the room. My courage was now elevated, so this time I volunteered to lead the way from the room into the second new tunnel. With anticipation of discovering something like the Dead Sea Scrolls, I wormed through the small tunnel which soon started getting smaller and tighter. It had a slight slope downward and then a slot or slit that required me to turn on my side to pass through.

I got through the slot then back on my stomach, and I hadn't moved forward more than five feet when my shoulders touched each side of the tunnel, and my back touched the top. I couldn't go any farther. That was okay with me because I was starting to get spooked and claustrophobic. I tried to slither backward but immediately realized I couldn't. I wasn't able to push backward with my hands or pull with my feet, I was stuck. Swamped in panic, I screamed out for help. Harry, who was directly behind me on the other side of the slot yelled back that he didn't think he could get though the slot because he was too big. Even if he had been able to get through, there wasn't enough room for him on my side of the slot. The harder I wiggled, the more I could feel the walls of the tunnel, and the more I panicked. In my panic I accidentally turned off my flashlight. In the pitch darkness I started to see a troubling image. For a lack of anything else to call it, it was like an apparition. It was something that I thought I had seen before, but I wasn't exactly sure what it was. It wasn't like I wasn't frightened enough from being stuck, now I was hysterical. I sure wanted to bawl, but for some strange reason, I was too afraid to cry. Trembling and praying, I began to hyperventilate. Knowing that I had to get my situation under control, I took a deep breath to get my breathing regulated. When I did, I realized that my flashlight was simply turned off. When I turned it back on the apparition was gone.

I found a sudden calm that gave me a moment to think. I reasoned that I didn't have to go backward at the speed that I had come in, and if I could simply jiggle backward one half inch at a time I would be able to get out. It seemed to take an eternity, but I was finally able to free myself and get back the five feet to the slot. Moving backward proved much harder than going forward. With no room to turn around, my flashlight was useless except to keep the so called apparition at bay. It was 100% by feel, and that wasn't easy. Maneuvering through the slot backward took about five times longer than it did going forward, and it was difficult not to revert back to panicking. Eventually reaching the room was a blessing, and I wasted no time sliding through the original tunnel out to the orchestra shell.

Something happened to me in that cave that would haunt me for years. I knew one day I would have to face that image again, and I thought it was a curse. Harry, Gary and I would often reminisce about our courageous adventure over the next couple of years. They both knew that I had become frightened when I got stuck, but I never told them about my biggest fear. Thankfully the subject of returning to San Souci never came up.

## Bulls Eye

Halloween was as much fun for me as any other holiday, but trick-or-treating had some type of magic flair. We didn't have money to buy costumes when I was little, so Mom always got out her sewing machine and created costumes that I thought were better than store bought.

As I got older, it wasn't hard to give up the treats, but it was hard to give up the tricking. It was a warm dry evening on October 31, 1965, as I rode in the back of a pickup truck with three other teenagers. We had a wash tub filled with water balloons, and we knew this night was going to be special. As we slowly drove through residential areas, it was fun to toss water balloons toward kids that were trick-or-treating. We were certainly mischievous, but at the same time we didn't want to be cruel. It was our goal to land the balloons close to the kids but not so close that we soaked them with water. We pulled out of one subdivision onto the highway heading for another subdivision when one of the teens said, "Watch this," and then lobbed a water balloon at a passing car. I think he was aiming for the windshield, but he waited too late to launch, and the balloon hit the car's rear fender. The driver may not have even known he had been hit.

We were about to turn into another subdivision when I spotted another set of headlights coming our way. With a windup similar to a major league baseball pitcher, I waited until the headlights were right on top of us, then I threw a fast pitch balloon directly into the center windshield of the car. It was a special night all right, as the car passed, I saw a reflective emblem on the side of the car, and I instantly knew I had assaulted a police car.

I dropped to the floor of the truck bed thinking "Out of sight, out of mind." Moments later I heard a couple of bumps of the police car siren, and our truck pulled to the side of the road. There were four boys in the back of the truck, but the officer didn't have any trouble in the darkness picking me out as the guilty party. Maybe he had seen my face, maybe he had seen my red hair, or maybe I just looked guilty, but it didn't matter anyway because I wasn't going to try to pin my crime on anyone else. It was about as up close and personal as it could get and the first of many future times that I would experience the big heart and professional demeanor of a police officer.

At the officer's direction, we popped all the balloons and headed home. In the past when I got in hot water, my dad always knew about it, but this time I was at home with my tail dragging but not my tail hurting.

## Chapter 9

## Newspapers- Verse Two

My neighbor, Gary, listened intently as I described the newspaper shower the cheerleaders gifted us in our last town. We decided together that it would be fun to reenact the stunt on Scott Allen and his mother. Scott was the leader, singer, and keyboardist in a rock 'n' roll band, and I was the drummer. Scott was very talented in more ways than one, and he worked hard to find gigs for our group. He was one of my closest friends, so I am not exactly certain why I thought it would be okay to share the same misery with him that my family received from the cheerleaders. I guess I just wanted to give him some admiration.

Gary and I shredded newspaper on and off for days and hid the grocery sacks full of shredded paper behind his living room couch. I only had my learner's license, but Dad had allowed me drive to Scott's house for band practice a couple of times because either he was busy with school business, watching sports on television, or because he already had had a nip. I didn't ask to use the car that night, but I slipped the car out, and I drove Gary to Scott's house with our grocery sacks of armament in the back seat. It didn't take but a minute to empty the sacks in Scott's yard, so we were back in the car headed home in short order. About two minutes after we got back to my house, the telephone rang. Scott's mother was on the phone and told me she discovered our loving prank, and she knew that Gary and I were the culprits. She said she found an envelope with Gary's return address in her yard. We both assumed Gary's mother found one of the grocery sacks earlier and pitched in an old envelope thinking the sacks were full of trash. It never crossed my mind, however, to wonder why Ms. Allen would call my house if she found an envelope with Gary's return address. I now think Mrs. Allen was as wise as King Solomon and out foxed Fox. I confessed.

Gary and I spent the next few days with rakes and sacks undoing what we had so daringly done. I can say emphatically that it was not near as much fun as the doing. That wasn't the last time anyone tricked me, but it was the last time I *newspapered* a yard.

## Driving Solo

Like most young people in those days, I insisted on taking my driving test the day I turned sixteen. I had studied the driver's manual from front to back and back to front, but I wasn't sure about the driving part of the test. A friend who had taken the test before me told me he failed because he couldn't parallel park. Another told me he failed because the examiner told him to turn around on a side street and he did it incorrectly. He said he drove forward onto the side street and backed out rather than backing onto the street then pull forward.

My fifteen minute wait to take my test felt like hours, but when my number was called, I hurried to Dad's Buick. The examiner got in and gave me a brief outline of what to expect. I cranked the car and pulled onto the road. I wasn't sure if the examiner could tell I was an excellent driver or if he was in a hurry to use the bathroom, but I didn't have to parallel park or turn around on a side street. As a matter of fact, all I had to do was drive around the block at twenty-five mph then I was issued my driver's license.

## Stinking Up Mom's Car

Being the loving lad that I was, I decided it was time to show more admiration to my buddy Scott. I drove my mother's 1965 Chevrolet Corvair toward Scott's house one night carrying a Cherry Bomb just for him. Driving slowly, I pushed the cigarette lighter in so it would pop out just as I got to his house. I stuck the fuse to the red hot lighter element, and the sparks started spewing. I swung the Cherry Bomb toward my open window with my left hand, but in my excitement to get the explosive out of the car, I misjudged the clearance, and my hand hit the vent window first. The Cherry bomb bounced out of my hand and across the passenger seat and landed between the seat and the door. With the car still rolling, I jumped out. A second later the Cherry Bomb exploded. I chased the car down and got it stopped just as it was about to strike a stop sign. It was full of smoke, paper debris and hopelessness for my future. I had just destroyed my mother's new car.

On the way home I came up with all types of excuses, but I didn't think any of them would fly. When I got home, I made sure the inside of the car was spotless, and I tried to make it odorless. The Cherry bomb landed between the passenger seat and the seatbelt anchor point. It blasted a hole about the size of a fist in the side of the passenger seat. I don't know if someone was looking out for me or I had dumb luck, but the hole was not visible unless the seatbelt was swiveled all the way backward.

When Dad finally sold the car, my unintentional incendiary damage had not been discovered.

# The Cornfield

In 1975, U.S. Federal Regulations were passed to limit all consumer-grade fireworks available for general sale to the public to be reduced from two hundred milligrams of pyrotechnic flash powder down to fifty milligrams. In 1966, however, M-80s were more powerful and caused a lot of property damages and bodily harm. I suppose I could have blown off my hands or worse, but I always had a fascination with fireworks. The larger the better. If one M-80 could blow up cans and things, I wondered what five or even ten M-80s would do if they worked in concert.

M-80s were made of cardboard, so they were easy to take apart and get to the flash powder. I found an empty plastic medicine bottle that I thought would be about the right size vessel to hold the flash powder from ten M-80s. I was surprised that the powder didn't completely fill the bottle, so I stuffed the remaining space with cotton. I tried hot candle wax to fuse ten fuses end to end but that proved to be a little problematic. Scotch tape, however, worked just fine. I firmly believed that a fuse that long would give me plenty of time to light, toss and safely escape to cover.

I tightly taped tiny pebbles to the outside of the medicine bottle and used a nail to poke a hole in the medicine bottle cap. After inserting the elongated fuse and wiggling it through the cotton down to the flash powder, I was ready to detonate, but where?

Foolhardy I wasn't, or so I thought. I didn't want to get hurt or to hurt anybody, but I sure wanted to see what my Little Boy could do. Timing would also be critical because I knew the explosion was going to be loud. I normally rode home from school with Dad, but in order to detonate my new bomb without his knowledge, I needed to beat him home. I picked a detonation day and rode the school bus home and beat Dad by forty-five minutes. Formulating a story why I needed to ride the bus wasn't so difficult. After all, I already knew everything by age sixteen.

I got home, and then quickly retrieved my homemade bomb, which I had carefully stored in a dark corner of Dad's metal Sears building. The thought suddenly hit me that if my device did what I hoped it would do, I would need a witness to prove it. Gary next door was the logical choice, so I knocked on his door, and he readily agreed to join in my pyrotechnical chemical research.

Behind our house was a fairly large corn field. Who would it hurt if I detonated Little Boy in the middle of nowhere? When Gary and I reached the corn field, I started having second thoughts about throwing the bomb, so I carefully placed it in the field and got ready to strike a match. I started getting cold feet, but I remembered that Gary was watching close by and there just wasn't any way I could chicken out now. I lit the match, placed it on the fuse, dropped the match box, and ran. The density of the corn stalks was not part of my calculated escape plan, and I learned that running across the rows toward Gary much harder than running down a row. I tripped and fell, and I knew my time was up. I started wishing I had thrown the bomb instead of lighting it in place. I buried my face in the dirt and put both hands over my head just as the megaton bomb exploded. The explosion was much louder than I expected, and the number of corn stalks destroyed by the flying pebbles left a clean spot large enough to park a small car.

It was not in my grand scheme that day to be a vandal, and I felt awful for destroying the corn stalks. I was already wearing a scar on my upper lip from the casing of an exploded cherry bomb I lit four years earlier, but today I would walk away unscathed. I had my witness and I had accomplished a great feat. Now I figured I would grow up to become a nuclear physicist, but there was a tiny little hiccup. I couldn't let anyone know that I was responsible for destroying part of the corn field, so I had to make Gary swear to secrecy. I threatened him with a similar bomb detonation in his bedroom if he ever spilled the beans. He never did.

## Crazy Cracker Balls

I guess I was always a little naughty, but I never thought of myself as being bad. Since the mid-1950s, I had been purchasing Cracker Balls at a variety of stores. Cracker Balls were tiny fireworks about the size of a pencil eraser that would explode with a little pop and smoke when they were thrown against a hard surface. Cracker Balls could easily be mistaken for candy by a child, so they were ultimately taken off the market because children put them in their mouths.

Cracker Balls became a very big part of my secret arsenal for fun in mid 1960s. Austin High School had a tradition of honoring the senior class by allowing them to leave the auditorium first after each assembly. I am not sure if I really wasn't in favor of the tradition, or perhaps I was just being naughty. During one assembly the lights were turned off in the auditorium, and I reached for my arsenal. I always tried to sit in a seat next to the aisle, and this day would be no different. I removed a small triangular package of the multicolored Cracker Balls from my pocket, removed the cellophane packaging and rolled all ten down the aisle. This day I was a little extra naughty, and I opened a second pack and let them join the first ten.

Lights on, seniors dismissed, and the fun began. I didn't count the pops, but I really don't think all twenty were detonated. The reactions and facial expressions of the seniors that stepped on the little balls were priceless. The laughs and giggles from underclassmen were simply icing on the cake, and I laughed until I snorted snot.

## Bringing A Knife to A Gun Fight

High school football games were always a big deal in my family. Dad played in high school and college, and I played in high school for a couple of years. As assistant-principal of the high school, it was Dad's responsibility to take the gate receipts to the bank night deposit after every home football game. One night Dad was pretty sick and not up to the Friday bank deposit, so he asked me if I would mind helping him out. Any opportunity to drive was a thrill for me, so I quickly said yes. He told me to use Mom's car, and she could ride home with him.

Before I left the stadium I pitched the bank bag in the back floorboard. Making a quick stop by my house, I ran inside leaving the car unlocked. We lived in a quiet community, and the thought of someone stealing the bank bag didn't cross my mind. Reaching inside a box hidden behind some blankets in our hall closet, I borrowed Aunt Martha Jean's derringer that Dad had gotten from Uncle Joe. I didn't have a premonition; it just felt like the thing to do. Dad didn't know that I knew about the derringer, but I accidentally found it months earlier while rummaging through the closet. I always had a penchant for going through closets, cabinets, and boxes just to see what was there, and I often found great hidden treasures and deep dark secrets. I figured that I would be able to put the derringer back without Dad ever knowing I had taken it. This move would prove to be something that would affect me for the rest of my life.

While stopped at a red traffic light about two blocks from the bank, a man jumped in the passenger side of the car. I didn't see where he came from, but I was shocked and alarmed. The nearby street light illuminated his disheveled hair and clothes, but the light came from his back which made his face harder to see. I wondered if he knew that I had a bag full of cash, but when the light reflected off a knife in his hand, I pretty much knew that he did. He must not have seen the bank bag on the back floorboard. If he had reached between the bucket seats, snatched the bank bag and then ran, I probably would not have been able to stop him. He told me he wanted the money. I thought about the derringer that I had tucked away on the floorboard between the driver's seat and the driver's door, but I was afraid to move. The red light turned green and he said again, "I want the money." His voice was scratchy and determined, and I was frightened. I eased down on the accelerator, let go of the steering wheel with my right hand and reached the bank bag. When I started bringing the bank bag forward, I used it to distract his view of my reach for the derringer. With the derringer in hand, I brought it up and across my lap then discharged a twenty-two caliber bullet into the man's left side.

He opened the door, fell out, and then ran. I was afraid to go to the bank because I didn't know where the man went, so I drove home. Dad was in the living room watching television when I slipped into the hall and re-placed the derringer in the closet. Hurrying into the living room, I relayed the incident to Dad, but I accidentally left out the part about the derringer. I guess he was so taken back by the thought of me being in danger, he didn't ask why the robber retreated without the money. He called the po-lice, and after a few minutes he put me on the phone to give a description of the suspect. From the officers response it sounded like he knew exactly who the man was and knew exactly where to find him.

Dad was upset and maybe feeling a little guilty. He and Mom both hugged me. As we talked about the incident, I thought I could see some-thing in Dad's eyes. Was it indeed guilt, or did he suspect I wasn't being honest? They both told me how thankful they were that I hadn't been hurt. Dad finally got around to asking how I got away. As I stammered while debating whether or not to spill the beans, the telephone rang and Dad answered. I could hear only one side of the conversation, but it sounded to me like he was talking to a police officer. He talked less than three minutes, and when he hung up his body language made it real clear that he knew. He stormed out of the room and returned a moment later with the derringer. After he sniffed the barrel his eyes spoke volumes. Then he said, "What in the hell is a sixteen-year-old doing with a gun?" He called Uncle Joe and fussed at him for several minutes, and I knew my turn was next. Mom was crying, so Dad consoled her for a bit then went back to his television. My turn never came.

The attempted robber was captured that night and he confessed. That worked out really well for me because I never had to face him again, and I never had to go to court. I don't know what became of the derringer, but I never touched another gun until I started my law enforcement career six years later. I've looked back on the incident many times over the years, and I always wonder how things might have turned out if Dad had made the drive to the bank. I also wondered how the man knew that I had the bank bag because it had never been transported in Mom' car.

## Chapter 10

## *Eastward Bound and Down*

*I*n 1967 Dad took a school principal job in Georgia, and after seventeen years, it was time for me to leave the beautiful state of Alabama. I am not sure if he was busy getting prepared for a new job or he finally realized I was growing up, but he sprung a surprise on me that still shocks me to this day. After we loaded up the twenty-five foot U-Haul moving truck and a trailer, he pitched me the keys to the truck. I had never driven anything larger than his 1964 Buick deuce and a quarter (224), but I figured what the hockey puck, I can do anything.

We left Decatur, Alabama, for Decatur, Georgia, and I didn't have a map. It was decades before the GPS or cellphones, and everything trucked along just fine until it didn't. I had never been in Georgia, so driving through Rome was uncharted territory. The traffic was thick, there were dozens of traffic lights, and if there was a sign that said, "Right lane must turn right," I guess I just missed it. Dad went straight, and I went wrong. I had no clue where I was, and I had no way to contact Dad. It was an awful feeling, and I feared I was never going to see my family again; I was hopelessly lost forever.

*Should I stop at a phone booth and call the police, should I call home, or should I turn around and go back to the point where we separated*, I wondered. I don't know if it was stubbornness, fear, or a rare case of brilliance, but I just kept driving. It was probably about six minutes into my predicament when I drove up to an angle intersection, and my only option was to merge with traffic. I couldn't believe my luck when I saw Dad's car just one car ahead of me. I flashed my headlights and sounded my horn in delight, but he didn't signal back. I guess he had simply taken everything in stride.

After we settled in Georgia, Dad asked me to go back to Alabama to get the metal Sears building that we left behind. The next day I was Alabama bound and proud as I could be. Upon arrival, I rented a U-Haul trailer then started taking the building apart, screw by screw. It didn't take very long for my pride to transform into painful, pitiful me. It was tedious, monotonous and painful work unscrewing a couple of hundred rusted screws using a slotted screw driver.

There must have been eight to ten screws per panel. Counting the sides and roof, there were enough panels that it took me almost a half day to disassemble. It only took one quarter of that time, however, to grow some mighty big blisters. This was years before cordless screwdrivers, and it was a task I might only wish on my worst enemy. Before the day was out, I began to think about my abhorrence for the person that invented the slotted screw.

I loaded all the panels and screws in the trailer and headed back to Georgia. Right outside of town I got behind a slow semi-trailer truck. There was too much traffic and too many driveways to pass, so I dawdled behind the truck waiting for the perfect opportunity to go around. We were approaching some small mountains, and I feared that if I didn't get around the truck soon I would be behind him for days. Easing the car to the left to check for oncoming traffic, I saw a very long straight-away and no cars in sight. I activated my turn signal and started around the truck. Dad's Buick was no slouch, so I gunned the big engine and easily zoomed around the truck like it wasn't there. When I got back in my lane I quickly noticed I hadn't done my homework very well. There actually was a car that I hadn't noticed, and it was fast approaching from the rear.

When I started around the truck I hadn't realized there was a road that made a T junction on the left, and I hadn't noticed the double yellow line. The car behind me belonged to the Alabama Highway Patrol, and the driver and I soon had a little powwow on the side of the road, but it didn't involve feasting, singing, and dancing. He gave me a bon voyage in writing, but it wasn't good wishes for my journey.

## Country Players

That summer, my family was living in an apartment in Clarkston until our builder finished our new house. One afternoon I met a man named Robert who lived next door, and we struck up a conversation which eventually got around to music. Robert told me that he and his brother had a country western band called the Country Players, and they were looking for a drummer. When I told him I was a drummer he said, "Hot damn." I told him I had experience drumming with my high school band, a symphony orchestra, and a rock 'n' roll band. I also mentioned that I previously taught private drum lessons, but I didn't know anything about country western music. He said that was hunky dory with him, and he wanted me to try out with his band.

The following Saturday night I loaded my drum set into Mom's car and met Robert at the Duluth American Legion Hall. There were a few people in the hall, and I thought that was a little odd for an audition. But what did I know about country western music? Robert's band had two guitarist, a steel guitarist, a bass guitarist, a drummer, and they claimed to play country western music.

My drums, called a trap set, were set up, and I was ready to audition, but Robert and the other musicians were in the back of the Legion Hall mingling with folks. They didn't seem to be in any hurry to get started. About ten minutes later, Robert came to the stage and told me we would get started exactly at seven. Just before seven the other musicians came to the stage and started tuning their instruments. The Legion Hall was starting to fill with people, and I was starting to fill with anxiety.

Precisely at seven, Robert nodded his head, struck a note on his guitar, and the band started playing. It was very different from the syncopated rhythm of my familiar rock 'n' roll music, but I found this simple boom-chick-chick rhythm easy to play. People started dancing, and I suddenly started realizing that my audition was going to be all night. We played song after song about falling in love, heartbreak, crying and being sorry. We took a fifteen minute break every forty-five minutes, and the last song we played before our last break was more rock than country. This really got my blood stirring, and I started double tapping my base drum, flam stroking my snare drum, whaling my hi-hat cymbals and generally getting into a groove. When the song ended, Robert grinned at me and said, "Hit it, Charlie." For the next several minutes I used every drum rudiment in my repertoire and every drum and cymbal in my trap set to play a ripping, bopping, cadenced solo that brought people to the stage to watch. When I stopped playing, I twirled both drum sticks in the air as the crowd erupted in applause. When the crowd started to quiet down, Robert walked over to his microphone and said to the crowd, "Give our new drummer, Charlie, another round of applause." I figured I had the job.

During the break, one of the ladies in the crowd walked up to me and asked me my last name. Still keyed up after my five minutes of fame, and after seventeen years of having people mispronounce my last name, I told her my last name was Fox. When we finished our last set at 11:00 p.m., the other band members welcomed me aboard and gave me pats on the back. For the next several years, in some circles, I was known as Charlie Fox. The Country Players continued to play at the Legion Hall every Saturday night for the next year until we took a gig at the Stone Mountain VFW. About a year later Robert was killed in a car accident and the band dissolved.

## New to Fast Food

The start of my senior year at a new school, Clarkston High School, was a couple weeks away, but marching band practices started early. At the first practice, I met a new friend, Jerry Hawkins, who was the drum major, and since I was a drummer, we hit it off big. Jerry introduced me to a few guys then introduced me to my first McDonalds restaurant. When we finished eating, I got up to leave, and Jerry told me we would have to police our table. When I was growing up our only fast food restaurant was Krystal, but we always got take-out. I just didn't have a concept of eating in a fast food restaurant, so I found this notion of cleaning my own table quite bizarre.

Jerry also introduced me to Burger King where he said we could get a well-balanced meal. He deduced that we satisfied the four major food groups by ordering a milkshake, fries and a whopper. The bread on the whopper satisfied grain requirements, the ketchup and pickle satisfied the need for vegetables, fries provided starch, and the hamburger patty offered protein. Then, if we topped it off with a milkshake we satisfied our dairy product needs.......voilà.

## Kicked Out

After my senior school year started, it didn't take me long to get in hot water with the band director. Jerry Hawkins showed me that we could climb the shelves in the band room closet, lift a ceiling tile and smoke a cigarette without getting caught. Looking back on it there were a lot of bad habits that Jerry taught me. During band rehearsal one day, I had a tiny device that I could put in my mouth and make whistle sounds without moving my lips. I thought it was funny as heck when I made it tweet, and the band director jerked his head trying to locate the source. I could see Jerry grin with every tweet, and naturally, that made me want to do it more. I made one tweet too many, and the band director pointed his finger in my direction and sternly shouted, "Charlie Sewell, get out."

I was very embarrassed that I had been caught and more embarrassed that I was scolded in front of the entire band. But worse was the fact that I had been suspended from a class that I needed the credits to graduate. I didn't dare tell my parents, and I had no idea what I was going to do. I could see my world crashing down. The next day during band class I sat in the woods near the school and contemplated my options. I finally concluded that I needed to apologize. When the bell rang to change classes, I waited until all the band students had left the band room, and then I went inside with my head down low. The band director accepted my apology, and I became a compliant student for the remainder of the school year.

## A Walk in My Shoes

One day I got to thinking about an old friend of mine from Hanceville, Alabama, who had a creamy yellow muscle car. He was quite dapper and a ladies' man. I remembered his saddle oxford shoes that he painted the white part the same creamy yellow as his car. The car/shoes combination was a big hit with teenagers around town.

Since I was a fairly new guy at school and it was my senior year, I decided that I needed something to help me be more popular. I went to the store to buy some creamy yellow shoe dye. The store didn't have creamy yellow dye, so I bought baby blue. I didn't own a car that I needed to match the color, so I thought the blue would accomplish the same thing. My saddle oxford shoes were dyed and dried and ready to wear to school the next day. I dropped Mom off at her school then drove two blocks to the high school. I proudly parked Mom's car in the parking lot and started up the steps to the back door of the school.

I heard someone shout, "Hey Red, your blue shoes look like shit." Without giving it a second thought I flipped a bird, and before I could reach the top step, I was so popular I could hear what sounded like a heard of buffalo charging from behind. I turned around to face a huge football player who was foaming at the mouth. "Did you shoot me a bird?" he asked. Mom and Dad always taught me to be honest, so I simply said, "Who me? Well, no." He told me that if I ever did he was going to stomp me in the ground. I never did know if anyone bought my baby blue saddle oxfords from Goodwill.

## Wildmen Wannabes

With Jerry and gang, it wasn't long before we created a pseudo-social club called the Wildmen. We did most everything as a group, but we didn't realize that when teenagers got together they were capable of doing really stupid things.

The Wildmen, Michael, Ben, Jerry, Greg, Ronnie, and I planned our first weekend adventure at Lake Lanier. I used Mom's Plymouth Belvedere to pull my 1967 model fourteen-and-a-half-foot Larson Shark ski boat. Michael Edwards took his Dad's ski boat. Dad likely allowed me to buy my boat before I owned a car so he could use it to go fishing. We loaded our provisions then launched the two boats. We were having a nice tour of the lake, but it wasn't long before we found the perfect tiny island with a perfect tiny beach where we could camp for the night. We unloaded our gear, popped a top, and promptly christened our discovery as "Wildman Island." No phone, no lights, no motor cars, not a single luxury; it was primitive indeed. It turned out to be a sporting weekend, and our favorite event was the flotation toss. The driver of a boat would get close to the beach in order for his skier to ski outside the boat's wake and try to throw up a rooster tail of water on the beach goers. The beach goers' challenge was tossing floatable seat cushions at the skier trying to knock him off his skies.

It started getting a little late in the afternoon, and Michael tied up his Dad's boat for the evening. We all had a little experience sipping on a beer or bottle of table wine, but none of us had ever sampled whiskey. One of the men in my country-western band had purchased a fifth of cheap whiskey for each of us, so we were all set. While the rest of us were still playing king of the skis, Michael and Ben pulled out their fifth of whiskey and engaged each other in a guzzling contest. Naturally, it didn't take long for the novice imbibers to get slap-happy.

The afternoon turned evening and time to think about dinner. Ronnie White had brought along a whole chicken that we put on a skewer over our camp fire. It had only been cooking about fifteen minutes when Ben stumbled too close to the fire and caused the chicken to fall into the red hot coals. Ronnie was furious. He grabbed the skewer and threw the chicken into the lake.

Greg Hathaway darted into the water and retrieved the chicken. He quickly replaced the upright sticks and put the skewered chicken back over the fire. Michael said, "All that chicken needs is a little disinfectant," and then he poured some whiskey on the ole bird. Ronnie had settled down by this time and walked over to the fire and said, "I think it just needs a little butter," and he inserted a stick of butter in the open cavity. This proved to be a flaming issue when the butter dripped in the fire. Ben said, "No, it just needs some barbecue sauce," so he did some doctoring as well. This played out over and over while we all sipped a little whiskey, told tall tales and waited for the bird to be done.

When the time came to eat, we gorged ourselves on lake chicken, green beans, potato salad, and bread. Because it was long past supper time, or perhaps it was because we had a few sips of whiskey, we all said the lake chicken was the best chicken we had ever eaten. Year after year, we would reminisce about our escapades at Lake Lanier until one day the lake chicken became a legend.

I was considered a top notch water skier because I was the only one of our group that could ski out of the water on one ski. The other guys had to get out of the water on two skis then drop one in order to slalom ski. The next morning we had fun using both boats to take turns skiing. I was a show off as well as a good skier, so I thought I would mimic a trick that I saw on television. My plan was to ski onto the beach and jump out of my ski. I was sure none of the other guys could do it, and the compliments I would get would be terrific. The boat came close to shore, so I swung wide outside the boat's wake. I let go of the ski rope, but when I neared the beach I was going much faster than I anticipated. When my ski hit the sand it was like super glue in fast motion. My ski stopped suddenly, and I sailed through the air wobbly. I hit the ground hard, rolled through our camp fire, and into a pile of canned food sitting on an old plank. I got my compliments just as I planned. Jerry said, "You did good, Charlie. That was the funniest thing I have ever seen."

The Wildmen weren't really all that wild but rather just a little imprudent at times. Lake Lanier became our favorite splashing grounds. The various roadway bridges were not very large, but they offered about a two-story drop from the top of the rails to the water. When the powerhouse gates were closed on February 1, 1956, and Lake Lanier started to fill, the water covered farm houses, fence posts, trees, cemeteries, businesses, a racetrack and more. A reasonable and prudent person would certainly scout out under the water to make sure it was safe to dive or jump, but we knew the folks that built the lake had done a fine job. After all, I had previous experience jumping into unexplored waters.

One Saturday we climbed on a bridge for a fun plunge. Greg jumped first, followed by Jerry, Ronnie, Ben, and me. Michael waited until the next round of jumps before he decided it looked okay to take the leap. It wasn't long before we had people watching from fishing boats, ski boats and houses boats. A two-story jump wasn't really that far, but we knew to be careful to hit the water correctly to avoid injury. It was exciting fun, but the swim to shore and the climb back up the hill to get back to our launching point grew tiring rather quickly. We called it a day after about forty-five minutes.

It might have been a week later that Michael stopped by the house to pick me up for an outing, and my dad walked into the kitchen and said, "I have something I want to show you." He showed us a color picture of teenagers in mid-flight wearing only blue jeans jumping from the top of a bridge at Lake Lanier. He said to me, "Is that you?" I was caught red hand-ed and redheaded, so I just shrugged my shoulders and didn't say anything. Dad didn't act angry, but I wasn't sure his eyes sent the same message. He never mentioned it again until he gave me that picture about forty-four years later, about two years before he died.

## Chevy Biscayne

Dad took over payments on my speed boat so I could buy my own car. He took me to a used car dealer, and I selected a pretty two-door, red, 1964 Chevrolet Malibu that had bucket seats, four-on-the-floor transmission, and a 327 cubic inch engine with a four-barrel carburetor. What I bought was a faded blue, four-door, 1966 Chevrolet Biscayne that had bench seats, a three-on-the-tree gear shifter and a straight six-cylinder engine. Dad said he thought the newer car was the better deal, but I think he probably thought the newer car was less of a hotrod and a safer deal. Whatever his reason, he was my dad, and I usually did what Dad said. It took me a day or two to get over not buying the sportier muscle car I wanted, but I quickly learned to love the Biscayne.

I wanted my new car to be cool like a lot of other teenagers' cars, so I decided to modify the muffler to make it sound a little deeper throated. With a ball-peen hammer, I knocked several holes in the muf-fler, and I couldn't wait to crank my car and hear the new muscle car sound. I put the key in the ignition and did a three, two, one count-down, and when it fired up it sounded not like a muscle car, but more like a Cushman scooter, or three dozen house flies in a tin can. It was awful and nothing like I envisioned. It was an expensive lesson because I had to buy a new muffler.

In another attempt to make my lean machine a mean machine, I bought a used set of five-point mag wheels. After the mags had been installed for about a week, I noticed the alignment of the wheels was a little off, and none of the five points on each wheel pointed in the same direction. To correct this obvious mistake, I jacked up the car, removed the wheels, and remounted them with each of the five points aligned with the others. A couple of days later I went to get in my car and noticed the wheels were out of alignment with each other. I was mystified at first. Then it was like someone turned on a light switch. Tires turn at different radiuses when rounding curves and going over bumps, so the wheels could never stay aligned with each other. I never told that story to my buddies, because I figured they would tease me about being a meathead.

## Crystal Lake

There was an abandoned rock quarry filled with crystal clear water a short distance into the adjoining county, or so I thought. I heard rumors that it was one hundred or more feet deep, and it was a depository for stolen cars, guns and safes. On a Friday night, I hooked up with a couple of guys to go to Crystal Lake to enjoy a few beers. We had almost a case of cold beer in the trunk of my Biscayne, and each of us had a beer in the car. I was about to turn onto the tiny dirt road that that led to the lake when I noticed a police car coming in the opposite direction. I made the turn hoping the police car would continue on, but as my luck would have it, the police car turned in behind me.

I figured I needed a distraction because I assumed the police officer was going to pull me over. I stopped and got out of my car, and the police car had no choice but to stop behind me. A DeKalb County Police Officer got out of his car and approached me, so I asked him if I could borrow a flash light. I told him I needed it so I could see how to change a blown fuse under my dash.

The officer said he would loan me a flashlight, but I needed to pull further down the road to get more out of the way. There wasn't any traffic. We were on a single lane road with grass growing in the center, and I was so nervous I didn't recognize that once again I was being hornswoggled. When I first stopped, I was in Gwinnett County, but when I drove further down the road to supposedly get out of the way, I crossed into DeKalb County and into the police officer's jurisdiction.

He spotted a beer in the back seat and knew that we weren't old enough to be in possession of alcohol. He let us go, but not before confiscating all the beer including the beer in my trunk. It wasn't until I became a police officer years later that I wondered if the officer improperly kept our beer for himself.

## A Great Teacher

Social studies was one of my favorite subjects my senior year, and my social studies teacher was my favorite teacher. Don Hill wrote a song called

"Why Do We Always Hurt the Ones We Love." Well, I didn't *love* my social studies teacher, David Ragsdale, but I did like him a lot. He was a fairly new teacher and probably not more than twenty-three years old. He was cool.

One school day, I left the lunchroom a few minutes early and took a Fudgsicle into Mr. Ragsdale's classroom. I climbed on his stool and unwrapped and strategically placed the Fudgsicle on top of a hanging florescent light fixture. Shortly thereafter, the bell rang, students entered the room and class began. Before Mr. Ragsdale sat down, the Fudgsicle started slowly dripping on the stool and spattering on the floor. When he finally noticed the melting mess he started walking toward the stool, but as he got close the entire Fudgsicle slid off the light fixture and onto the stool with a smack. The expression on his face was priceless, but I was suddenly thankful that he skipped his tradition of starting class from his stool. Several different students were suspects, but the crime was never solved until right now. A week later it was like it had never happened. I hoped Mr. Ragsdale assumed it was a student from another class, but I stopped worrying about it rather quickly.

He was being Mr. Cool one day telling us about marriage rituals in other cultures where men would slip into the hut of their future bride late at night. There was a girl in class named Laura that everyone liked to tease. She had long brown hair and this day she wore it in a ponytail. I couldn't keep my eyes off her ponytail because I had seen one just like it somewhere before, or so I thought.

Just as planned, and on cue, six of us guys simultaneously said "phew" and slid our desk away from Laura. Her desk became a tiny island in the big classroom. The entire class, even Mr. Ragsdale, giggled at the suggested notion that Laura had passed gas. She must have been a good sport because she rolled her eyes, shook her head and said, "Boys."

## Broke Two

Greg Hathaway, a charter member of the Wildmen, was one class behind me. He was helping the basketball coach with some type of project which required him to climb above the ceiling in the gymnasium. Greg misjudged his step and fell through the ceiling, landed on the gym floor, then landed in the hospital with two broken arms.

The remaining Wildmen went to the hospital the next day for a visit. We had an unremarkable conversation which probably dealt with driving, beer, girls and school. Greg interrupted the conversation with the announcement that he needed to go to the bathroom. We didn't think anything about his declaration until he held up both casted arms and said he would need some help when he finished. I am not sure which one of us bolted out of the room first, but I particularly remember everyone shouting, "Nurse."

## The Dead-End of I-285

Right after I graduated from high school, in 1968, I landed a part-time job as a full-service gas station attendant, I earned $1.65 per hour. The owner seemed to like me, and it wasn't long before he allowed me to double as a wrecker driver. The station had a contract with the local police department to handle all their towing needs. I felt really big and important and was excited to turn on the yellow rotating lights when I was called out to hook a car in the middle of the night.

One wet night I was contacted by the county police radio operator and told to meet the city police at the dead end of Interstate 285. I was there in no time, but I couldn't locate a police car or police officers. The wrecker wasn't equipped with a radio, cellphones had not been invented, and I had no way of calling the radio operator, so I went home. I had no more gotten back home than the telephone rang again. I explained to the radio operator where I had been, and she explained there was a second dead end to Interstate 285.

On arrival, I found the officers sitting in their police car which was stuck in the mud about twenty-five to thirty-five feet off the pavement. I was driving a small Holmes 440 sling wrecker with winch, and as I started to unreel the winch cable one of the officers told me to back my wrecker up to the police car and hook it up. I explained my concern about driving the wrecker in the wet red clay, but the officer wouldn't take no for an answer. "I will take responsibility," he said, so I obeyed.

Of course the wrecker got stuck just like the police car. The same officer pointed to a construction contractor's water truck on the other side of the road and told me the keys were likely inside. He told me I could use it to pull the wrecker and the police car out of the mud. I started a mild debate about getting the water truck stuck, but he was an officer of the law and he was determined to be right.

As I expected, the water truck also became stuck. The police officer then radioed for a county police car to come pick us up. I was dropped off at home, and I giggled for the longest time before I could go back to sleep. The next day, the city had to pay for a large diesel wrecker to go to the scene and winch out the water truck, the wrecker, and the police car. I guess karma struck again, huh?

## Chapter 11

## Yellow River

As an eighteen-year-old, I was very much into drag racing, girls, beer and having fun. It was a beautiful Sunday, March 2, 1969, when I attended the drag races at the Yellow River Drag Strip between Covington and Conyers, Georgia. I had no idea how dangerous it was, and I didn't realize the drag strip had little or no safety features. I stood with a couple of buddies just past the finish line drinking a Budweiser and watching the stock cars run. We were real close to the track with only a chain link fence on top of a small dirt bank separating us from the fast cars.

One of my buddies, Frank Watters, said the funny cars were starting up, and we could get a better look if we walked up to the starting line. We walked up and gazed at the dragsters, and I was particularly drawn to the "Dixie Twister" that belonged to Huston Platt. After a few minutes, Frank said we should go back to our previous spot because the funny cars would be racing soon. Walking back, we spotted a couple of guys we knew, and it was real easy to notice they each had a Budweiser in their hand. Since we were out of beer, it was the natural thing to chum up to our new best buddies. We gladly accepted when we were offered a beer, and we didn't want to be rude by accepting the gift and then walk away.

Huston Platt was staged at the starting lights along with Frank Oglesby. Their burn-outs and revved engines were electrifying. The lights, called a Christmas tree, started moving down the starting pole, and when the green light lit, the two dragsters shot down the track with a thunderous roar. At the finish line Huston deployed his parachute, it swayed from side to side, and scooped up a man who we heard later was trying to get a beer can off the track. It all happened so fast that I wasn't sure what I had seen. Huston's funny car left the track just feet down the track from me. It went up the dirt bank, through the chain link fence and into a large crowd of people in the exact same spot where I had originally been standing. I saw the funny car slam into a crowd of people. Bodies flew everywhere. A four-year-old child was killed when the dragster knocked him off his father's shoulders. The "Dixie Twister" landed back on the track, but only as a twisted metal frame. Forty people were injured that day, and eleven people were killed, including the man in the parachute who had been decapitated. Seeing a human being without a head is a gruesome spectacle and a mental image that can never go away.

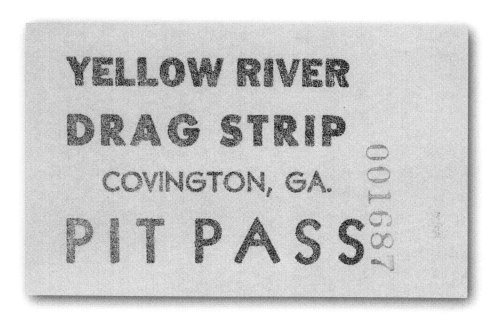

Some spectators fled while others rushed to see the mayhem. People were thick on the track. I remember very vividly the announcer on the PA system pleading, almost crying, and telling people to clear the track so the ambulances could get to the injured. I wanted to help, but people were so packed around the casualties, and I had no idea what to do, so I stood to the side shaking, and trying to make sense of what I had witnessed.

Looking down at one of the dead, I saw a fleeting image. It was an image that I had seen more than once. I realized it was an unwanted memory, a flashback of something horrible from my past, but it was distorted. It was fully preserved in my brains unconscious and it hurt, but I couldn't get it to fully materialize.

Seeing the sea of dead and injured was deeply disturbing, but I was also disturbed by what I couldn't see. Some of the dead bodies didn't look like they had ever been human, a couple looked like they were asleep. When the ambulances did arrive, it seemed to me the drivers quickly tossed the injured onto stretchers and drove off.

It was a beautiful day of sunshine that turned suddenly dark. We had a sobering and somber ride home. Over the years I have retold the story many times about how Budweiser saved my life. But I have never been able to express to anyone how much that day changed my life.

The track closed for good that awful day and ultimately became the main street for a mobile home park. I revisited the old drag strip with my daughter, Erin, a few years ago, and I could still see the actual track, and the approximate area where I stood and watched many people die instantly. That was not my first glimpse of death, and it certainly wouldn't be my last, but at that time, I believed it was one of my most difficult.

## Renewing My Driver's License

Five months later I turned nineteen, and it was time to renew my driver's license. It was relatively easy to fill out the form for my new license and write down my wrong date of birth. By writing 1948 instead of 1950, I instantly had a temporary government document that said I was twenty-one years old. I received the permanent but incorrect driver's license in the mail a short time later.

About a week later I received a letter in the mail from the state telling me there was an error on my driver's license. They instructed me to come to the Driver's License headquarters on Confederate Avenue and bring the incorrect driver's license. When I went, I was interrogated for about an hour by a Georgia State Trooper about what I had done with the incorrect driver's license. I maintained my innocence and repeatedly said that I never got the incorrect driver's license in the mail. I probably would have told the truth except I was afraid that would have gotten me in deeper trouble. Leaving with a feeling of being beat-up, I still had a driver's license that indicated I was twenty-one years old.

Before one of our weekend outings, I went into a package store to buy beer for the Wildmen since I was the only of the group that could do so. I always kept my accurate driver's license in my wallet where it was easily accessible and the inaccurate driver's license in a place that was harder to reach. I didn't want to accidentally hand over the inaccurate driver's license to a police officer in the unlikely event that I got stopped.

I am sure I didn't look twenty-one, so the clerk asked for my identification. Instinctively, I handed him the driver's license with my correct age. I immediately realized my error, I jerked the driver's license back, and I came up with the laughable statement, "Sorry, that is my brother's driver's license." The clerk then asked, "So what are you doing with your brother's driver's license?" I was surprised that the clerk didn't shoo me out of the store with all my stammering, but I eventually said, "My mother asked me to keep it because my brother had gotten in trouble." I guess I made a good liar because he sold me the beer after I produced the driver's license that indicated that I was twenty-one years old.

I took the incorrect driver's license out of my billfold only one other time. I attended a bachelor party for a friend named Lou, and of course, the party involved a little beer drinking. About ten o'clock that night we ran out of cigarettes, and Lou wanted to go to the store for more. Michael and I thought why not, we are not driving. Lou seemed to be driving fine, but after he was stopped by the police and told he had pulled up sideways on a railroad track, I guessed perhaps my judgment wasn't all that good.

Lou was arrested for driving under the influence, and it seemed like it took a long time for the police officer to complete his paperwork and for the tow truck to arrive. Michael and I needed to get rid of some beer we had consumed, so I called out to the police officer to let him know we needed a bathroom. He said, "You can go over there in the woods, but you have to go one at a time because I only have one bullet."

In hind sight, I know he was kidding, but as an almost intoxicated nineteen-year-old I wasn't taking any chances. I went first then Michael, but when he returned to our car, the officer approached us and said since we had been drinking and had gotten out of the car, we were considered publically drunk. We all three were taken to the local police department for a breath test. I am not sure if only Lou was placed in handcuffs because the officer only had one pair, or if the officer didn't consider my crime to be a big deal. The officer opened the back door of the police car when we got to the station, and he led Lou by the arm. He told me and Michael to follow. I noticed a small shrub next to the sidewalk, so I hurriedly removed my incorrect driver's license from my wallet and stuffed it in the shrub.

After taking a breath test we were all taken to the county jail. I was told that I *had* to call a parent to come and get me. I found out later that anyone could have posted my bail. It was my first and last time behind bars because there wasn't anything about that experience that I wanted to repeat. Mom came to get me, and she let me know how disappointed she was, but being my mom, she loved me unconditionally.

The following day I was agonizing about the incorrect driver's license stuffed inside the shrub. I was sure that a lawn care person or an eagle-eyed police officer would find it. The police department was housed inside city hall, and the building was occupied all day long. I still knew that somehow I had to get my hands back on the incorrect license.

I owned a 1969, Ford Mustang with a 351 Cleveland engine, and a three-on-the-floor gear shifter, and I had been in the process of teaching my girlfriend, Sally, to drive it. I figured that if I ran to the shrub and re-possessed the incorrect driver's license I could be back to my waiting car before anyone inside city hall could catch me. Sally pulled up to the curb in front of city hall, and I jumped out in a full sprint. The incorrect license was easy to grab, and I was back in my car much quicker than I had imagined. Sally revved the engine to leave, dumped the clutch too quickly and stalled the car. In her panic, she couldn't get the car to restart. *We were both now going to jail*, I thought. We played a quick game of Chinese fire drill, and I managed to get the car started and rolling before anyone came outside of city hall. It might have been possible that I wasn't even seen running to the shrub, but I wasn't taking any chances.

I found the first building I could drive behind, and we hid out for about a half hour before driving on. While in seclusion, we used Sally's nail clippers to make minced meat out of the incorrect driver's license and scattered the tiny pieces a pinch here and a pinch there. I never went for a trial, and my arrest never showed up on my driving record. It wasn't until I became a police officer years later that I learned my arrest was not legal. A few years later the public drunk law was considered unconstitutional and removed from the books.

# The Raiders

One day I answered the telephone and a man asked to speak to Charlie Fox. He said his name was Danny, he had a band called the Raiders and he was looking for a drummer. He said their drummer had quit, and he heard me play at the Stone Mountain VFW. He told me he thought I would be a good addition to his band. I wasn't listed in the telephone book as Charlie Fox, and I didn't think to ask him how he got my telephone number, I just quickly said yes.

The next Saturday night I hooked up with the band at the Loganville VFW and enjoyed a great night of what I would describe as upscale country music. The Raiders had a bass guitar player, a keyboardist, two six string guitarist, a great singer named Rick Lane and of course a drummer.

That first night we were playing a popular country tune, and Rick started singing the modified lyrics, "*We don't smoke marijuana in Muskogee, except the drummer*." At first, I thought he was just joking. Later, I wondered if he had a false impression of me because I had long hair and wore bell-bottomed jeans. Either way, I wasn't too happy about it. Over the course of a few weeks of hearing it, I slowly started to think it was funny.

We became a local favorite, and we were featured twice in the local newspaper. We even played a couple gigs in Underground Atlanta. I supplemented my income with odd jobs and stayed with the band until I landed a job with Eastern Airlines.

## Beach Bound

A year out of high school and it was time for a road trip, so the Wildmen headed out for Panama City Beach. We used walkie-talkies to communicate between cars, most of which was silly teenage babble. Jerry and I led the way in my 1969 Mustang with Michael and others following in his Dad's station wagon. About an hour into our trip, I gave Jerry a paper sack containing several packs of firecrackers. He unraveled a couple of packs and placed them in his lap on top of the sack. Using his cigarette lighter, he lit them one by one and tossed them out the window back toward the station wagon. We were having more fun than should have been legal; it probably wasn't.

Something caught my attention, and I looked toward Jerry and noticed the paper bag in his lap was on fire. About the time I shouted, Jerry threw the entire bag out of the window. The station wagon stopped, and one of the guys got out, extinguished the fire, and took possession of the firecrackers. When Michael got his first opportunity, he passed us, and Jerry and I then became the recipients of incoming firecracker explosions.

With the station wagon now in the lead, we started using the walkie-talkies in an unprecedented way to race to the beach. If other cars got between us, the station wagon would round a curve first, and Michael would radio to let me know if a car was coming. When there were no reports of incoming traffic, I would pass cars in the curve. It was very unnerving, but we were getting to the beach in record time.

We were outnumbered two to one, but the station wagon warriors soon ran out of firecrackers and the bombardment was over, or so we thought. The station wagon was carrying all the groceries we had purchased for the week. One of the guys climbed into the rear of the vehicle and ripped off a large piece of a brown paper grocery bag and shoved it in his mouth. It almost had to gag him because the size of that spit ball when it hit my windshield was so large that Jerry had a hard time seeing. It was an all-out onslaught with spit balls coming one after the other. They had the perfect attack wagon because the rear glass rolled down into the rear door. When the paper bags were used up, they opened a five pound bag of sugar and started slinging the contents. Jerry said they needed to stop before they used up all of our food. He keyed up our walkie-talkie and called for a truce. Thankfully, they agreed.

The trip was a lot of fun and the time passed quickly. As typical tourists, we stopped for pictures at the State of Florida welcome sign. I had never seen moss hanging in trees, so this sight was helping make my first Wildman road trip mystical. The city limits sign for Panama City Beach was a welcome sight, and it seemed like seconds before we were pulling up to our cottage.

Budweiser Brewery employees were on strike when we left Atlanta, so we brought along another brand of beer, a brand that we didn't like as well.

With our dreams bigger than reality, each of us had prepared for marathon beer drinking by purchasing a plastic juice pitcher and decorating it with our Wildman nicknames- Fox, Snake, Worm, Walrus, and Little O. We probably should have been nicknamed Larry, Curly, Moe, Shemp, and Curly Joe. We found out that we had overrated our ability to drink beer because a sixteen ounce beer didn't come anywhere close to filling up a juice pitcher.

The back bedroom in our cottage had a double bed, a full size kitchen table and two benches. We were drinking beer and telling tall tales when Jerry noticed a Budweiser delivery truck drive by the cottage. I suppose it was in childish celebration for the end of the company's strike, but Jerry said, "I am going to get drunk on my ass." Michael replied, "Yes, you are," and reached for the back of Jerry's belt and poured the remaining contents of his beer laden juice pitcher down Jerry's pants.

This started a hilarious beer brouhaha. I was propped up against the headboard of the bed watching my goofball buddies shaking beer after beer then pulling pop top tabs to spew beer in each other's hair, face, clothing, and all over the room. I watched with delight, but kept my mouth closed. Suddenly, someone shouted out, "Charlie doesn't have any beer." Like mechanical clockwork, the entire group descended on me, soaking me and the bed with beer. Our bragging about consuming mass quantities of beer turned out to be more like consuming mass quantities of imagination because we learned that we were quite light-weight imbibers.

A couple of fun days at the beach passed, and since I was a fair complexioned redhead, I only stayed in the sun for short periods. Jerry made a chain out of the used pop-top beer tabs and strung it across the front bedroom. The Wildmen left for the beach one afternoon and I decided to take a nap. About the time I snoozed off, I thought I was dreaming about rain, but when I fully woke up I realized someone was squirting water on me. I jumped up just in time for an eye-level firecracker to explode. That, of course, made me mad. Jerry had removed the filter from a cigarette then stuffed the fuse of a firecracker inside the tobacco, lit the other end and hung it in the pop top chain. I can only guess that he sat and giggled for a few minutes with his squirt gun until the cigarette burned down enough to light the fuse. Jerry ran out the front door with me in hot pursuit. I wasn't able to catch him, but I knew that I would be able to pay him back someday.

Jerry taught me many useless things, like how to put a lit cigarette in my mouth backwards. Once, he showed me how to make a grilled cheese and pineapple sandwich using aluminum foil, an iron and ironing board. He didn't hesitate to implicate me when he got caught the year before with hard apple cider in his high school locker, and he denied being the owner when I got caught at school with his switch blade. Jerry was the only person I ever knew that could put the butt of a beer can in his mouth. He was also the only person I ever knew that wanted to. There were many good and bad things I learned from Jerry, but one great thing I did learn from him was friendship.

## The Mildmen

Ronnie died in Vietnam, and Jerry died from cancer a few years ago. For the remaining Wildmen, a better name for the group today would have to be the Mildmen, even though back in the day, we really weren't wild. We still get together every few years, but communicate more frequently through e-mail.

## Swallowed By A Shark

A friend named Matt Millirons wanted a scuba diving partner, so he decided to teach me that skill. We went to Lake Lanier for my first dive, and I knew it was going to be great. I was using Matt's spare diving tank along with my personal and official handy dandy Lloyd Bridges diving knife and a genuine monogramed Jacques Cousteau diving mask. Matt had been talking about diving for days, and I was ready for the plunge. With the air tank turned on and the regulator in my mouth, I slipped from the boat into the water. I immediately thought I had jumped into a barrel of coffee. It was so dark that I couldn't see my hand in front of my mask. Thankfully, we were only in a few feet of water, so my head broke the surface when I stood up. I am certain that if we had been in deeper water I would still be there today.

Matt admitted that the lake was not the best place for diving, and he said for our next dive we should go to the ocean where the water was clearer. The next month we were off to Panama City Beach with Matt's sixteen foot runabout in tow. Our first day at sea found us anchored at the jetties. Matt was a spear fisherman, and he knew that selling fresh grouper locally would help offset the cost of the trip. I slipped into the ocean and went about fifteen or twenty feet straight to the bottom. It took a few moments to get accustomed to breathing through the regulator because I thought I had to suck the compressed air hard rather than breathe normally. Once I got the hang of it I was able to enjoy the great view. Large and small fish were everywhere, and I was finding scuba diving delightful.

There wasn't anything but sand on the ocean floor where we anchored, and I noticed the anchor was moving. I knew if the anchor was moving the boat was too, and if the boat slammed into the jetties, it would receive significant damage. Matt was holding his spear gun and intently looking for fish. I knew that I needed to tell him about the boat, so I headed in his direction. To get his attention, I grabbed him around his ankle. With a sudden jerk Matt turned around with his spear gun in my face. In an instant I could see the expression through his mask change from fear to anger. He reached and unbuckled my weight belt and pulled off my mask. I bobbed toward the surface.

I am not sure I had ever had a lecture from a buddy like the one I got from Matt. In his spitting rage, he said he thought his foot had been swallowed by a shark. He told me if I needed to get his attention in the future, I should take out my diving knife and rapidly tap my air tank. That proved not to be a problem in the future because I never went scuba diving again.

## Chapter 12

# Another Tragedy

It was my first date with Sharon. She had just started her second year of nursing school. We were on I-285 in May of 1970, heading to Alfie's Fish and Chips in Forest Park when we came upon stopped traffic. A few people were getting out of their cars and walking toward Moreland Avenue, but the weather was nasty, so we stayed put. We sat in my car for a while chatting and listening to music on the radio. We thought there must be a car crash ahead, and our curiosity got the best of us, so we changed radio station to see if we could get some news. About the time traffic started to creep, we heard on the radio that an airplane had crashed just ahead of us on I-285. I had to drive onto the right emergency lane to get around a couple of driverless cars, but we inched along until we started seeing the aftermath of what happened.

We exited onto Moreland Avenue, but we couldn't turn to go to Alfie's because a portion of the airplane was crossways on the bridge over the interstate. I saw an ambulance on the interstate and pointed it out to Sharon telling her it made me think about an incident at the Yellow River Drag Strip. She said they had been talking about ambulances in school, and she wondered if what we were seeing wasn't a converted hearse. According to Sharon, in 1966, the Federal Government started establishing minimum standards for ambulances, but only a few had attendants with Red Cross first aid training and basic first aid equipment. She said funeral homes had been providing emergency ambulance service in our area for a long time, and she wasn't sure if these ambulances met the minimum standards.

We found out later that the airplane was a chartered twin-engine Martin 404, with thirty-four people on board. It lost power shortly after taking off from Peachtree-DeKalb Airport then crashed. The airplane clipped one car, but landed on top of another car killing a family of four and a neighbor's child. One wing of the airplane and the tail section was sheared off, and it landed under the interstate bridge. A female passenger riding in the tail section was killed, and thirty people in the main section were injured.

The next day, I overhead a couple of guys talking about the crash. One theorized that the driver of the second car saw the airplane coming down, and his natural instinct was to stop, so he applied his brakes. "If he had used his accelerator he could have gotten past the airplane before it hit the ground," he said. I spoke up and told him he could speculate all he wanted, but what we should be doing is praying for the families who lost loved ones. I think that perturbed him just a scooch.

## Straddled

On our second date, Sharon and I were following a motorcycle down a winding road approaching a sharp curve. When I started slowly braking, Sharon pointed out that it didn't look like the motorcycle was slowing down. The motorcycle entered the curve, and it looked like the rider was leaning into the curve hard, but the motorcycle left the roadway and flipped sending the driver sailing through the air. The event could not have been scripted more graphically by a screen writer, but it looked like the rider straddled a telephone pole about six feet up then fell to the ground. I pulled to the side of the road to render aid, and when I ran up to check on the rider, it was clear that he didn't actually straddle the pole. He had apparently rammed his right foot into the pole first. His blue jeans were ripped, and the bone in his right leg was sticking through his skin in two places. His helmet had been knocked from his head, but I didn't see any head trauma.

He appeared to be unconscious, and I didn't know what to do. I knelt by him and said, "Hey buddy." He partially opened his eyes which startled me. I thought his eyes were as deep blue as any I had ever seen. I felt rather peculiar, but I could not help starting at this man's eyes. It was as thought I had seen them before, but I knew that wasn't the case.

His breathing was raspy, he couldn't talk, and I started babbling. I told him not to worry because he was going to be okay, but I had no clue if I was correct. I told him the ambulance would be here in a second, but I had no idea if anyone had even called. The more I thought about his crushed body, the more I started remembering scenes from the Yellow River Drag Strip from two years earlier. Then I remembered the fleeting image that had that never fully materialized. I knew I was mentally disconnected with something traumatic from my past, but I didn't think it was Billy's brother, Aunt Martha Jean, Carolyn Massey or the Yellow River tragedies themselves. I started to tremble. But today wasn't going to be the day of revelation, a dark cloud still hovered, and I had to think about something else. My mind drifted toward Sharon, and I wished she was alongside me helping. I assumed that since she was studying to be a nurse, she would be better equipped to handle the situation, but I noticed she was still sitting in my car.

Time moved slowly, and I continued to babble until an ambulance finally arrived. As the ambulance driver approached, the man's eyes closed, and his breathing became shallow. There was no triage, no IV, no oxygen, just a rush bam thank you man, and he was on a stretcher. The ambulance sped away with a tiny red light turning on the roof, and I began to think they had just put a small bandage on a gushing wound.

When I returned to my car, I asked Sharon why she hadn't come out to help me, and her only comment was that it looked nasty. That made me question her affinity for being a nurse, and then I began to question my affinity for dating her. I have no idea what happened to the motorcyclist, and I have no idea what happened to Sharon.

## Chapter 13

# What Goes Up

Danny, of the Raiders, was also a flight instructor. He told me that he wouldn't charge me for flying lessons if I would pay for an airplane rental. He said that was a good way for him to record flight time. I was always anxious when we left the ground, but there was something about flying that kept me coming back. We were airborne for about thirty minutes one day in an older two-seater Cessna 170 when we heard a very loud pop. The single-engine was still running, but we didn't have enough power to stay airborne. Danny took control and told me to start looking for a suitable place to land because he didn't think we could make it back to the airport. I pointed out a large field. I suggested that was the place to land because there wasn't any traffic. He didn't like the idea but didn't say why. I tried a second time to convince him the field was the right spot, but he didn't seem to be listening. We were losing altitude, and I was losing my nerve.

Danny pointed out to the left and said, "We are going down on the interstate." From my vantage point traffic looked thick. I couldn't speak. I really wasn't thinking about dying, but it did cross my mind that we might get hurt. I knew Danny was a skilled pilot, so I just sat still. As we neared the ground, I could only guess the truck drivers and other motorists knew we were in trouble because by the time we touched down, there weren't any vehicles close behind us. The traffic in front of us was going faster than we were anyway, so they were not in our way. Danny made a perfect landing, but he must have rolled off the interstate into the deep median at the wrong angle because the nose of the airplane tipped forward. The still-spinning propeller started striking the dirt causing damage to the front of the small airplane. The rental company brought a trailer, removed the wings, and carried the airplane back to their hanger. The official investigative report said that a spark plug exploded in the engine.

The following Saturday I went back to the area to find the field where I wanted to land. I couldn't be certain, but I thought I found the correct place. As soon as I got a good look at the field, my knees got weak and I dropped to the ground. The field was covered in tree stumps, red ant mounds and barbed wire, and there wasn't anything about it that I could call level or smooth. I realized that if I had gotten my way, it might have been the last time I ever got my way. I never flew in a small airplane again.

## Two-Day Rent-A-Cop

Taking a job as an armed security guard at age twenty-one promised to be the exciting career that I had dreamed about since I was five. I was proud wearing the baby blue uniform shirt, the navy blue pants with a baby blue stripe down each side, and carrying a 32-Caliber Rossi revolver on my belt.

My first assignment was guarding a small hospital on the west side of Atlanta. Many of the employees were picketing at the hospital because of their claims of unfair labor practices. About three hours into my first day at the hospital, a fellow security guard and I were standing outside, and we waved at an approaching car. Before the car passed, a passenger in the back seat stuck a gun out of his window and opened fire. I can't exactly tell you how many rounds were fired, but I can say that we both hit the concrete sidewalk as bullets struck the bricks behind us. The car was gone before we could return fire, and the police never located the vehicle.

That afternoon I requested and received a different assignment for the following day. The next day, my shift started at 11:00 p.m. at an apartment complex under construction off of Flat Shoals Road in DeKalb County. When I arrived, a supervisor told me I could sit in the small construction office trailer and watch television as long as I walked the complex once each hour. The trailer had an office desk with a thirteen inch black and white television, and a rolling swivel chair. *This was going to be a fabulous job getting paid to watch television*, I thought. At midnight, as directed, I made my rounds through the complex. Back inside the trailer, I settled in to watch the tail end of the Johnny Carson Show. A few minutes later I detected something moving in my peripheral vision, so I jerked my head to the left, but nothing was there. Thinking it had to be my imagination, I resumed watching television. It couldn't have been more than thirty seconds later that I detected the movement again. Turning to my left, I saw the largest rat I have ever seen. It was just staring at me, it didn't move, and it had to be the size of a cat. In total disbelief and alarmed, I jumped unbalanced from the chair and the rat started running across the room. Grabbing my Rossi as I stumbled toward the door, I fired two rounds at the fleeing rodent, but I only managed to shoot two bullets into a filing cabinet. It was a cold winter night, but I spent the rest of my shift in my car. I turned in my uniform the following day.

## Plumes of Self-Rising

Just over a week later I took a job working in the distribution warehouse for a county school system. It was a great job. I started out loading trucks then quickly moved up to driving a delivery truck. It was easy to get to know the cafeteria workers at various schools because I delivered most of their staples. More importantly, I got to know the ones who were the best cooks. Lunch menus were posted weekly, and it was my daily task to determine which lunch looked the best so I could schedule my route to be there at lunch time.

I had complained twice to my supervisor about the bad brakes on my truck, and he assured me both times that he would take care of it. After the third time I complained, he told me he would take care of it that afternoon, but I needed to go ahead and make my run because several schools were running low on flour. My helper and I loaded my truck halfway to the ceiling with twenty-five pound bags of flour and started our rounds.

After several deliveries, we stopped at that day's choice of lunch rooms. We enjoyed fried chicken, green beans, mashed potatoes, gravy, and a delicious roll. After lunch we headed to another school, and as we started down a steep grade I applied the brakes to slow down, and the pedal felt spongy. There was a rough railroad crossing at the bottom of the hill, so I applied the brakes again to slow down even more, but this time the brake pedal hit the floor. The lights on the crossing arms started flashing, and of course, that started my mind flashing thoughts of hitting a train. I tried the emergency brakes, and when that didn't help, I geared down, but the truck just wasn't slowing down fast enough.

It was all happening too quickly to think clearly, but I knew instinctively that we were going to crash. My helper obviously recognized our situation because when I pulled close to the right side of the road and yelled jump, he didn't hesitate. There was a small ditch and embankment on the left side of the road and a small pond close to the railroad tracks on the right side. I thought about steering toward the pond, but I thought I had a better chance to stop by opting for the ditch. The truck was probably moving at twenty to twenty-five miles per hour when it hit the ditch, but instead of stopping, it rolled over the embankment like it was slow-jumping a ramp. As soon as I found a good spot, I jumped. The truck crashed through a wooden fence and bounced sideways into the moving train. The impact destroyed the truck and the busted flour bags sent plumes of flour into the air.

My helper and I both received minor injuries but nothing to write home about. The following day I was assigned a different truck, and my supervisor was assigned a different job. My new truck was better than his new job, but a month later I gave it up for a more lucrative career.

## Knock, Tonk, Four Eyes and A Body

Dad had a friend who was an aircraft mechanic, and he helped me land a job working on the ramp for Eastern Airlines at the Atlanta Airport. It felt like the coldest place in winter and the hottest place in summer, but working for an airline felt prestigious. I was also earning my largest salary ever.

I was assigned to a freighter crew, and every day we flagged in a few Boeing 727QC airplanes to load them with freight. The letters Q & C stood for quick change, meaning the seats could quickly be removed, and the airplane could be converted from a passenger airplane to a freighter. On the front left side of the airplane there was a huge door that opened to expose a couple of rows of passenger seats. A group of seats were bolted to a pallet, and the pallet sat on rollers attached to the floor. When a pallet of seats was unlatched from the floor, it was easy to roll the pallet out of the airplane onto a loader lifter and lowered to a waiting dolly connected to a tractor. When all the pallets of seats were removed from the airplane, the process was reversed, and we loaded Fiberglas packs full of freight. The Fiberglas packs reminded me of pointy top igloos

As I gained experience, I gained responsibility, and one of my proudest moments was when I was allowed to "wand" out my first 727QC. Wanding an airplane was also called aircraft marshalling which is visual signaling between ground personnel and the flight crew on the airplane. A ground crewman acts as an external set of eyes for the captain and directs the captain how to pull the airplane out of the gate safely.

My supervisor told me to walk under the nose of a particular airplane and plug in a headset and microphone which had direct communication with the captain. He told me to say "ground captain" and wait until the captain responded so I could make sure he was ready to leave. I was excited to be the ground captain, and I felt very important waiting to communicate with the captain of the airplane. Keying up the microphone, I said, "Ground captain," and the captain responded. He sounded a little like he was laughing when he told me he was ready to go. I wanded out my first 727QC and I felt proud. Trying not to brag, I told my supervisor about my experience, and he burst out laughing. He told me that I wasn't the ground captain, but rather the "ground," and I was supposed to say "ground to captain." It made perfect sense to me, but I wished that he had told me that earlier.

It was more fun than it was work. I got to drive tractors, loader lifters, and other motorized equipment, and it was even fun doing manual labor. The shifts, however, tended to drag a little because we only serviced about three or four airplanes each night. When an airplane arrived for us to convert it to a freighter, the actual time spent working with the airplane was called a push. Between pushes we usually gathered in the break room for a game of Knock or Tonk. I was usually a little on edge because I was told during orientation that gambling was against company rules, and I knew if I got caught, I would be fired. I never got caught, I never got fired, but I did learn how to be a better gambler.

Now that I had a classy new job with the airlines, I thought I needed a classy new pair of eyeglasses to match. I picked out a pair of eyeglasses with a thin metal rim instead of the thick plastic type I had always worn. I noticed that when my eyes moved to the side and my vision passed from the prescription lens to my peripheral vision, the large plastic frame wasn't there to remind me that I was looking outside the prescription. One evening I was walking by one of the igloo-looking freight packs with a co-worker, and I turned my eyes to my left to read a tag on the freight pack. It appeared as if the freight pack was moving. I jumped like a rabbit, barked like a dog, and my co-worker laughed like a clown. The freight pack had not moved, but when my vision changed from prescription to nonprescription, it looked like it had. I got used to the new frames, but I never got used to the ribbing about being afraid of freight packs.

Many professions have their own jargon, and some may be funny while others may be thoughtless. A cashier at the Varsity restaurant tells the cook to prepare a naked dog when a customer orders a plain hotdog. Pilots call their cockpit the flight deck, and a person speaking on a CB radio might call a police officer on a motorcycle "Evel Knievel."

It wasn't a daily event, but we did ship a corpse in a coffin from time to time. The coffin was always staged on a set of roller pins before it was rolled onto a dolly and taken to the airplane by tractor. I don't ever remember seeing any non-airline people in my work area, but there was a first for everything. During a push, my supervisor told me to load a coffin that was staged on the rollers. I didn't notice the civilian standing nearby when I yelled out, using typical jargon, for a co-worker to help me get the coffin off the meat rack. The brother of the deceased, who was accompanying the coffin, stood within ear shot of my comment. I wouldn't have hurt the man for the world, and I really felt bad about the situation. Matter not, the man told a supervisor, and I received a reprimand.

## Mr. Westbrook

It had been six years since I skipped out on my debt at the hardware store, and that was something that had bothered me since. I had gotten an early start one Saturday driving to a family reunion, and like so many other times, I thought about nice Mr. Westbrook at the hardware store. I dug out my Alabama map, changed my route to Hanceville, and drove about two hours out of my way to pay him a visit. Relieved that he was still in business, I walked in the store, and he instantly recognized me. He asked about me and my family, but he never mentioned my debt.

After a fifteen-minute visit, occasionally interrupted by a customer, I wished him well and prepared to leave. Before I turned to walk away, I handed him a $20.00 bill. I told him I was making my last installment with interest. He smiled, took the money, and handed me a $10.00 bill in return. He said he enjoyed our visit and that my bill was paid in full.

## My Fine Ride

I had a new 1973 Pontiac Sport Coupe for my everyday car, and I bought a 1960 Black Cadillac Fleetwood Sedan to play around with. It was a comfortable, sweet ride, and I decided it would be great for our weekend road trips. The young woman next door, my roommate, and I were close friends, and we enjoyed going to the mountains on weekends. Once in a while we enjoyed it so much we got home after bedtime.

I remembered how Dad filled the rear floorboards with suitcase and blankets to make a large bed in the back seat area of his car. That gave me an idea. I removed both pieces of the Cadillac's back seat and used a hack saw to remove the cross member that kept the back of the seat from being pushed into the trunk. With some wood and padding, I made the back floorboard of the car and the floor of the trunk one large bed. I had more fun piddling with the project, and I couldn't imagine that I would be able to enjoy driving it half as much. It was a project that would go on for weeks, and sometimes it would take me all weekend to get nothing done. I went to the junk yard and got a couple of really funky interior car lights off an older car and installed them in the sleeping area.

The renovations to my "Land yacht motel" was finally complete, so the next Saturday morning the three of us loaded some provisions and headed to north Georgia. As we expected might happen, we only made it half way back home by bedtime, so we stopped at a closed business and got some shuteye. The next morning when we woke up, we were all feeling great from a good night's sleep, and we headed home. I recognized that I had created a fine ride and a wonderful novelty.

The following week a friend called me to say his car had died, and he needed a way to get to work. Being the kind soul that I was, I told him he could use my novelty until he could buy another car. One week led to two, and two weeks led to three, so I called him to ask how his car search was going. He gave me a sad story about running into financial hard times, and he said he would appreciate it if I could let him use the novelty a little longer. I said yes.

My roommate and I moved into another apartment complex, but we stayed close friends with our former neighbor. Trips to the North Georgia Mountains weren't the same without my novelty, so about six weeks later, I called my friend to make another inquiry. He said it broke down right after we last talked, and he left it parked on the street in a neighborhood nearby. He apologized and said he had been meaning to call me and let me know, but he had been very busy.

After letting out a few choice words, I jumped into my Pontiac and drove to the neighborhood, but I couldn't locate the car. If thoughts could kill, my former friend's funeral would be starting at any minute. Two days and several telephone calls later, I learned that the police had impounded the car the day after it was abandoned.

I learned two valuable lessons that day. The first was to think twice before I loaned anything, and the second was to notify the post office when I move. The wrecker service said they mailed me an impound notification letter, but it was returned in the mail, and they sold my novelty fine ride at auction a month later.

## Roadshow

I was pleasantly surprised when I received a telephone call from the manager of a country western roadshow. He said the roadshow was a subsidiary of a popular weekly television show, and they needed a drummer. I was already making good money at Eastern, but he floored me when he told me he could pay me a lot more. I told the manager I would have to think about it because Eastern provided insurance and job security and he couldn't. He said he needed to know right then because he only had until the end of the week to find a drummer. My head was spinning with visions of becoming a star, but in a rare flash of good judgment I told him no.

## The Elusive Brew

My sister Gail lived in Dallas, Texas, and she invited me for a visit. Since I could fly for free, I thought it was a great idea. I was anxious to see her, and I was also anxious to get my hands on a can of Coors Beer that wasn't sold east of the Mississippi. I took a taxi from the airport for what I thought should be about a twenty to twenty-five minute ride to Gail's apartment. I was enjoying new scenery and after a while it seemed like the drive was taking longer than I had expected. I looked over to my right and spotted a building that I was certain we had already passed. Shortly, after engaging the driver in a rather warm discussion about a circular route, we arrived at her apartment. The taxi driver quoted what I owed him, and that sparked another warm debate. He ultimately settled for two thirds of the price shown on the meter.

After we visited for a while, Gail drove me to the store, so I could buy some Coors. I stayed for a couple of days, the visit was grand, and I enjoyed the Coors so much that I decided to take some home to share with my Georgia buddies. We went back to the store, and I bought two cases. I didn't think the airline would let me take two cases of beer in the cabin of the airplane, so I emptied my suitcase and loaded it with beer. Gail promised to ship my clothes, so I called a taxi and enjoyed a quick ride to the airport. When we arrived, the taxi driver picked my suitcase out of his trunk and the handle broke. Toting a large square suitcase without a handle, loaded with two cases of beer, to the baggage drop off proved to be no easy task.

Back in Georgia, I was a sensation because I had something to share that no one else had. The beer only lasted a couple of weeks because there was no shortage of guys willing to suck down a free beer.

## Temper

My entire life people poked fun at me about me being quick tempered, unpredictable, feisty, and a couple of folks even said I was a firecracker. While I admit I have my moments of sudden anger, I don't believe it has anything to do with the color of my hair.

One day I pulled into the parking lot of a convenience store and got out to go inside. A woman parked her car beside mine, and as I reached for the front door handle of the store, I heard a familiar bang. I knew instantly that the woman had hit my car with her car door. I walked over to the woman and asked, "Did you just hit my car with your car door." She said, "Yes," then opened her car door and flung it into the side of my car again. She shrugged her shoulders and walked away. I was madder than a mosquito in a mannequin factory and too stunned to react properly or timely. She entered the store, and as I fumed I exploded. I had never been a vindictive person, and I had never hit a woman, but in this case I wanted to make an exception.

She was driving a brand new expensive two-door luxury car, and it was beyond my comprehension why she didn't care about it. I thought if she didn't care about her car, or mine, then I didn't need to care about her car. Turning with my back to her driver's door, I pulled my foot forward, and then brought it back swiftly leaving a nice large dent in her door. Feeling a little better I did it again, and I left an even larger dent in her fender. I felt like a cocky jockey winning his first Kentucky Derby as I strutted to my car and drove away. Did I go on to have regrets? Yes. Did I lose sleep over it? No.

## Chapter 14

# Putting on A Different Blue

I am not certain how I landed my first position as a reserve police officer because the qualifications back in those days seem to be more about being a veteran or being big and burley. Most police officers were tall, heavy, and rough. I wasn't a veteran, I weighed 165 pounds fully dressed, but I had an advantage. I worked at Eastern Airlines with a guy who also worked as a reserve police officer. He had a lot of seniority with the airlines so he was able to get weekends off. Every Monday night when he returned to work, he told me about the fun and exciting things he did on patrol. Because I had dreamed about being a police officer since I was five, his police stories were gripping. I loved Eastern Airlines, but I really wanted to be a police officer.

At my request, he arranged for me to be interviewed by a lieutenant with the police department where he worked. The interview was rather odd because it took place in a restaurant booth. We sipped coffee, we chatted, and the entire interview took less than ten minutes. Most of that time he talked about the department, and he only asked me a couple of questions. I was really surprised when he told me he could use me as a reserve police officer. With my long curly hair and small frame I didn't look like most police officers. The next day, after I got a haircut, I stopped by the police department and picked up my uniform. Then life happened.

# Surprise, Surprise, Surprise

I took a Friday night as a vacation day from Eastern so I could enjoy my first experience as a police officer. After putting on my uniform and thirty pound gun belt, I found it awkward to walk because I didn't know what to do with my arms. The gun belt with gun, holster, handcuff case, etc. provided obstructions along my waist, and it made me feel like I needed to walk with my arms lifted from my sides. In my car and headed to the police station, I was as thrilled as I was when I got my first driver's license.

After arriving at the police station, I walked in and shook hands with the lieutenant. He introduced me to a veteran officer in his late thirties named Bobby Northcutt. Bobby was intimidating with his large size, his rough mannerism, and his crude language. He took me outside where he quickly inspected a police car, and I was surprised that the department still had a police car with red emergency lights.

Bobby told me to hop in, and no sooner than I had closed my door, we pulled onto the highway. It was almost as if Bobby was in a hurry. I couldn't believe that I was actually riding in the front seat of a police car. About a minute after we left the police station, I realized we were following a woman in a small green car. Turn by turn we followed her until she turned onto a dirt road and stopped at the dead end. Bobby stopped behind the car and got out, and then he started taking his gun belt off. The woman got out of her car and climbed in the back seat. She looked like she was in her late teens or early twenties. Something wasn't right about this because I had never seen anything like this when I watched cop shows on television. Bobby said, "Red, listen out for the radio, and I will be back shortly." I didn't know one end of a police radio from another, so I had no idea what to listen for, but I sat intently listening. Bobby also climbed in the back seat of the woman's car. I may have been one donut short of a dozen, but it didn't take a genius to see the green car rocking and know that Bobby and the young woman were doing what comes natural between a male and female. At that moment, I had a new and unrealistic view of police work.

# Through The Ditch

About a month later, I was riding with Bobby again on the night shift, and we heard on the police radio that our lieutenant was engaged in a pursuit. A fourteen-year-old boy had commandeered his mother's Mustang, and the lieutenant observed him burning rubber. When the lieutenant turned on his red emergency lights, the teenager took off at a high rate of speed. The lieutenant recognized the Mustang and the teenager because his mother worked as a radio operator for our department.

When the Mustang and pursuing police car passed us, we pulled in behind the lieutenant and followed the pursuit which was primarily in a residential area. The fourteen-year-old drove like an experienced NASCAR driver, and we weren't making any progress getting him stopped. The Mustang approached a T intersection, but instead of turning, the teenager drove straight through it and crossed a small ditch into a field. In the field was a small trail that led to the back of his mother's apartment.

I didn't see the Mustang hit the ditch, but I did see the undercarriage of the lieutenant's police car when it bounced across the ditch and into the field. As we approached the T intersection, Bobby accelerated instead of slowing down, and I braced for impact. We hit the ditch like two amusement park bumper cars hitting head on. The impact caused our red lights and siren to stop working. Bobby said to me, "Roll down your window, Red, and stick your head out and rotate it." I thought that sounded stupid as hell, but since my window was already down, and I was a rookie, I did what I was told. Bobby reached over and grabbed my inner thigh and pinched me hard which made me let out a scream like a siren. Looking back on that night, I am amazed that Bobby could think humorously at the same time he was engaged in serious police business, and I am amazed that I would do something illogical while engaged in serious police business.

The teenager made it to his apartment and abandoned the Mustang out front. He ran around the left side of the apartments toward the back.

The lieutenant ran after the teenager, and Bobby and I ran around the right side of the apartments hoping to intercept. When we reached the rear of the apartment, we found the teenager lying face down on the ground. He was running so hard in the dark that he didn't see his 400-pound neighbor until they collided. The neighbor, who had been out back having a smoke, told us it was a regular occurrence for the teenager to take the Mustang out for a drive. He also said the teenager's mother knew about his regular trips. The mother and the lieutenant had words, and the mother resigned from the police department the following day.

## Look Out for The Dog

Bobby was not a good influence on anyone, especially a green police officer like me. We arrested a man for D.U.I., and as we were transporting him to jail, in typical fashion for a drunk, he started calling us every nasty word in his vocabulary. Bobby tapped me on the leg and said, "Put both feet on the floor, Red." I had no idea why, but as soon as I did, he yelled, "Look out for the dog," and then slammed on the brakes. I don't recall if the rear seat of our police car had seatbelts, but the drunk sailed through the air and smashed his face on the mesh cage that separated the front and back seats. There was no blood, but I suspected the next day the drunk felt like he had been hit in the face with a waffle iron.

Bobby moved on to another police department, and sometime later I stopped a woman for D.U.I. Her speech was slurred, she was unsteady on her feet, but she was very sweet and complimentary. When I told her she was going to be arrested, she started a barrage of name calling and profanity that would embarrass the most hardened sailor. I placed her in handcuffs and put her in the rear of my police car. She got louder and louder, but when she started saying nasty things about Mom, I admit she pulled my string. Without a conscious thought I briefly bumped the brakes hard sending the inconsiderate bitch into the cage. She was no worse for wear, but it still made me feel bad, and it was an action that I never repeated. I am not sure which was worse, the fact that I lost my temper, or the fact that I forgot to yell, "Look out for the dog."

## The Attack

It was around ten o'clock in the morning when sirens woke me from a deep sleep. I looked out of my bedroom window and saw several police cars and an ambulance across the driveway from my apartment. Because of my badge, I had been hired to provide security for my apartment complex in exchange for rent, so I figured I needed to find out what happened.

I was dog tired because I had recently gotten off from working the midnight shift at Eastern, but I got dressed, grabbed my police badge, and headed across the driveway. An elderly woman with an amputated leg who lived alone recounted that an unknown man entered her unlocked kitchen door, grabbed a barbecue fork from her kitchen drawer, and stabbed her stub leg. She said he stabbed her in the left hand twice when she tried to defend herself from the fork. When she refused to obey his commands to undress, she said he shoved the barbecue fork through her panties into her vagina.

There were no claims of rape and her statements and answers about the entire incident didn't add up. Her kitchen was heavily spattered with blood, and it was a gruesome sight, the apparent scene of an intense struggle. I had seen a huge amount of blood like that numerous times before, but this time the sight of the blood was trying to wake up a memory. Was I unconsciously blocking a past event due to something traumatic? I distinctly remember going through an array of emotions that ranged from guilt because I had not protected the woman, concern that someone that diabolical was roaming our complex, sorry for her pain and suffering, and even a little anxiety that I would be criticized and lose my free apartment. Moreover, something from my past was still haunting me.

The woman was transported to the hospital to be treated for her injuries. The next day a detective visited her at the hospital to continue his investigation. During the detective's interview, the woman admitted that she inflicted the injuries to herself for attention because her adult children had little to do with her.

# The Chase was On

It was serious business when the bell rang in the fire house followed by a radio broadcast of a fire. The fire engine started pulling out of the bay one evening with police officers and firemen clinging to the outside rails. The police and fire departments were small, and we shared a small building. When it was firefighting time in 1973, it was an all call for everyone to pitch in.

Pulling onto the street, we could hear someone shouting for us to stop. Looking back toward the fire house, we saw a police officer running toward us waving his hands. We found out later that when the alarm sounded, he had been in the loo taking care of business. The old 1950s model fire engine wasn't very fast, and before the engine got out of first gear, the officer caught up and sprang like a gazelle toward the rear platform on the engine. The engine driver must have realized the officer was there and momentarily braked for him, but in doing so, he caused the officer to slam into the back of the engine then drop to the pavement. The motor revved as the engine resumed its run to the fire, and the officer was back in pursuit.

With much dedication and determination, the officer caught up once again and leapt toward the back of the engine. It was a one-two punch when the driver applied the brakes, and the officer smacked the back of the engine then the pavement. Again we started rolling and the sound of the officer's shoes striking the pavement was unmistakable. I assumed the driver must have noticed the officer in the large side mirror of the engine and once again hit the brakes just in time for the officer to have a close encounter of the third time with the rear of the engine. It was a remake of the Keystone Kops, Barney Fife and the Little Engine That Could all in one movie. As the engine rounded a curve, we could see the officer walking toward the fire house with his head down and his hat in his hand.

## On Impulse

A few months later the lieutenant and I, along with a couple of other officers, were sitting in a Waffle House drinking coffee. I noticed one of those triangular-shaped coffee creamers sitting on the table. Without brains or forethought, I raised my hand and smashed the creamer into the table. I am not sure if it was my luck or my dumb luck, but of the four officers at the table, the cream only spewed on the lieutenant. I jumped from the table with the lieutenant in pursuit, and I ran until he gave up. I never heard another word about it until he reminded me about it when he interviewed me for a full-time position a couple of years later. I still got the job.

## Chapter 15

## I Was Serious

Sometime around September of 1973, my brother Jim and his girl-friend, Mary, decided that they should be match makers. They invited a young woman who lived across the street from Mary to come to my apartment complex to go swimming. Pam was very attractive and smart, and we got along quite well, until I made a comment about being different from the average guy. Pam adamantly disagreed and said I was a typical hippie. I became indignant, and she stood her ground. Words flew, and I am sure I must have lost my temper. Jim quickly left with the two women.

One week went by, and the match makers were at it again. Jim called me to say that Pam was interested in me, and at the same time Mary called Pam and told her I was interested in her. *Well, if I have an admirer I need to give her a call*, I thought. The call went well, I was careful to avoid the topic of being different, and that week we enjoyed our first date.

About a month later, we were in Pam's parent's home, and I was try-ing to propose to her. Every time I tried to pop the question, her younger brother, Pat, would interrupt. He was about twelve and thought it was funny to sneak into the den and crawl directly behind the couch where we were seated. When I would catch him, he would laugh and run off. It didn't look like I was going to get the opportunity I wanted with this little brat in the way, so I devised a plan.

I had a large red multi-tool Swiss Army knife in my pocket. I really liked that knife, but I really loved Pam. The next time I caught the brat behind the couch, I offered him my knife if he promised not to return. He did leave the room, and he didn't return. I collected my nerves and finally asked her the big question. This was going to be the greatest moment of my life. I really was not expecting her to burst out laughing, and I never dreamed that she would say NO. I had lost out on my Swiss Army Knife, and I lost out on Pam. It wasn't easy to keep my emotions in check, so I ended our date early and went home.

I kept my distance for a few days, but I loved Pam more than cars, trains, and airplanes, I couldn't get her off my mind, so I gave her a call. We began to date again, and it didn't take us long to become a couple. I was still working in ramp services at Eastern Airlines as a reserve police officer. I shared with Pam that I wanted to leave Eastern and go to work full time with a different police department. She told me she loved me and would support any decision I made.

## I Got What I Asked For

In late January 1974, I landed a full-time police job in a much larger police department, and I gave up the financial security of the airline. When Dad found out that I quit my job at Eastern he was upset. He told me that when I was one years old, he took a summer job as a police officer. He said that he once tried to stop a man who was drunk, and when the man would not obey his commands to stop walking away, he shot him in the leg. He said he resigned that day. The look in his eyes clearly told me that he was disappointed, but there was something else. He went on to tell me that he knew first hand that I was giving up a lucrative career for a life of low pay, lousy working hours, and years of misery, heartbreak and ridicule. Law enforcement was already in my blood, and a locomotive could not have stopped me from fulfilling my dream of becoming a full-time police officer.

Pam and I eloped on February 2, 1974, which was three days after I was sworn in as a full-time police officer. It was also six months after I first asked her to marry me. We were married in the office of a motel owned by my former lead singer, Rick Lane, who was also a Justice of the Peace. Later that evening, we celebrated in Underground Atlanta with another couple. Six months later when I could get time off for a honeymoon, we spent a few days in Panama City Beach, Florida.

Being married took some real adjusting for me. Pam quickly informed me that the proper names for our meals were breakfast, lunch, and dinner. For twenty-four years I had always heard breakfast, dinner, and supper. She said pyjamas and I said pajamas. She said Atlanta and I said Allana. I said dawg and she said dog. She was smart as any woman I ever knew next to my Mom. She was very smart, and she was sure opinionated.

Pam was born and raised in Missouri to a chemist father and a dietician mother. She had five siblings. Her youngest brother was stuck by a car and killed in March of 1973, when he was ten years old. That was about six months before Pam and I met. She enjoyed regular political debates with her Dad, whereas my Dad and I never talked politics, and my mom took care of all the housework.

One day Pam told me we needed to talk. She said that she went to work every day just like I did, and she wanted to know where it was written that it was her responsibility to take care of all the housework. She was so smart, and I quickly learned that if we were going to stay married, I would have to learn to compromise. We became a great team, and we would go on to raise two wonderful daughters. As of this writing, we have shared over forty-two wonderful years together.

## The Bird

The state mandated training for new police officers had just been increased from two weeks of instruction to three weeks, so I knew I had gotten exceptional training. Fresh out of the police academy, and after one week of field training, it was my first day to patrol alone. In the squad room at shift change, the lieutenant gave out beat assignments and assigned each officer a police car number. I was as giddy as a newlywed on his wedding night, and I was about to champion the world. I carefully inspected my assigned police car making sure to check all the fluids, the tires, the caged compartment, the police radio, the blue emergency lights, and I think I even checked to make sure the AM radio antenna was on tight.

I adjusted the seat and mirror, fastened my seatbelt, and lifted the police radio to notify the radio operator that Officer Sewell was now on patrol. Exiting the parking lot of headquarters, I eased onto a side street driving about twenty miles per hour. Suddenly and without caution, I slammed on the brakes, put the police car in park, exited the car, and ran to the side of the road.

Staring at the police car that I abandoned in the middle of the road with the driver's door open, I thought, *What in the hell am I doing? I'm not a cop, I'm just Charlie.* The exceptional instruction at the police academy ill-prepared me for policing alone, and I thought I needed a partner to tell me what to do. I stared at the police car for a moment and thought at least I need to return it to headquarters before I quit. I got back in the police car and started back, when a man in a pickup truck passed and waved. When I got to my final turn, a woman standing on her front porch waved. *Well now*, I thought, this may not be all bad, so I decided to give it a few more minutes. A few minutes turned into a few minutes more, and then fifteen minutes passed. I settled down, started initiating the waves, and everything was going smoothly. I was starting to enjoy the benefit of working during the day, which is something I had never done as a reserve police officer.

Driving slowly in a quiet neighborhood, I saw a maroon Cadillac approaching. I had already taken my left hand off the steering wheel with anticipation of waving to the driver. As it got close, I could see the driver was a teenager, and the passenger was an elderly man. When we were about two car lengths apart, the driver threw his hand out of his window with his middle finger extended. My rage was instant, and I returned the gesture even higher. Then I said to myself, *Charlie, you are in a highly-marked police car. What the hell are you doing?* I can't swear to you that I have never lost my temper or shared my middle finger with anyone since that day, but I can attest that I never did it in uniform again. I made it through the shift and continued to work for that department for eleven months.

# Bagging The Bear

Shaking door handles at closed businesses night after night would eventually result in an officer finding one unlocked. When a door came open in an officer's hand, it was usually followed by a lump in the throat and tightening of the stomach muscles. It really didn't matter if there were any signs of forced entry; the officer would turn on a flashlight, quietly ease inside, and check for burglars.

Anytime I was dispatched to a business because of an alarm, I knew the chance of an alarm malfunction was possible, but I was always taught that no call should be considered routine. When an officer considered a call routine, it was a possibility the officer could get hurt.

It felt like another routine call when the radio operator notified me of an alarm at the local junior high school. It was protocol to send two officers to an alarm call, so the officer on an adjoining beat was also dispatched. We arrived about the same time and started the process of shaking door handles and inspecting all windows for damage. My backup officer, Larry Boyd, walked around one side of the building, and I walked around the opposite. About the time we lost sight of each other, Larry contacted me on the radio to say he found an unlocked door. It was highly likely that a teacher, custodian, or principal forgot to lock the door when they were closing school for the day, but the alarm had sounded, so we took extra precautions.

I jogged to Larry's location, we turned on our flashlights, and we entered the unlocked door. Room by room we checked for intruders, and as was customary back in the day, the officer in the back frequently looked to the rear to make sure no one was sneaking up from behind. We came to a larger hallway which we would later find out was the entrance to the school. As I turned around to check our flank, I heard a thunderous boom, and saw what looked like a bolt of lightning reflecting off the walls. I didn't know if there had been an explosion, or a vehicle had smashed through the front doors, but just to be safe, I drew my weapon.

My ears were still ringing, but I distinctly heard Larry say, "Oh shit." The school mascot was a Grisly Bear, and Larry had successfully placed one 357-magnum bullet center mass in an eight foot Papier-mâché model of their mascot. The bullet went clear through the model and out through the glass of the front door.

Larry was sent home early that night and never returned to work. Rumors had it that Larry had been fired, but most of us knew that leaving was his choice. I admit the Papier-mâché bear looked lifelike and intimidating, especially in the darkness. I always felt sorry for ole Larry. I also admit that I might have been sorrier for ole Charlie if I had been in front.

## Butts on The Road

On patrol one afternoon, I was stopped behind a car at a red traffic light. I couldn't believe my eyes when the female driver, in the car in front of me, opened her driver's door, and emptied a full ashtray of cigarette butts onto the pavement. Blue lights activated and siren bumped, I was having an intimate conversation with the butt-littering driver before the traffic light turned green.

The first thing I wanted to say was, "Are you stupid?" My second thought was, "Have you lost your mind?" What I came out with was asking her if she had a fire in her ashtray. She instantly belted out an apology saying her husband hates the cigarette smell and cigarette butts in the car, and she was about to be home. I gave her an option of picking up all the cigarette butts instead of me taking her to jail. Thankfully, she didn't know I didn't have the authority to incarcerate her for littering, and she very quickly picked up every single cigarette butt.

## Tactically Wrong

One sticky August night it was near the end of our tour of duty when my partner, Joseph, and I responded to a domestic violence call. We entered the living room of a house, and I started taking notes as the woman recounted how her husband was drunk and had slapped her, grabbed her hair, and thrown her to the ground. Joe looked down the hall and into the kitchen, but he failed to look in the living room closet just behind him. This was a move we both would soon realize was a huge tactical error.

I heard a commotion, and I lifted my eyes from my note pad. The woman's husband had jumped from the closet, he had his arm tightly around Joe's neck, and he had sliced Joe's arm with a butcher knife. We would learn later that the woman knew that her husband was in the closet, but didn't give us a clue. Joe was struggling violently to escape, but he was overpowered. I drew my weapon to shoot the husband, but I couldn't get a clear shot for fear of shooting Joe. Joe's screams were piercing. Before I could reach Joe, the husband had sliced Joe's chest. I could see fear in Joe's eyes. I knew that if I didn't do something quickly, he was going to be dead. I had never been in such a life threatening dilemma. I holstered my weapon as I jumped on Joe with all the force I could bring. This knocked him backwards, which in turn knocked the husband into the kitchen door jamb. The impact caused us all to fall, and it caused the husband to lose his grip on the butcher knife.

It became a three-way fight for life, and the woman screamed for us not to hurt her husband. Joe was able to kick the butcher knife away, and after a brief but intense struggle, we were able to put handcuffs on the assailant husband. I came out with only a small scratch on my neck, but Joe was transported to the hospital where he received thirty or more stitches. Joe took a few days off to recuperate, but ultimately decided that he wasn't cut out to be a police officer; he never returned. I learned a very valuable lesson that night about handling domestic violence calls. I learned to ask the complainant the location of the other party, if the other party is armed, and I learned where to position myself when responding to a domestic violence call.

## Two on The Floor

Several officers responded to a call where a man was threatening suicide. The first officer waited to go inside until two additional officers and I arrived. Up a staircase and into a kitchen, we were confronted by a friendly man in his late twenties. The senior officer engaged him in conversation, and everything seemed to be going well until a fifth officer, George Eubanks, entered the room. George was small in stature and served in a special unit that didn't normally answer calls for service. I'm not sure if George was a distraction, or if the man didn't like George, but the man quickly reached on top of his refrigerator and retrieved a double-edged razor blade. With both hands raised in the air, he started vertically slicing his left arm. We rushed the man and easily took him to the ground with what I am sure sounded like a clap of thunder. Then we heard another clap of thunder, but it was softer. We recovered the razor blade and I radioed for medical personnel.

When I turned around, I instantly knew the source of the second clap of thunder. George was out cold with his face on the floor. I hated it for the ole boy, but I sure was glad there was someone in the room that was more squeamish about watching flesh being cut than me.

## Ice Cream and The Baby

A reserve police officer named Ralph Whatley and I were on patrol one afternoon, and we both decided we wanted a milkshake. We stopped by an ice cream store, and Ralph stayed in the police car because we didn't have portable radios and someone needed to listen out for dispatched calls. I was paying for the milkshakes when I noticed blue lights reflecting off the stainless steel ice cream mixer.

I ran out to the police car, handed Ralph his milk shake, and asked him what type of call we had. "Signal sixty-two," he said. I acknowledged, then backed the car out of the parking space, and turned south onto the highway. As I made the turn from the parking lot, I lost my grip on my milkshake. It bounced across the radio console toward Ralph. He tried to grab it, but in the process he lost control of his too. Milkshake went all over the passenger seat, floor, radio, siren box, dash, and of course, Ralph.

In my excitement to get to the blue light call, I failed to ask Ralph the location of the call, and Ralph was so upset about the spilled milkshakes that he failed to tell me I was going in the wrong direction. After I got clarification about the location, a gas station one mile behind us, I made a one-point turnaround and sped northbound with blue lights turning, siren blaring, and milkshake running everywhere.

Seconds later, I asked Ralph what a signal sixty-two was. He replied, "A woman having a baby." My immediate thought was to turn off the blue lights and siren and slow down because I didn't know anything about "birthing babies." My second thought was about my oath of office and my responsibility. We arrived at the gas station, and the attendant met us at the street. He shouted, "She's in the back room."

I ran inside and found a woman, Karen Valentine, sitting on cases of oil cans. I was a married man, but up to that time I had never seen anything like the image that has been forever etched in my mind. Her water had broken, and much to my dismay, she was about to drop a tot. This was her fourth child, and she had a good idea what to expect; she was prepared, but I wasn't. It was a sweet sound when I heard the siren of the approaching ambulance, but it was coming too slowly to suit me. I heard Karen scream, and I looked down and realized the baby was coming faster. The baby's head was crowning, and I knelt down with the inane notion that I could keep the baby right where it was until the ambulance arrived. My heart was racing, and Karen began to scream louder. Before I had time to think, a tiny little girl slid right into my hands. I raised my head to ask Karen the question, now what? But I couldn't speak, I was immediately drawn to her deep blue eyes-- they looked so familiar. I was excited about the little baby, but I was sad. I looked around for Ralph to get me something to wrap the baby in, but he was nowhere in sight. I guessed he was still slipping on ice cream trying to get out of the police car. Just moments later, the paramedics arrived and took control.

Karen and the baby were taken to the ambulance, and I stopped by to take another look at the precious marvelous bundle. When everything looked okay with the baby, I was drawn once again to Karen and her eyes. I asked her if we had ever met, and she told me no. She also told me she was going to name her baby after me, but I never knew if she did.

Ralph and I both went home early that day because of our soiled uniforms; he rather miffed, and I rather elated. We remained friends, but he never wanted to patrol with me again. I would go on to catch two more babies in the next seven years, one of which was my own. As exciting as it was, I will always be satisfied to leave that total at three.

## Chapter 16

# Meatloaf Surprise

Pam and I were ready for our first mini-vacation, so we headed to West Virginia to visit friends. She cooked a meatloaf which was my favorite, and we made two sandwiches each for our trip. We packed our cooler and picnic basket and headed out as soon as I got off work at 7:00 a.m. Pam drove while I tried to sleep through a magnificent storm. The morning sky was black as the night, and oceans of rain made it hard to see how to drive. The windshield wipers could barely keep up with the demand as it poured, and the water pounded the car with a tumultuous din. Lightening tore through the air in huge bolts, and the thunder echoed forever then more. At times, the wind seemed to be going faster than our car, and Pam gripped the steering wheel tight and in fear. Her speed fluctuated between thirty-five and forty-five mph. There came a loud roar.

The weather slowly improved, I finished a short nap, and we turned on the car's radio. It was then that we learned that she had just driven through a tornado that damaged the Georgia Governor's Mansion. She would tell me later that the only way she could see how to stay on the road was to follow a semi-trailer truck with a large triangular yellow sign on the back of the trailer.

Pam was mentally exhausted, so I took over driving. Before we knew it, it was time to stop for lunch. We pulled into a rest stop, and I found a great parking place. Out of habit, I reached for the police radio microphone to call out of service. Pam laughed because, of course, we weren't in a police car.

We took the cooler and picnic basket out of the trunk, and selected a picnic table. Pam set out the table cloth, paper plates, plastic cutlery, and napkins, while I set out the drinks, lettuce, tomatoes and condiments. When I looked for the sandwiches, I couldn't find them, so I asked Pam to look for them because I thought she had packed them. She said to me, "You put them in the cooler, and you don't remember where they are?" We took everything out of the cooler, and surprise, the sandwiches were not there. After eating a bag of chips, a couple of pickles and two cookie, we were back on the road. When we got back to our apartment four days later, we could smell our mistake the moment we walked in. The entire apartment was filled by an awful stench, and the sandwiches were right where we left them on the living room couch.

## Another Trip

Friends of ours, Jake and Margaret, invited Pam and me to go to Gatlinburg for a nice weekend get-a-way. Money was tight back in the day, so we decided the four of us would share a motel room with two double beds. It was winter time, and the temperature was around the freezing mark. Pam decided to take a shower, and I decided to walk around the corner to the store for a load of firewood. When I got back into the motel room, Jake immediately told me he couldn't wait until I had my film developed. That sounded a little curious to me, so I asked him why. He said he was just interested in pictures, he was having a good time, and he was anxious to reminisce. I took him at his word, and I thought nothing more about it. We all had a nice weekend playing in the snow and knocking about in the mountains.

The following week, I took my film to the developer, and I picked up the prints a couple days later. I sat in my car in the parking lot slowly looking at the pictures remembering a great weekend, until I came across a picture that I didn't take. While Pam was in the shower, and I was gone to the store, Jake had dropped his pants, and his wife used my camera to snap a picture of his exposed derriere. I drove straight home and called Jake. When I told him I found his lily white gift in my stack of pictures, he busted out laughing. As a matter of fact, he continued laughing for the next two weeks every time he saw me.

Enough was enough, so I took the negative that Jake and his wife created with my camera to the film developer. A couple weeks later, Pam and I went to Jake's twenty-sixth birthday party. Words can't express the look on his face when he unwrapped our gift in front of a room full of people. He was the proud owner of a poster showing his exposed derriere. Jake wasn't laughing.

## Chapter 17

## The Saber

M y department had some very strict policies that were probably brought about because of officer abuse. The strictness and enforcement of the policies, however, created a dangerous situation for everyone. We were not allowed to leave our assigned beat, under any circumstances, without permission from a supervisor.

I was working a normally busy beat late one Friday, and I received a domestic call in reference to a man armed with an axe. My previous experience with domestic calls taught me that two officers should respond. For reasons unknown to me, I was the only officer dispatched. I arrived at the apartment complex, and before I could get to the apartment door, I could hear the bone-chilling screams of a woman. I ran to the door, turned the knob, and it opened. When I swung the door back, I could see the screaming woman on her back with a man straddling her on his knees. The man was striking the woman directly in the face, and with each blow came a large squirt of blood. I ran toward the man to knee him in the shoulder, but I missed and squarely hit him in his head. When he hit the floor I was able to roll him over to start applying handcuffs.

Before I could get my handcuffs out of the leather case on my gun belt, the woman grabbed a handful of my hair and started pulling. "Let my husband alone you bastard," she said, and things quickly turned into another three-way fight for life. The axe turned out to be a decorative saber which had fallen off the wall, and thankfully had not come into play in this setting.

I knew backup wasn't coming because of the strict departmental policies. I stood up and jerked around to get the woman off me. It was the first time I ever hit a woman, and I hit her so hard in the shoulder that she looked like a pillow being tossed across the room. The man grabbed my arm and jerked me to the floor. He struck my face with his fist, and crushed my eyeglasses into my face. I am sure the entire fight lasted less than three or four minutes, but it seemed like the time between first and twelfth grade. I had often seen movies where an iconic police hero got into a fight that lasted for ten minutes, then after a few seconds of rest, fought for another ten minutes. Ha! It was mostly a three-way wrestling match with an occasional violent slug, but I was finally able to break free and run to my car to call for help.

Two officers arrived. Both the man and the woman were taken into custody. I was covered in blood, mostly hers, so I planned to go see the desk lieutenant to get permission to go home and change uniforms. As I was leaving the scene, one of my backup officers approached me with some disheartening information. He told me that the patrol sergeant was also responding to my help call, but when he passed him on the road, he was driving way under the speed limit. Policing is a very dangerous job, and it deeply disturbed me to know my supervisor had no concerns about my safety. As a matter of fact, he never even showed up at the scene.

I went to see the desk lieutenant, but instead of asking to go home, I took my badge off my uniform shirt and placed it, along with my gun belt, on his desk. In a very angry and not so subtle way, I told him where he could put the badge. I got home that day before Pam and washed the bloody uniform so she wouldn't see it. My cut face was easy to cover up (to lie about) by explaining how easy it was to trip when chasing a burglar.

It would be more than thirty years later before I fessed-up. I turned in my remaining equipment and uniforms the following day.

It took about a month, but I landed another police job as a full-time police officer. This department was very small. I didn't enjoy the overly-relaxed atmosphere and the lack of policies, so I resigned after only four months. In May of 1975, the lieutenant, who I previously squirted with coffee creamer, hired me at the department where I started my law enforcement career as a reserve police officer.

## All Expenses Plus Music

My new police chief approached me and asked me if I wanted to take a police car to Jekyll Island for the weekend. Naturally, that intrigued me, so I asked for details. He said it was the State Jaycee Conference, and the president of our local chapter of Jaycees was running for state president. They wanted a local police car to lead a campaign parade, because that would be name recognition and good advertisement. When he told me all expenses would be paid, and I could take Pam, I was all in.

Before we left that Friday morning, the chief warned me to take very good care of the police car. He said there would be a lot of beer at the conference. The police car was equipped with a citizen band radio (CB), so I turned it on to monitor traffic. Pam had previously made it real clear that she didn't like CB radios. Today was no different. She was wearing a short sun dress, which I am sure looked a little odd for the front seat of a police car. Somewhere south of Macon, we slowly started passing a semi-trailer truck, and I noticed the driver looking down at Pam's sun dress. Before we could completely pass the rig, we heard on the CB radio, "If I had known there were police officers that looked like that, Hell, take me to jail." The next thing I heard was Pam saying, "Maybe we ought to get us one of those CBs."

When we arrived, I parked and locked the police car under a palm tree near the ocean. Pam and I joined a group of Jaycees and walked to the beach. One of the Jaycees offered me a cup of something they called Purple Jesus, which I think was a concoction of a couple types of juice and two or three types of liquor. I told him that I couldn't drink alcohol because I had the police car. He told me, "Don't worry, little buddy, the parade isn't until tomorrow." Under those circumstances, I thought it would be okay, so I accepted his offer.

After a couple of small sips of the drink, someone hollered "Parade," and my heart skipped a couple of beats. I ran up to where the police car was parked, and I was horrified when I saw that it was filled with Jaycees all waving beer cans out of the windows. I still had the keys in my pocket, and I never did find out how they got inside my locked police car. I ordered everyone out of the car, made it through the parade, and was not called upon to use the police car again.

The highlight of the conference was a dance/concert at the convention center. I was really excited to hear the original Drifters play. About half way through the night, I told Pam that I was going to play the drums. She laughed. I walked over to the stage and got the attention of one of the musicians. I told him I wanted to play the drums. He said, "Can you play drums?" and, of course, I said "Yes." Before they started their next song, I was invited to come on stage and take the drummers throne. For a long time, my claim to fame was that I played drums with the Drifters. Every time I told this story, I always got a chuckle, particularly when I include the lyrics, to the one song we played, "Play that funky music white boy."

When we got back to police headquarters, I started moving our belongings from the police car to our personal car. Along with suitcases and accessories, I removed about a dozen beer cans from under the front seat. A couple of weeks later, one of the Jaycees brought me a framed picture of my police car at the beach in front of the palm tree. When I had my own office years later, I proudly displayed the picture on my credenza. I was always thankful the picture was a little grainy, because it made the beer cans impossible to identify.

The local Jaycee president was elected State Jaycee president, and later that year, the local chapter gave me a plaque for being the *Outstanding Young Law Enforcement Officer of the Year*. It must have been a lean year.

## The "All Call" and The Volunteers

Volunteer firefighters are fantastic. They offer a very valuable service all over the country. Our volunteer firefighters, back in the day, were a force to be reckoned with, and in some cases, a force to avoid. When an all-call went out to the volunteers, any rational and prudent person knew to get off the street. With teardrop red lights on their dashboard, a few volunteers were recklessly determined to be the very first volunteer to the scene of any fire. These few always let their foot take control of their intellect and the thrust of their accelerator outmatch their brain. As a result, it was not uncommon for a volunteer firefighter to slide his car into a ditch.

During one structure fire, our full-time firefighters used new ramps to allow traffic to slowly drive over the water hose without causing damage. The ramps had a channel for the hose to nestle, so the hose could be stretched across the street. When cars drove over the ramps, the hose was protected. When the all-call was sounded, the volunteers came like pouring sand out of a bucket. Four volunteers arrived in safe fashion, but one slid into the back of the fire truck. Another volunteer was driving so fast, when he tried to drive over the ramps, the impact of his wheels caused one ramp to shoot out from under the hose like a cannon ball. The fire hose then got tangled around his rear wheels and damaged the hose. That caused the water supply to be interrupted, and the firemen had to pull out another section of hose to extinguish the fire. A few years later our fire department became a 100% fulltime fire department, and we said goodbye to some great volunteers, and a couple of whackos.

## Down With A Boom

While on patrol one afternoon, I noticed a Cadillac backing into a parking space in front of a small business. A middle-aged woman got out, opened the trunk, but looked bewildered as she stared inside. I drove over to her and asked if everything was okay. She told me she was trying to figure out how to get a motor out of her trunk. I looked inside to see a Briggs and Stratton lawnmower motor deep in the well of the trunk. I was young, I was male, I was a police officer, and I had an ego that rivaled my gallantry. "I'll get it out for you," I told her. With the weight of the motor, and the depth of the trunk, there really wasn't a good way for one person to lift it out except to bend at the waist. I snatched it hard. I didn't snatch up the motor, but I did snatch out a disc in my lower back. I hit the ground with a thud. I'm not sure who was more freaked out, me or the woman, but I couldn't get up. An ambulance arrived shortly, and I was taken to the hospital.

The emergency room doctor prescribed x-rays, then ten milligram Valium twice a day. He told me to say at home for a couple of days and to get an appointment with my regular physician. I went to see my regular physician the following day. He showed me a couple of exercises for my back and he prescribed ten milligram Valium twice a day. I told him that I already had a prescription for ten milligram Valium, and he said that I needed to do what my doctor's ordered.

I assumed that since he was a doctor, he understood what I told him. Forty milligrams of Valium the first day kept me in a mild stupor, but it did little to ease the pain. I guess the medicine took the rational out of my thinking, so on the second day I opened a beer. After a third beer, I went to sleep in bed with a cigarette in my hand. Pam put my cigarette in the ashtray and my pills in the toilet. I was angry at first, then thankful she cared.

We lived in a two-story townhome, and on the third day Pam's sister Debbie and her two-year-old son Brian came for a visit. I was still in bed upstairs, I heard a loud boom like an explosion, and I heard Pam scream. Jumping from the bed, and taking every other step down the staircase, I reached the kitchen to find an incredible sight. The upper kitchen cabinet, totally loaded with all our dishes and crystal glasses, had fallen off the wall. The upper kitchen cabinet was on the floor leaning up against the lower kitchen cabinet. This left a small triangular shaped space between the two cabinets. Pam, and our nephew Brian, were both lying in the triangular opening amidst shards of glass. Both were unhurt, not even a scratch. It was almost like the triangle was sized just for them; any smaller, and they would have been crushed. Even when I think about it today, I realize it was nothing short of a miracle.

The only pain was in my back, and our only suffering was to our nerves, so our only compensation was for the loss of our dishes. Management wrote us a check to cover our loss, and they replaced the cabinets. I went back to work two days later, but I have experienced recurring and debilitating back pain since.

## The Exorcism

"Think outside the box" is an over-used cliché that refers to novel or creative thinking. It also illustrates a required mind-set for police officers who respond to unusual calls for service. One day the radio operator dispatched me to a house I had previously been warned about the quirks of the elderly resident. When I arrived, I walked toward the front of the house, a woman threw open her front door, and she whisked past me rambling excessively. "They are here, they are here" she kept saying. She told me that a commercial airlines was dive bombing her house, and each time the airplane passed, small aliens snuck into her attic. In my short career I had already been exposed to some weird stuff, but this instantly elevated to the top of my list.

I told the woman that I was sorry, and then I quickly retreated to my police car. As I drove away, I remembered my sergeant telling me that if he had to make decisions for me, he didn't need me. I made a U-turn and went back. Still in her front yard, the woman approached my police car as I pulled into her driveway. Her eyes were mesmerizing, they were deep blue, and it was almost like I had seen them before. She continued her rant, but her eyes clearly told me she was frightened.

I told her everything would be okay, and I offered her my hand. She gently clasped her frail fingers around my hand, and gave me a very slight squeeze. When I returned the squeeze, the woman relaxed and started to hum. I am not exactly sure why, but I asked her if she felt the spirit, and she said, "Oh yes." We must have looked like four-year-olds holding hands and swinging arms in rhythm to her purring. I joined in her melody, and we both got louder and louder. At a point when I thought she seemed excited, I clenched her hand harder, stopped our arms from swinging, and she became still and silent.

It wasn't until that very moment that I knew how the event would end. I said to her, "They are gone," and I could instantly see the relief as I looked deep into her eyes. She said quietly and almost in a murmur," Yes." I have repeated this story about exorcising a house many times in my career. The account is most often received with skepticism as well as laughter. There were no rule books that gave me play-by-play instructions on how to handle every call, so sometimes I had to make things up as I went along.

The police report I gave my sergeant was stranger than fiction, but subsequent telephone calls to the woman's family provided her with the true professional help she needed.

## Chauvinism

Chauvinism was steeped in tradition in a rigid and powerful social structure in 1976, and breaking tradition seemed like fun. My female police partner loudly and vocally debunked the idea that men were superior in terms of ability and intelligence. She had a bumper sticker on the back of her personal car that said, "The best man for the job is a woman." We particularly found it fun when she drove the police car, parked in front of a business, then walked around and opened the door for me. We had lots of fun imagining the thoughts of people who could not wrap their fingers around this conflicting act of chauvinism.

We pulled this stunt over and over for a few weeks until we responded one day to a call from a woman complaining about someone shoplifting at her business. When we arrived, my partner opened my door, and I approached the complainant who was waiting for us outside. She said to me, "Oh, I didn't know they let handicapped people be police officers." I couldn't laugh, I wanted to hide, and I wanted to leave, so I did. My partner took the shoplifting report while I pouted in the police car.

## The Trick

Small town politics may not be much different from large town politics, but at the time, it was daunting to me. I was on patrol with a reserve police officer one Saturday night when we spotted what we were sure was an intoxicated driver. We executed a traffic stop on a gray truck, I quickly got out of the police car, and I opened my driver's side rear door in anticipation of arresting a drunk. Before I could reach the truck's driver's side door, the driver jumped out and told me he was going to "kick my ass. *Whoa*, I thought as I started backing away from his staggering lunges. I reached the passenger side of the police car and found that my partner had opened the rear door. I jumped in the rear caged compartment with the drunk closely following. There are times when I did things using logic, and other times, well, let's just say there were other times. Instantly sliding out the open driver's side rear door, I slammed it shut. My partner closed the door on the other side. The well-oiled suspect was enraged when he realized he had been outfoxed and confined in the rear of a police car. We led that horse to water, but he didn't get another drink! I was taught to pat-down subjects before placing them in the back of the police car. To this day, I can't tell you why I didn't follow the proper procedure.

When we removed him from the back seat to search and handcuff, I realized my quirky maneuver was ill-conceived. Nonetheless, the lesson learned was quick thinking can sometimes overmatch muscle. The drunk was charged with D.U.I., and booked into the county jail. It was right with might on a Saturday night.

The following day I received a visit from one of the city councilmen. He was a next door neighbor of the D.U.I. suspect, and he asked me to drop the charges. When I told him I couldn't do that, he told me he would have me fired if I didn't. I was only twenty-six, and I unquestionably lacked the councilman's maturity, communication skills, and political prowess. The councilman, however, lacked something that I didn't, which was an understanding of Georgia law. I wasn't sure how this would play out, but I told the councilman that if he continued with his demand, the next time I saw him would be at the district attorney's office. Dropping charges was never mentioned again.

## It Was Real

I was on patrol in the vicinity when I heard the sound of the radio operator broadcasting an armed robbery alarm at the bank that was located just inside the main entrance to the new mall. I was the closest uniformed officer, so I headed toward the call. One of our detectives just happened to be walking into the mall when the call was dispatched. He passed a man wearing a trench coat who was walking out of the mall. This looked odd because it was August, so the detective turned around, pulled out his weapon and called out to the man. We had responded to many alarms about armed robberies that turned out to be nothing, so I assumed this would be the same. I arrived just in time to see the detective in the process of placing handcuffs on the suspected robber, then remove a shotgun from under the suspect's coat.

I grabbed the police radio and announced in a very excited, and probably high pitched voice, that this was a REAL armed robbery. Generally speaking, I was always calm and collected on the radio even in emergencies. On this day, however, I must have sounded as excited as a small girl riding the Six Flags Scream Machine. Later that day, some of my fellow officers started ribbing me about my high-pitched and animated Mickey Mouse radio broadcast. Thankfully, the moniker didn't stick.

## Yet Another Threat

While I was walking through South DeKalb Mall, a man came up to me and asked me if I remembered him. I had no clue who he was, and he didn't look the least familiar. He told me I had arrested him, and, because of me, he spent a year in jail. He started reaching in his pocket and said, "I am here to pay you back." I was off-duty and unarmed, and at that point quite concerned. Looking over the guys shoulder, I spotted a DeKalb County Police Officer, so I called out, "Hey, officer." The man turned around, saw the officer, and started running.

In my mind, there was no rhyme or reason for what happened, but when the officer approached me I identified myself, and told him what had occurred. We tried to locate the man to identify him and determine his motive, but he was nowhere to be found. I never found out who he was, but it taught me a lesson about leaving home unarmed.

# The Box

In June of 1977 our radio operator would broadcast all medical calls for service to both the police and the fire department. One day I was the closest officer to a dispatched call, so I told the radio operator I would be responding. I arrived moments before the paramedics, and I soon wished that I had never arrived. A fifteen-year-old boy had been tossing his machete trying to make it stick in a large cardboard box. He would later tell me he missed the box completely, every time he threw the machete, until his last try.

What he didn't know was his twelve-year-old brother was hiding inside the box. The machete pierced the box, and then pierced the younger brother's neck. He was gurgling blood when I arrived, and I used one hand to try to stop the flow of blood. With my other hand I held his hand, and I could see sadness and fear in his eyes. I told him everything was going to be okay, but he died in my arms before the paramedics arrived.

The deaths that I witnessed at the Yellow River Drag Strip eight years earlier were horrible and traumatic enough to last a life time. Even the death of the four-year-old child from his father's shoulders tore at my heart, but I thought this twelve-year-old's death was different from any others that I had experienced. It hurt really badly. I had touched him, held him, talked to him, and then he suddenly closed his eyes and was gone. I reflected on my brief law enforcement career, and I could not remember ever seeing a dead child. Sadly, it was a peek into a window of many grim deaths to come.

## Chapter 18

## I Can Cut Down That Tree

We bought a split-level house just outside of town, and we really enjoyed our new neighbors. One day the man next door and I were talking, and he mentioned that he had a fifty foot tree that he needed to take down. He said he dreaded what he would have to pay a professional tree service. Before I thought about consequences, I said, "Ben, you don't need to pay a professional, I can take care of that for you....NO PROBLEM."

The next Saturday I took my chain saw down to Ben's, cut a notch on one side of the tree, and started sawing the other side. The tree started to fall slowly, and exactly in the direction where I planned for it to go. It was less than half way down when it started to turn. I had never cut down a large tree, but I had seen it done on television several times, and not a single one ever turned. This one was certainly going to crush Ben's house, so I started running toward the tree. I had no clue what I planned to do, catch it, I suppose. Just as the tree was about to hit the house, it stopped turning, and it landed just inches from the house. I guess the old adage is true, "God looks after fools and babies." With a sheepish grin, I turned to Ben and said, "See, I told you I could do it."

## Foxtopography

In 1978, I bought a single-lens, reflex camera, and quickly got good at taking pictures. Before I knew it, people started asking to buy some of my pictures. My success led me to start a part-time business. My business needed a name, and since I had grown up with the nickname Fox, I called my new business Foxtography. I was soon doing outdoor portraits, and that led me to shoot my first wedding.

The bride was beautiful, the music was great, the preacher was brief, and time passed rapidly. I wasn't exactly sure of the customary order of taking pictures, but I started with the bride and groom, then the bride and her parents, followed by the bride and her bridesmaids, and so on. The bride's mother was as anxious as a woman with diarrhea in gridlocked traffic. She asked me to hurry because the guest were waiting in the reception hall for the wedding party to arrive. I told her I would go as quickly as I could, but I didn't want to miss any of the wedding party.

The bride held her anxiety in check until I started taking pictures of the groom and the groomsmen. She walked up to me and said very snootily, "For God's sake, can't you hurry?" It was clear to me that the bride and her mother wanted me to shoot an hour's worth of pictures in five minutes. I finished the shoot, and we moved on to the reception. The pictures turned out great, and the newlyweds were well pleased with the lovely album I delivered.

After four more successful wedding shoots, I started wondering what I would do if by chance any wedding pictures I took didn't look good. When I was asked to shoot another wedding, I decided to get a little insurance, so I invited a friend named Joy to accompany me. Joy had a camera just like mine, and she had a little more experience with photography. The church sanctuary and the wedding party were both very large, and the service was the nicest I had seen up to that point. By this time I had gotten a little more experienced handling other people's anxiety. My organizational skills had improved, and when the service was over, we worked our way through the shoot expeditiously.

When I got the telephone call that my pictures were ready, I dropped what I was doing and drove to the film developer. When I arrived, there was a car already at the drive-up window, so I had to wait. I was very anxious about seeing the pictures, but my anxiety started turning to something different, something upsetting. I started seeing in my windshield what I thought had to be an apparition; it was a brown pony tail, but I could not see the person who wore it. The car in front of me drove off, and the image vanished. I knew an image in my windshield couldn't be real, and I couldn't make sense of it, so I pulled on up to the drive-up window.

I got my pictures, then hurriedly drove to a parking spot to inspect my work. When I opened the envelope of pictures, I became numb. Had I jinxed myself by bringing along another photographer? Most of the pictures were too dark. I couldn't believe what I was seeing. I had an earthquake in the pit of my stomach. I had taken thousands of pictures and this had never happened. I was devastated. In disbelief, I thumbed through the pictures a second time and noticed that one of the bridesmaids wore a long brown pony tail at the rehearsal dinner. I wondered if this could have been the vision that I saw in my windshield. Anxious to talk to Joy, I dismissed the thought, and hurriedly drove home.

When I got home, I immediately called Joy and told her what happened. The phone got really quiet for a few seconds, and I thought she had hung up. When she finally spoke, she sounded discouraged. With a slow soft voice she told me that most of her pictures were also dark. Then she said something that made the hair on the back of my neck stand up. "Who is she?" I thought she was asking about the brown pony tail that I saw in my windshield. But then, I realized I had never mentioned that to her. I asked her what she was talking about. She said, "The bride, what is her name." She told me she was labeling the pictures and wasn't sure she wasn't confusing the bride with her sister.

I stewed for three days, and put off calling the newlyweds. On the fourth day I got a call from the bride. She was excited, said she couldn't wait to see the pictures, and she asked me when they would be ready. With great trepidation, I told her I would drop them by the next day. When I was face to face with the young couple, I gave them back their check and some cash to cover their deposit, then the pictures. The cheerful bride opened the envelope and saw the pictures. She was obviously crushed. She started to cry, her mascara quickly flooded her cheeks, and my spirit hit rock bottom. The groom shared some words with me that lacked sophistication and good taste. I apologized profusely, then apologized again. There was nothing I could do to ease their pain, so I left.

Joy and I went back to the church the next week to see if we could determine what happened. We reflected on the previous weddings I had shot, then I mentally compared those sanctuaries to the one we were standing in. I realized the other sanctuaries were much smaller and the lighting was different. Joy pointed out that it may also have had something to do with the size of the wedding party. She said, "Our flash equipment isn't very strong, there were quite a few people in the wedding party, and we took most of the pictures from a good distance back." I had been lucky at shooting the other weddings, but I knew right then that I lacked the knowledge, and perhaps equipment, to be a professional photographer. I received other calls for photo shoots, but each time I told the caller that Foxtography was out of business.

## Trypanophobia

In 1979, when Pam was eight months pregnant with our first child, she got extremely sick. I took her to the doctor, and he put her directly in the hospital. After a few tests, he told her she had hepatitis A. He said that since she was an elementary school teacher, she probably picked the disease up at school. The next day, I was in Pam's room when her doctor came in. When he saw me, he immediately told me he was concerned about the disease being passed along to me. He wanted me to get a gamma globulin shot to temporarily boost my immunity. Since I had a needle phobia, I was less than excited to hear his words. He said I should go downstairs to the hospital lab for the injection.

When I arrived at the lab, a young woman who appeared to be about eighteen greeted me, and asked me how she could help me. I told her what the doctor had ordered, but I also told her about my phobia. I mentioned that I was a police officer, and I could handle it if someone came at me with a knife, a gun, a flame thrower, or a hand grenade, but I couldn't handle a needle. She said, "Oh, you have Trypanophobia." I had never heard the term, and I had no idea that twenty percent of the population had the same issue. I thought I was one of a few.

It was bad enough that the young technician was going to inflict extreme pain on me, now she was going to inflict extreme embarrassment on me. She told me to drop my trousers. I unbuckled my belt and unbuttoned my jeans, then lowered them a couple of inches. I was expecting some additional conversation, but she grabbed my jeans and underwear, jerked them down, swabbed my hip and let it rip. Before I knew it, I was a grinning gamma globulin survivor. Pam came home six days later, and three weeks later our beautiful five pound daughter, Jennifer Anne, was born.

## Chapter 19

# In Less Than A Year

*O*ur department had bad hiring habits that resulted in the occasional hiring of a police officer who could mess up an anvil with a rubber hammer. It seemed like we were hiring and losing officers faster than we were making arrests. One day the police car I normally drove was in the shop for repairs. I got in another police car, and after I cranked it, I noticed a piece of black electrical tape stuck on the instrument panel. Out of curiosity, I removed the tape, and saw the check engine light was on. I turned the car off, went inside the police department, and telephoned the officer who normally drove that car. He told me the light had been on for about a week, and it bothered him, so he covered it with electrical tape. I created a maintenance ticket and selected a different car. The officer resigned a couple of weeks later to work in his brother's landscape business.

We hired one officer who had experience with a large metropolitan city. Everyone seemed impressed with him because he had been in a shoot-out. It was about 2:00 a.m. one shift when he called the radio dispatcher saying he was making a traffic stop on a car without a tag. Moments later, he screamed into the radio, "Shots fired, shots fired." He gave a vague description of a brown car that he said was heading southbound, out of town, in an industrial area. What he didn't know was a county sheriff's deputy was parked on the side of the road about a mile south of his location. There were no side streets between the deputy and our officer, we were still using the county radio frequency, so the deputy was keenly aware of the situation. After several minutes, and the brown car hadn't passed the deputy, he drove northbound to our officer's location. The deputy knew our officer's claim of the brown car was fictitious, so he reported his observation to our on-duty supervisor. The dishonest officer was terminated the following day.

Our city was always borrowing money from the bank to make payroll, then paying it back a week later. Everyone knew the city was not flush with money, but no one could ever claim that the city skimped on taking care of safety issues. On another occasion, I started driving out of the police department parking lot in a police car that I didn't normally use. When I got to the end of our driveway I applied the brakes, but the brake pedal went almost to the floor, and the police car rolled into the road. I backed up, parked the car, and then went inside to telephone the officer who normally used it. He said the brakes had been that way for a while, but he was careful, and he spent most of his time sitting behind a shopping center. I created a maintenance ticket and selected a different car. The officer was terminated a short time later for sleeping on duty.

About two months later I tried to call another officer on the police radio, but he didn't answer. I was concerned that my own radio was not working, so I called our radio dispatcher. She answered quickly, which let me know my radio was working. I told her that I was trying to contact the unresponsive officer. She told me he was okay, that she had just gotten off the telephone with him, that his radio was not working. A few seconds later, another officer radioed me to say he had located the officer outside a fast food restaurant. I drove to the restaurant and spoke with the officer. He told me his radio was not working, but he planned to telephone the radio dispatcher every thirty minutes to see if there were any pending calls for service. I told him I thought it would be wise if he created a maintenance ticket and selected a different car. The officer resigned a month later to take a job as security manager at a major metropolitan hospital.

Dunderheads came in all professions, and thankfully they were rare in law enforcement. But it wasn't always a fellow police officer who gave me consternation. Our department, with the desire to save money, started using a shade tree mechanic who made repairs on police cars at his home. He was always doing things like using coat hangers to hold up mufflers, or tighten bumpers. It was not uncommon for an officer to pick up a police car after an oil change, drive it back to the police station, then find a puddle of oil on the ground because the oil drain plug or oil filter had not been tightened. Probably the strangest thing that I experienced with the mechanic was when I picked up my assigned police car after having the carburetor worked on. When I applied the brakes, the AM radio came on. Thinking this was a fluke, I reached up and turned the radio off. When I got to the stop sign at the end of his street, I applied the brakes again, and again the AM radio came on. Every time I touched the brakes, the AM radio came on, and when I released the brakes, the AM radio went off. I drove the police car straight to the police station to show the handiwork to the police chief.

A bad twelve month period came to a close, and the police management amended their ways. The police department started using a different mechanic the next day. We also drastically changed our hiring practices by including in-depth background checks, polygraph test, physicals, psychological exams, and more. The results were great.

## The Sting Operation

It was just another routine call to assist a stranded motorist, but the poetic justice that followed has given me numerous chuckles over the years. A semi-trailer truck pulling a flatbed trailer stalled on an interstate exit ramp causing traffic to become snarled. I positioned my police car behind the trailer so my blue lights would notify motorists of the traffic hazard. It was a steamy summer day, and the trailer was carrying perhaps as many as 400 beehives. The extreme heat and lack of shade caused thousands of bees to swarm around the trailer.

It was rush hour, and some motorist must have assumed I was conducting a traffic stop and was causing the traffic to back up onto the interstate. I guess I will never understand the wisdom of antagonizing a person who has a gun and the power of arrest, but a few people blew their horns, shouted foul language and raised their fists as they passed. The truck driver wasn't able to let his rig roll backwards onto the shoulder of the road, so he called a mechanic and a wrecker. The wrecker was twenty minutes away, so I asked the driver to raise the truck's hood to signify to other motorists that his truck had mechanical problems. I couldn't help but notice the windows were down on the car of a foul-mouthed driver as he passed, and seconds later I saw him fanning himself. My first giggle came when I realized he was actually swatting at bees that filled his car.

This scenario repeated itself several times before the wrecker arrived. I waited in my police car with windows rolled up and enjoyed the air conditioner and FM radio. My amusement intensified when I noticed drivers swatting at bees in rhythm with my music and moving their arms and swaying like conductors for a symphony orchestra. I felt sorry for the calm and patient drivers, and I do hope no one got seriously hurt. I also hope most people noticed the raised hood and recognized the incident for what it was. Benjamin Franklin said: "Believe none of what you hear and half of what you see."

## Lions and Tigers and Bears

The Atlanta area wasn't known for lions and tigers and bears, but we often saw squirrels, and rabbits, and raccoons, oh my. Varmint handling was not on the curriculum when I attended the police academy. I knew I might confront two-legged vermin, but I never fancied being called upon to deal with four-legged and legless critters. I usually had no clue what I was about to encounter when responding to a call for service because what a caller told my radio operator was often drastically different from what I found when I arrived..

It was amusing being dispatched to a report of a squirrel attacking a house. It was bewildering upon arrival. I assumed the caller was a whack-a-doodle, but when I got there I discovered a squirrel was repeatedly ramming a closed sliding glass door on the back of a man's house.

The only tools available for me to deal with a dangerous animal at that time was my standard issued firearm, and any tool I found in a home storage shed. Animal control would only respond to dog and cat issues, and this terrorist squirrel was clearly not intimidated by my gun, so my options were limited.

A sudden brainchild, which some might say was a brain spasm, prompted me to grab a nearby sofa cushion and open the sliding glass door. When the squirrel charged the door again, my sheer dumb luck made me feel like a professional wildlife trapper when I caught the squirrel under the cushion. I have no idea what I would have done if I had missed.

Having unexpectedly arrested the angry varmint, I had no clue what to do next. Fortunately, the homeowner had a pair of extra thick gloves that allowed us to move the now fiercely fighting squirrel into a burlap sack.

The police academy taught me how to respond to an armed robbery, but I was in shock the first time I had to deliver a baby. A call to remove a twenty-five foot python from a bathroom, however, gave me more jitters than delivering a dozen babies or facing two dozen terrorist squirrels.

At first sight of the mammoth and menacing monster curled under a small hot water heater, I considered pinning my badge to the police car seat and walking home. Luckily, a nearby pet store owner with a police scanner heard the call, and he came to my rescue. The docile and cozy reptile was actually only five feet long, but it wouldn't have mattered if it had been five inches long, I didn't do snakes.

I had a written job description that listed my typical work activities, but it wasn't possible to predict every type of incident that I had to face during a tour of duty. I encountered many crazy incidents that I had never previously handled, and it was a paradox to call my workday "routine."

## In and Out

When the fourteen-year-old boy who had previously commandeered his mother's Mustang was nearing his twentieth birthday, he got arrested by my department for D.U.I. He went to jail for a short while, and during his incarceration, he apparently had time for his anger to fester.

The police department, fire department, and city hall were all housed the same building. It had a set of tall, heavy, double glass front doors on both sides of the front wall, and our radio room was just a few feet inside the right side double doors. Around 11:00 p.m. one evening, the radio operator started screaming on the radio frequency that a white male had run through one set of double doors and out a second set of double doors. For the life of me, I couldn't imagine what the big deal was to make her so excited, but I headed to the police department post haste. Upon arrival, I realized the operator meant a white male ran *his car* through the double doors. In the middle of the lobby, just feet from the radio operator's window, I saw a dark-colored Volkswagen Beetle resting in a pile of glass under a hanging door frame.

At the far end of our parking lot, I found an empty plastic cup and liquid on the ground that smelled like alcohol. I theorized the driver dumped his cocktail, then dumped his clutch and sped toward the building. There was adequate space for the Volkswagen to drive in through one set of double doors then drive back out through the other set, but I believe the driver hadn't counted on his car getting tangled up and stuck in the heavy metal door frame. I was sure his intent was to drive the Vega in and then out of the building.

The now twenty-year-old ran out of his shoes in his escape, and I was amazed that I didn't find blood on the floor. The explosive crash through the front doors had to be tremendously loud and exceptionally shocking. The radio operator asked to be relieved to use the rest room, and I always wondered if she needed to answer the call of Mother Nature, or if Mother Nature had already paid her a visit.

I didn't know until the next day that the twenty-year-old passed out in a grassy field just a few feet from where I found his cup. He was later captured, tried and sentenced to prison where he ultimately committed suicide.

## Take Me Directly To Jail

It wasn't hard to detect an intoxicated driver, and I had little doubt about the condition of the driver that I had pulled over. He got out of his car, and was so upright and polite, I wondered if I had made a big mistake. He had a slight odor of alcohol on or about his person, so I decided to administer a field sobriety test.

I asked him if he could count to ten, and before I finished the word ten, he said, "One, two, three, four, five, six, seven, eight, nine, ten," I was really starting to question my instincts, and I asked him if he could recite the alphabet, to which he replied, "A B C D eight nine ten, hell, take me to jail." I did.

## Up Close and Personal Hands-On Training

Training was something that we received only occasionally, but when we did, we were always sitting in a classroom. Even when I attended basic training at the police academy, our defensive tactics training consisted of watching a state trooper beat the snot out of a fellow student.

No one in my department had any real hands-on training, yet we were supposed to respond in text-book fashion when we were called to handle a serious crime. When I was promoted to sergeant and assigned to the evening shift, I often provided realistic training for my officers when our call volume was slow. I invited a couple of off-duty officers to join us one evening because we needed role players to help stage a mock armed robbery. I selected a local motel as the setting, primarily because I had a good relationship with the night manager. As I had instructed, the two role players entered the motel lobby with guns drawn. Unfortunately, I hadn't considered that they would be clearly visible from the street through the large plate glass windows on three sides of the lobby.

We had previously practiced responding to burglaries, traffic stops with felony takedowns, and various scenarios without alarming anyone. It never occurred to me to post a sign outside that said training in progress, and I certainly should have clued in our radio operator.

Four police cars staged outside the motel, and four police officers with guns drawn must have looked daunting to anyone driving down the road. The plan was to order the role players outside by using the public address system on one of the police cars, but in doing so, we alerted a cashier at the fast food restaurant next door.

The cashier called the police department, and told the radio operator what she heard and observed, and said she thought the police officers at the motel needed help. The radio operator called the county police dispatch center, and the county radio operator broadcast a help call to the entire county police department. I heard the call being broadcast, but it took me a moment to realize the radio operator was talking about us. When I realized what was going on, it took me a moment to get a clear channel to cancel the call. Unfortunately, I wasn't quick enough. A dozen or more county police officers had already activating their lights and sirens, and were heading our way. It was also unfortunate that my chief didn't think the benefit of hands-on training outweighed my little slip up. He put a letter in my personnel file, and prohibited me from providing any future hands-on training.

## The Report

At the end of shift, it was customary in our department to put all our paperwork in a large folder and slide it under the door of the chief's office. The chief liked to see the reports early each day in case the city manager, the district attorney, or a citizen had questions about something that happened the night before. After our tour of duty one evening, an officer asked me if I read his miscellaneous report. I told him I signed it. He asked again, but this time he said, "I know you signed it, but did you read it?" I told him "No," and he suggested that I fish the envelope from under the chief's door and read the report. I fished it out and read the report which said in part, "Sergeant Sewell and I found an opened door at the Apostolic Church. We went inside where he played the drums and I played the guitar." While this was a true statement, it wasn't something that I wanted the chief, or anyone else for that matter, to read. The officer then handed me a replacement report that I read in its entirety, then placed it in the envelope, and slid it back under the chief's door.

I learned a valuable lesson that evening about reading reports. A couple of months later I read a miscellaneous report about an officer removing a car that stalled on a state highway bridge over the interstate. The report read, "Mr. Jackson's car stalled, so I pushed it off the bridge." I made him rewrite the report to show that Mr. Jackson's car stalled on the bridge, and he pushed it to the side of the road.

## Meals On Duty–A Comparison

We never knew when we might receive a call for service, so sitting down in a restaurant to order a nice meal was always a gamble, and something we almost never tried. Meal time usually meant eating fast food in the police car, and most of the time we could gobble a bite before we had to respond to a call. Sometimes we had to re-sack our food and eat it cold later. There weren't any drink holders in the cars, so if we bought any type of beverage and got an emergency call, the beverage usually had to be poured out the window.

It was an unusually slow day, and I decided I would treat myself to a rare sit-down white-napkin meal. There wasn't a wait, so I was seated quickly. The server came to my table promptly, and the food didn't take long. I was barely three bites into a nice fish dinner when I got my first call for service. The radio operator said there was a holdup alarm activated at a local pawn shop. I jumped up, and I scurried out toward the front door telling the server that I would be right back. As usual, it was a false alarm, so I drove back to the restaurant. I had probably been gone about eight minutes, but when I got back to my table, it was occupied, and my food was gone. I found a manager and asked about my dinner. She snootily said, "Well, you left it," and she handed me a bill for $11.95. I guess she had never heard the adage, *The customer is always right.* I was out the $11.95 plus tip and another $5.00 that I had to pay for fast food. I never patronized that restaurant again.

About two years later I decided to treat myself again to something other than fast food. I went to a favorite restaurant, and I didn't have to wait too long to be seated. I was enjoying a fried chicken dinner, and had only one or two bites left to eat, when I received a call for service. As I was leaving, I told the hostess that I would return to pay my tab. When I completed my call for service, I drove back to the restaurant, and I asked for the manager. A couple of minutes went by, and the manager approached me holding a Styrofoam container. I told her what happened, and I was there to pay my tab. She said, "Your server noticed you had not finished your meal when you ran out, so I had the cook prepare you another dinner," and she handed me the container. Again I asked for my tab, and the manager said, "I have great respect for police officers, and the job that you have to do. Tonight is on me." I took the container, thanked the manager profusely, and took the food back to the police station. Over the years Pam and I ate there many times.

## Fate or Fortune

Every Tuesday night after work I joined three other officers for choir practice. Choir practice was simply an alternate word for social time. We would arrive just after 11:00 p.m. at our favorite pizza restaurant, and order a pitcher of beer, and sip on it until 11:40 p.m. At 11:40 p.m. we would order and pay for a second pitcher because the restaurant was required by law to close at 11:45 p.m. The manager, however, welcomed us to occupy the booth and finish our second pitcher past closing time.

One Tuesday night, we arrived at the restaurant for our usual weekly social and ordered our beer. When it was nearing 11:40 p.m., we ordered, paid for, and received our second pitcher. At 11:45 p.m. the manager approached us and said we had to leave because the store was closed. He was a new manager, and he clearly had a different agenda. We were quite miffed having to leave four full mugs of beer and the dregs of our pitcher on the table, but we bit our lips and left.

The following Tuesday we decided against having choir practice, and we all went home after work. As the new pizza restaurant manager was about to close for the night, an armed man entered the restaurant. He not only robbed the restaurant, but he forced all the employees into the walk-in cooler where he relieved them of their wallets, watches, and other valuables. My shift didn't find out about the robbery until Wednesday when we reported for work. We all agreed that it may have worked out for the best. There wasn't any telling what might have happened if four young police officers, drinking beer, with guns strapped to their ankles, had been around during an armed robbery. It might have been wilder than the gunfight at the O.K. Corral.

# Through Not Over

On patrol one afternoon, I spotted a car driven by a man named Gerrard whom I knew had outstanding warrants. We always thought of him as a police groupie, but he turned out to be more of a junkie who stalked police officers to steal their equipment. Garrard had recently been released from jail after serving time for breaking into a county officer's car and stealing the officer's gun belt, gun, and handcuffs.

Jockeying for position, I maneuvered my police car directly behind Garrard's car, and then put on my uniform hat in anticipation of initiating a traffic stop. As soon as I had my hat square on my head, Garrard accelerated his car, made an abrupt left turn, and started to flee. With my blue lights and siren activated, I notified my radio operator that I was in pursuit. After three-quarters of a mile, Garrard skidded his car to a stop in a gas station parking lot, exited, and started running. He was pretty heavy, so I was shocked at his speed and agility. In a single movement he placed one hand on top of a five-foot solid wooden fence and vaulted over. Following suit, I stopped my police car, exited and started chasing. When I approached the wooden fence, I placed one hand on top, and in a single movement, I vaulted into the fence breaking it into splinters.

Garrard had a good lead on me, and I didn't think I would be able to catch him. It didn't occur to me that I didn't need to chase him because I knew who he was and where he lived. I also knew we could pick him up later. As he gained ground, I drew my weapon and shouted, "Stop, Garrard, or I will shoot." Like a large tree branch falls, he hit the ground with a thud. When I got to him, I placed him in handcuffs and led him back to my police car. I told him I didn't think I would have been able to catch him, and I was curious why he stopped. He said he knew I would shoot him.

My threat to shoot Garrard was an idle threat made as a last resort because I was losing the chase. While transporting Garrard to the county jail, he told me he knew I was going to pull him over because he saw me put on my hat. He served additional time in jail for violation of probation and for fleeing and attempting to elude a law enforcement officer.

# The Squeeze

A couple of months later, the radio operator dispatched a call of a burglary at the same gas station. My lieutenant was on the scene when I arrived, and I noticed the front door glass had been busted out. We went inside and quickly saw the cash register open and empty. Two more officers arrived on the scene, and we systematically searched the entire building and came to the conclusion that a burglar left before our arrival.

It was around 1:00 a.m. when we asked the radio operator to call a key holder to come to the gas station to tell us what was stolen and to secure the building. The radio operator said the owner was on his way and would be there in ten minutes. We all stood around the front office area making small talk until the owner arrived. He looked around, said he couldn't see anything missing except some packs of cigarettes and mentioned that he always left his cash register open with no cash. We didn't know if the owner was psychic or because it was his business he felt something was out of place. He excused himself and walked between us to a row of cabinets barely twenty-two inches tall. He opened one of the cabinet doors, and lying there in the fetal position amidst packs of cigarettes, was our burglar. I can't speak for the other officers, but in a millisecond, a bevy of what-ifs crossed my mind. Our systematic search had been about as constructive as stomping the ground looking for landmines. We took the burglar into custody, learned he was twenty-two years old, and that he had a long criminal record including charges of burglary, larceny, resisting arrest, DUI, and possession of illegal narcotics.

## Chapter 20

## Flowers at The Pond

There was a stretch of road leading out of town that ran by a small pond, and on one bank of the pond, there was a large row of pretty orange flowers. On patrol one afternoon, I saw the flowers and thought how sweet it would be to pick a few and take them home to Pam. I thought, however, it might not look professional if someone saw a police officer picking flowers, so I decided to wait until dark.

During the evening, I thought more about the pretty flowers, and had second thoughts about picking them because I sure didn't want to be accused of stealing. As the night rocked on, I began to think about the flowers being wild because the area was wooded, and there weren't any houses close by. Pam worked days, and I worked nights. By the time I got home, she was asleep, and when I woke up, she was always gone. The next morning was Saturday, and I was going to be able to give her a nice surprise. It was nearing shift change, so I went back out to the pond to pick the flowers, but in the darkness, I couldn't find them. I used my spot light to no avail, and I went home that night empty handed. The next morning, I shared with Pam my story about the flowers at the pond. She said, "If you are talking about the pond on the road going out of town, honey, those flowers are day lilies."

## Something About Church and Funeral Homes

Our house was often a place for family to gather to cookout, play billiards, and shoot the bull. One Saturday, when family was visiting, an older man named David told a joke about remembering to zip up and unzip your pants when we reach his age.

The next day before Sunday school, I led a camp-meeting style singing in the church sanctuary in front of 300 people. Immediately afterward, and before the lesson, I led singing in my Sunday school class. When the bell rang for dismissal, I stopped by the men's room, and when I prepared to take care of business, I realized I was already unzipped. Naturally, I was mortified, but when I thought more about it, I hoped I had gotten away with it because I was wearing properly fitted pleated pants, and they were not gapped open. If in fact I had exposed myself, everyone was kind enough to keep it to themselves.

A few weeks later, I was with family attending a visitation at a funeral home. The double doors to the visitation room opened to a hallway that was about seventy feet long, and the restrooms were at the far end of that hall. I headed for the men's restroom, and as I got near, a woman exited the women's restroom dragging a ten to fifteen foot string of toilet paper from under the back of her dress. Quickly turning my head, I pretended to look at the pictures on the wall until she passed. I was embarrassed for the woman, and embarrassed for myself, but I couldn't help but turn around in disbelief to make sure I saw what I thought I saw. As the woman got closer to the visitation room, my mother rushed out and came to her aid.

Some months later after Sunday school, I made my usual stop by the men's restroom. When I walked out, I decided to get a sip of water from the fountain that sat between the men's and women's restrooms. I stepped up to get in line behind a woman who had just come from the restroom, and I noticed the back of her skirt was tucked inside her pantyhose. There really wasn't a good way to tell the woman her fanny was exposed, but I thought it would be worse to let her walk down the hall showing all to all. I Knew I had 100 times rather one person tell me that I had my pants unzipped, a pimple on my nose, or hamburger meat stuck between my teeth than displaying either to dozens of other people. I mustered up a little courage and said, "Ma'am, your skirt is tucked in the back." It became a contest of speed as she jerked around to pull out her skirt, while I quickly jerked around to walk away. The woman must have been a visitor because I didn't recognize her, and I am rather certain that I never saw her again.

## Chapter 21

# "Ribbit, Ribbit," I Didn't Meant It

At the time, we shared a radio frequency with the fire department, and professional radio etiquette was a regular point of discussion. We were told that the Federal Communication Commission (FCC) monitored our radio traffic, and we could be subject to losing our radio license if we didn't follow protocol.

The fire department conducted regular fire hydrant inspections, which had to be as much fun as watching corn grow. I had just completed a traffic stop when I heard a fire department sergeant key up his radio and say, "Ribbit, ribbit, bite my ass, dumb ass." The firemen were just trying to while away the day having fun as they completed their humdrum task.

The fire chief didn't think it was funny. He must have felt the breath of the FCC breathing down his neck, so he called the sergeant to his office. The sergeant explained to the chief that he accidentally picked up the radio microphone thinking he was using the public address system microphone. The chief didn't accept his explanation and said the sergeant shouldn't even use the public address system to talk nasty anywhere the public might be able to hear. Everyone guessed it wasn't going to work out very well for the sergeant, and indeed it didn't. He was sent home that day busted down to the rank of fireman.

## Breaker Breaker One Nine

CB radio popularity had peaked, and every police car in my department had one. Previously, our police chief had taken some heat from the city council about police cars parked side by side at shopping centers. It didn't seem to satisfy the council when the chief told them that what they were actually seeing was a supervisor approving a report, or counseling with an officer. He told them he didn't want the police cars at headquarters because then, the police cars wouldn't be visible to the public. Actually, the chief knew in reality when two police cars were parked driver next to driver, it was their time to tell war stories, jokes, or to discuss what the officers were going to do when they got off-duty. The CB radio was a great way for officers to have fun during the shift, and it also served as a way for personal communication without irritating the city council.

Each officer had a unique handle for use on the CB; mine was *Smokey Red Fox.* The microphone for our Motorola police radio was much larger, and it had a different shape from the microphone for the CB radio. One slow night my entire shift was carrying on a silly CB radio conversation about fast cars. I picked up my CB radio microphone and said, "Breaker-breaker one nine, I once had a car that was so fast I could get to my destination before I left." Our newest officer mistakenly grabbed his police radio microphone instead of the CB radio microphone and said, "Well, Smokey Red Fox, I guess you felt like big shit." The radio frequency became so quiet I think we could have heard a leaf fall on a bail of cotton. Luckily for the newest officer, it was around 3:00 a.m., and our shift lieutenant had left work early because he was sick. I should not have, but I let it slide.

## The Buck Stopped With Me

After being promoted to the rank of lieutenant, I decided I wanted to observe the work habits of some officers on my shift. When young police officers got together, I always knew to expect a little horseplay, but I didn't foresee the upcoming mishap. I was a passenger in a police car when another officer pulled alongside to chat. The two vehicles were parked in opposite directions, and close enough for the two drivers to shake hands. The drivers were horsing around pulling forward and back, and doing things like opening the gas tank covers on each other's car. After a couple of minutes of fun, the radio operator dispatched a burglar alarm call. Both officers immediately put their cars in gear to leave, but the other driver didn't remember that his tires were turned to the left, and when he accelerated, his car crashed into ours.

I wasn't driving, but the chief put a letter of reprimand in my file. He said because I was the lieutenant, I was in command, and I could have prevented the crash by preventing the horseplay. It took me a long time to absorb the totality of the situation, but I learned that the buck stopped with me.

## A Runaway

While on routine patrol, I noticed a semi-trailer truck parked in a turn lane on a state highway in front of a fast food restaurant. I had already made up my mind if the rig wasn't having mechanical issues, I was going to give the driver a ticket for parking on the highway. Just as I started to pull in behind the rig, it started rolling backwards. I noticed a man running toward the cab. A quick check of my surroundings told me if the truck went to the right, it would roll into oncoming traffic; if it went left, it might roll down an embankment onto the interstate.

There wasn't any time to think, and it didn't look like the driver was going to be able to get to the truck in time, so I pulled behind the trailer and stopped. Just before the trailer hit the front of my police car, I put my car in reverse gear and started backward trying to match the speed of the rig. My hope was to minimize the impending damage to the police car by trying to slow the rig to a stop gradually, rather than trying to stop it suddenly.

It worked. The police car received hundreds of dollars in damage rather than thousands. The truck driver had been in the fast food restaurant eating, so he received a ticket for parking on a state highway and failing to properly apply his brakes. I received another reprimand in my file. I appealed, and the chief rescinded the reprimand a few months later.

## Never Underestimate

While I was loading my gear into my police car at the start of shift one afternoon, my radio operator dispatched me to a shoplifting call at a large department store. When I arrived at the store's loss prevention office, I spoke with a female loss prevention officer (LPO) who told me she caught a man stuffing tools in his pants. The man was twenty-five years old and had not given the LPO any trouble when she handcuffed him and took him into custody. While I was jotting down some information for my report, the LPO left the room to retrieve some video footage of the shoplifting. My usual routine on shoplifting arrests was to call the radio operator to find out if the arrestee had any active warrants on NCIC or a criminal history. I can't rightly tell you why I did things differently on this particular call, but I can tell you that I would later wish I hadn't.

The man was quiet and cooperative, so I didn't think anything of it when I removed the handcuffs that belonged to the LPO to replace them with my handcuffs. That, as you might imagine, was a big mistake. As soon as I removed the LPO's handcuffs, the man spun around and slugged me in my face, crushing my eyeglasses. I staggered backward slightly and then instinctively lunged at the man. His right arm was the closest, so I gripped it with the intent of spinning him around to apply handcuffs. He was very quick and agile, and in an instant, he unsnapped my holster and removed my pistol with his left hand.

Letting go of his arm, I jerked around and grabbed the top of the pistol with my right hand then with my left. He was strong as an ox, and I had to constantly dance away from the receiving end of my gun barrel. I pulled him toward me to knee him in the groin, but I missed and hit his leg. I didn't know the LPO had returned until I heard a walloping sound and felt an impact. The LPO had picked up and swung a metal arm chair striking the man on the top of his shoulders and the back of his head.

He fell to the ground unconscious, so I applied my handcuffs and then called for an ambulance. It turned out that the man had an extensive criminal record, including several arrests for assaulting police officers. The man survived and pled guilty to his crime. I survived and pled guilty to my indiscretion. After a little research, I purchased a gun holster that provided a security feature. The lesson learned was always to apply my handcuffs before removing another set.

## Friendly Fire

There was a very large distribution warehouse in town, and when they housed pharmaceutical products, they employed armed security guards. Near midnight one shift, our police radio operator dispatched me and another officer to a suspicious-person call at the warehouse.

The warehouse was considered one of the largest in the southeast, and the grounds were huge. A security officer had radioed his dispatcher that he saw someone walking around the semi-trailers in the back of the loading docks. The security company dispatcher relayed the information to my radio operator. I arrived first, and I parked my police car on the left side of the building near the rear.

When my backup pulled into the parking lot, I prematurely started around the corner of the building toward the loading docks. Before I could reach the first trailer, a gunshot rang out, and a bullet zinged off the concrete just a few feet away. I ran to the closest trailer, and I took cover behind the rear wheels just as another shot was fired. It was too dangerous for my backup officer to come around the corner of the building, and that made me feel alone and vulnerable.

I contacted the radio operator and asked for assistance. Then I heard another gunshot, and a bullet hit the trailer. I felt like an old painted metal pig target at a carnival shooting gallery. I was able to see muzzle flash reflecting off another trailer, but I wasn't 100% positive from where the shots were being fired. My partner contacted our radio operator and asked if she could find out the location of the security guard because he was concerned that he had been killed by the shooter. A couple of minutes later, our radio operator responded that she had made contact with the security company and they informed her their security guard was in a heated gunfight with someone he caught breaking into trailers.

It didn't take a rocket scientist to know it was the security guard who was shooting at me. Our radio operator informed the security company dispatcher of our situation, and a minute later the security guard appeared under a nearby floodlight. Relieved and apologetic, he said he was frightened because he thought I was someone trying to break into the trailers. Numerous other officers surrounded the area, but they were unable to locate anyone else in the area. We never determined the source of the suspicious person that prompted his call to the police, but when the smoke cleared, the security guard was criminally charged, and a lesson was had by all.

## The Guillotine

About three months later I received a call to respond with paramedics to the same loading docks. On my arrival, I saw a group of people crowded around a man lying on the ground. His left arm had been severed at his elbow, and his severed limb lay just a couple of feet away. Coworkers were working to keep the man from losing too much blood. Paramedics arrived seconds later, and they immediately went to the man's aid. I removed a sheet from the back of the ambulance, picked up the severed arm with the sheet, and took it to the paramedics. They quickly stabilized the man, then put him in the ambulance.

I could not help but see the large amount of blood, bandages, and wrappings on the pavement. It wasn't like I hadn't seen it many times before. I stood there frozen in place, and gripped with the notion that this scene should be reminding me of something. My memory had never been as good as some people I knew who seemed to be able to remember every detail of every book they ever read. I remember being frustrated. I wasn't able to figure out what it was that I thought I was supposed to remember. The ambulance's siren startled me when the paramedics headed for the hospital, so I set about to see if I could learn more about the accident.

I walked over to a small group of the man's coworkers to see if they knew what happened. I learned that the man was using a forklift to unload pallets from a trailer. When he backed the forklift out of the trailer, the friction of the reversing wheels pushed the trailer forward because he had not properly chocked the trailer tires. When the trailer rolled forward and separated from the loading dock, the forklift started to fall backward. The forklift driver's natural instinct was to let go of the steering wheel and fling his arms. He threw his right arm to the right and his left arm backward. In doing so, he exposed his left arm which became pinched between the metal roof of the falling forklift, and the concrete edge of the loading dock. It was like a guillotine had cleanly severed his arm.

Over the next few weeks I asked the paramedics a couple of times if they knew what happened to the man. One of them told me the doctors took him into surgery and reattached the arm, but he didn't know if the surgery was successful for the long haul.

## Chapter 22

# A Tale of Two Hens

My cousin John and I decided to go on a motorcycle camping trip. He lived in Alabama, and I lived in Georgia, and we wanted to select a place to meet, leave his car, and take a ride on my motorcycle. I told John that space was limited, so anything he brought needed to fit inside his sleeping bag. We met in a small town, and found a good place to park his car, then rode my motorcycle to the local police department to see if an officer might tell us a good place to camp. The officer suggested a wooded area about thirty miles away. We thanked the officer, and happily headed in that direction. It was a nice fall afternoon, and the small back roads proved to be perfect for a ride.

We came across a forest stand, turned onto a small dirt road, and quickly found the perfect spot in the woods to stay the night. It was easy to pick up loose firewood, and we found enough leaves to build a couple of soft nests for the evening. The camp fire was lit, the sun went down, and we kicked back for an adult beverage. After a few sips I started getting hungry, so I told John we should get on my motorcycle and go get a couple of hamburgers. He said, "Don't be silly, it's twenty-five miles to the nearest restaurant, it is dark, and we already had a drink." I agreed, and I pulled a pack of crackers and two cans of Vienna Sausage from my sleeping bag. He laughed, lifted the end of his sleeping bag, and dumped out two Ziploc bags containing two still frozen Cornish Game Hens, two baking potatoes, plastic cutlery, folds of aluminum foil, paper plates and some butter.

Around 7:00 p.m. we stuck a couple sticks in the ground near the fire, put the frozen hens on a skewer, and then started the slow process of thawing. It seemed like it took a week, but the hens were finally thawed enough to cook. The foil wrapped potatoes were already on red hot coals, so we hung the hens directly over the fire and had another sip. Reminiscent of the famous lake chicken, we put a little butter and a little bourbon on the hens, and before we could tell all the jokes and tall tales we could tell, it was time to eat. We were both famished, so we chowed down on a meal that we felt to be on par with food prepared by Julia Child, or Wolfgang Puck. Not long after we finished eating, John was tucked away belly-up in repose, and my sleeping bag started to look lonely, so I called it a night.

## Something Fishy

Pam and I were with another couple, Mike and Gloria, at a nice fish restaurant enjoying fellowship and hoping to enjoy a nice evening meal. The server took our orders and soon brought out our salads. I pointed out to the server that I didn't have flatware, she apologized, and said she would be right back. The others started eating, and it wasn't until they were through with their salad that the server brought my flatware. Before I could finish my first mouthful of salad, my table mates received their entrées. Pam's entrée was missing a baked potato, and Gloria's entree was missing vegetables. We pointed out the missing food to the server, and we asked her for refills on our beverages. She apologized and said she would be right back. When the other three were half way through their entrée, I still didn't have mine. I quietly got up, found a manager, and made an inquiry. The manager apologized and said my food would be right out, so I went back to the booth and sat down. After the other three were through eating, the server brought Pam's missing baked potato, Gloria's missing vegetables, and our check. We still hadn't gotten refills or my entrée. I was totally flabbergasted and unable to formulate the words I wanted to say. As the server turned to walk away, Mike spoke up, but the server did not turn around.

After collecting my thoughts, I told my dinner dates that I was going to find a manager and complain. Gloria became visibly upset and said, "Please don't make a scene." I told her I had no intention of creating a scene, but the manager needed to know what happened. Gloria was wiggling in her seat and said, "Oh please don't embarrass me."

Ignoring what I thought was Gloria's weird response, I quietly walked away and found a manager. I told the manager the series of events, and she was very apologetic. She said it wasn't a good excuse, but they were very busy and shorthanded, and they could have some food ready for me in about five minutes. By this time I was too upset to eat, so I declined her offer, and told her I didn't think I should have to pay full price for the food we didn't receive. She agreed, she told me she was going to comp our meals, and she gave me four coupons for future dinners.

I wanted to be mad and ugly to the manager, but her demeanor took the mean out of my madness. I smiled, gave her my thanks, and went back to collect my dates. Incidentally, I stopped for a burger on the way home. I can't speak for the other couple, but Pam and I never used our coupons, and we never patronized the restaurant again.

## Chapter 23

## Much Ado

O ur radio operator dispatched the fire department and me to a call of a basement house fire. More times than not, those type of calls ended up being much ado about nothing. Often it was the smell of smoke, a small fire that the home owner extinguished before the fire department arrived, or some other minor issue.

When I arrived seconds before the fire department, I saw a young man walking slowly in his front yard dressed only in his underwear. He appeared to be dazed. He had his hands out to his side, and he was walking sort of like a zombie. I got out of the police car, and started walking over to ask him if he knew anything about a fire. When I got closer I could see that he had been badly burned. It looked like he had been peeled with a large potato peeler, flesh was hanging from him in strips. There wasn't anything I could do to help him except to assure him paramedics were on their way. He was obviously in shock, and I am not certain, but I might have been as well.

The fire department arrived on the scene seconds later, and firemen started running toward the basement to extinguish the fire. I flagged one of the firemen down, and he came to the young man's aid. Oddly and sadly, the fire department didn't bring an ambulance. Some of the firemen had recently finished training to be paramedics, but the fire department hadn't fully instituted their medical program. Every fireman on the scene was occupied with the fire or the burn victim. A fireman asked me if I could go to the fire house and drive the ambulance back; I readily agreed. I had driven lots of large vehicles in my time, but this was heavy, and it felt like it would flip over at every turn. I arrived safely, the fire was extinguished, and the young man was loaded quickly into the ambulance and taken to the hospital.

The young man had been in his basement cleaning motorcycle parts with gasoline, and the fumes reached the pilot light on the furnace causing a flash explosion. He was sixteen years old, and he suffered third degree burns over eighty percent of his body. I never had any more contact with him, but I understood he survived.

## The Gift

My department had an intoximeter (Breathalyzer) that would register if a driver had consumed too much alcohol to legally drive. I was a state certified intoximeter operator, and during one shift I received a radio call from my radio operator asking if I could assist another agency. The radio operator wanted to know if I could meet an officer from the adjoining town to administer an intoximeter test for someone he had in custody.

I drove to the police department and set up the equipment. The other officer arrived and brought in his suspect, and I administered the test. When the intoximeter indicated the test results, I relayed it to the officer saying the suspect's alcohol level was above the legal limit for him to drive. When the arresting officer stepped out of the room to get some paperwork, the suspect reached in his right front pocket and pulled out a thirty-eight caliber pistol. I jumped backward and reached for my own gun. Before I could unsnap my holster, the suspect handed his gun to me handle first and said that I had been very nice to him, and he wanted me to have it. I was stunned how quickly it happened; I was shocked thinking that I would have been shot if that was the suspect's intention.

I turned the pistol over to the arresting officer, and told him to find another place for future intoximeter tests. The lesson learned was: Always initiate my own pat-down regardless if the initial officer says he/she has already done so.

## How Slow Could They Go?

The county radio operator broadcasted a BOLO (Be on the lookout) for armed robbery suspects from the county just to my south. After robbing a small motel, two robbers left in a gold, two-door, sports car heading south-bound on the interstate. I previously lucked out finding the shooters who were said to be driving away from my jurisdiction, and I wasn't particularly busy, so I drove my police car toward the interstate highway. I parked on the northbound entrance ramp and waited.

About six minutes later a gold, two-door, sports car occupied by two white males passed me going northbound. I put the police car in drive and hurriedly caught up to the car. I radioed the county radio operator what I had observed, and I told her my current location.

The car changed from the left to the right lane then slowed down from seventy mph to fifty-five mph. I followed suit and the car slowed down again to about forty-five mph. I am certain they hoped I would pass them and go on, but when I didn't, they slowed down again to twenty-five mph. Now on that busy interstate highway, even though it was the middle of the night, the flow of traffic was whizzing. When they realized I wasn't going to pass, they increased their speed back to the speed limit.

We were leaving my city limits, and I was waiting for at least one back-up unit to reach me before I activated my blue lights to stop the car and investigate the occupants. I wasn't 100% sure that I was following the robbery suspects, but after their peculiar driving stunt, I should not have had any doubts. There was only one other police officer on duty with me in town that night, and he didn't recognize my voice on the county police radio frequency.

The suspects got off the interstate at the next exit and then turned right onto a state highway. I kept a slight distance from the car, and I continued to give the radio operator my location. I anxiously waited for backup. The car made another right turn then abruptly turned left onto a road that I had never traveled. We were going very slowly, and I could hear a multitude of police sirens in the distance, but before another officer could get to me, we came to a dead end.

It was a very awkward moment that I had not anticipated. I thought to myself, *what now Einstein?* I could only imagine what the two suspects might have thought when I turned on my blue lights. Exiting my police car with my gun drawn and pointed toward the driver, I shouted commands for him to get out of his car with his hands up. The approaching sirens were louder, but at that moment I was a one-man band. The driver followed my commands, then got out of the car, and lay face down on the pavement.

I turned my focus on the passenger giving him similar commands. I don't think I will ever forget seeing the business end of his breadbox-sized nickel-plated revolver as he exited the car and raised it toward me. If I was going to shoot this man, I knew I needed to be accurate. I had a good sight picture, so I started squeezing the trigger. I have no idea how far back the hammer on my 357 Magnum Colt Trooper Mark III came, but before I finished the squeeze, the passenger turned 180 degrees and threw his pistol into the woods. I eased up on the trigger and directed him to the ground.

One by one county police cars started filling the residential street. If I had wanted to leave, there wouldn't have been a way because police cars lined the street like eggs in a carton. The county officers took custody of the two suspects and started a search and inventory of their car.

I got out of their way and watched the activity from the sidewalk. I am not sure where they came from, but I suddenly realized a mother, and who I assumed was her young son, were standing a few feet from me. Talking to the son, the mother screeched excitedly saying, "It was just like in the movies, get out with your hands up." To this day, I really can't tell you what it was about those words that started me trembling, but my legs began to shake to the point they felt like rubber bands.

The county officers found the pistol in the woods rather quickly. They were told by the motel clerk that both robbers were armed, so they began searching for the second weapon. When they didn't find it in the car, they searched up and down the dead end street until they found it. I was not able to see the passenger side of the suspect's car as it made the last left turn, but apparently, the passenger tossed one revolver out of his window. Both suspects went to jail.

I received a letter of commendation for my actions from the adjoining county police chief. I was also criticized by two police officers because I didn't shoot the passenger who pulled his gun on me. I responded to both by saying, "I was in the process until I didn't need to anymore."

## The Curb and The Kindergartner

Speaking to school children was a regular event for me, and I was never sure who received the largest reward-- me or the children. A local kindergarten teacher was teaching her class about pedestrian safety, and she invited me to be a guest speaker. It turned out to be three classes combined, but the class went well.

It was time to leave, and each class, along with three teachers, followed me outside to my police car that was parked along the curb. As I stepped down from the sidewalk to the driveway, one of the teachers told the class to say goodbye to Officer Sewell. I turned around to wave goodbye, and a little boy ran up to give me a hug and kiss me goodbye. But since the tyke was short, he was standing on the sidewalk, and I was lower on the driveway. His aim was off. He hugged my hips and kissed me on my crotch. I am sure the teachers were accustomed to seeing kindergartners do unexpected things, but for me, well, I am still blushing.

## Something Was Wrong In Denmark

While patrolling one afternoon, I spotted a Georgia State Patrol Car parked in the mall parking lot. That wouldn't have been a big deal, except the car had a Louisiana tag. I did a double take then adjusted my eyeglasses and looked again. I didn't know what to think except something was wrong. I contacted the radio operator and asked her to check the tag number against the NCIC known stolen vehicle data base.

Normally, the radio operator responded with stolen and registration information from tag numbers within thirty seconds. After three minutes and I had not heard back from the dispatcher, I supposed that the patrol car, or the tag, or both were stolen. When I still had not heard back from my radio operator in another two minutes, I keyed up my radio microphone and inquired if she had a response. She told me she just got off the telephone with the registered owner and learned that the car was a prop for the cast of the movie *Smokey and the Bandit* that was filming close by.

## I Wasn't A Flirt

For three years, I worked part-time as an undercover security officer at a department store in the mall. The majority of employees were women ranging in age from eighteen to sixty. I could shop, talk to customers and employees, and generally hang out. I was hired for loss prevention, but the job turned out more like employee security. It was simply a great job, and I always enjoyed going to work.

I was twenty-six, married, and it wasn't hard to recognize obvious flirting. Flirting was something I tried to avoid because it could cause trouble, and that is something I sure didn't need.

One afternoon the security manager called me into his office, which wasn't unusual. When he closed the door, I knew something was up. He told me that one of the women who worked there had accused me of coming onto her. She claimed that I had invited her to spend the weekend at the lake. When he got around to telling me the woman's name, I was floored. Earlier that day, as I walked through the department where she worked, I noticed the forty-something-year-old woman looked particularly nice. I had spoken to her numerous times just like I had with all the store employees, so I told her she looked nice, and I kept walking. As I passed, I heard her say, "Flattery will get you anything you want." I guess she was angry that I didn't respond, so she made up a story to get me in trouble. I told the security manager my side of the story, and I never heard another word about it. I did, however, take caution to avoid the woman's department when she was at work.

## Taking It On The Chin

The county radio operator broadcast an all-call asking for any uniform police car near the interstate to assist three detectives in getting a vehicle stopped. They were following a suspected murderer from New Jersey, and they wanted a marked police car to initiate a traffic stop on the Buick Riviera he was driving.

As I drove down the southbound entrance ramp, the suspect vehicle, and the three unmarked detective cars drove past me running about ninety to ninety-five mph. I pushed the accelerator hard and caught up to them as they crossed the line into the adjoining county. What we hadn't been told was the adjoining county police had a roadblock set up across the interstate.

We topped a small rise and could see police cars in the road with all emergency lights activated and officers with rifles pointed over the top of their cars. When it looked like the suspected murderer was not going to stop, the officers at the roadblock opened fire. I swerved into the median, and spun out, then ducked on the floorboard. One bullet went through the windshield of the Riviera and struck the suspect center chin. He slammed on his brakes which caused the lead detective car to crash into the rear of the Riviera followed by the second and third detective cars to crash into the car in front. Two of the detective cars were struck by friendly fire, but no police officers were hurt. The suspect was critically injured but alive.

About ten minutes later a police car from my county came flying up to the scene with blue lights and siren activated. When the officer got out of his car he was tugging at his gun belt and trousers trying to pull them up. With a waddled gait like an old western gunslinger, he walked over to me and said, "You're a city copy, what the f&%# are you doing here?" I knew that I had responded to an all-call, and other than his desire to gawk, I had more reason to be there than he did. I also knew there was nothing to be gained by entering into debate with a dimwit. My job was over, so without uttering a word, I turned around and left.

## One That Got Away

One of the most exciting things a young police officer could do in those days was engage in a vehicle pursuit. That was something that didn't happen very often, but it was looked at as kind of a rite of passage. One young officer told me I couldn't be a real police officer until I had been in a pursuit. That concept was about as stupid as the notion a fifteen-year-old boy told me years earlier that I couldn't be a man until I had sex.

In the 1970s, a large Ford LTD with a 460 police interceptor engine could accelerate to 100 mph very quickly. The challenge, however, was learning not to outrun the brakes.

One evening I was driving down the main drag through town, and a souped-up Mustang pulled out of a shopping center in front of me. He stopped at the next red traffic light, but before the light turned green, the Mustang took off with tires spinning and the entire roadway filled with smoke. Blue lights on, siren on, the chase was on. I notified the radio operator of the tag number and type of car as we headed northbound on the interstate. Traffic was light, but our speed wasn't. One hundred twenty mph came quickly. A couple of minutes into the pursuit, the radio operator advised me that a vehicle matching the description of the Mustang had recently left the scene of a shooting.

It didn't make sense to me that any level-headed person who had just committed a crime would bring that type of attention to himself. Giving it no more thought, I concentrated on catching the red light, tire spinning bandit. The Mustang exited onto the beltway, and I had no trouble keeping up as our speed was nearing 130 mph. Surprisingly, the driver put on his right turn signal and started up an exit ramp. The Mustang turned left onto a state highway, but I was going way too fast to make the turn. I applied my brakes to slow down, but the harder I pressed the pedal, the softer the brakes became. Traffic was coming from the left, I was still going too fast, and I was certain a collision was imminent. When I reached the state route, I still had my foot pressed hard on the brakes, and I jerked the steering wheel to the left. The police car spun twice before coming to rest against a curb. It was evident the oncoming traffic saw me coming and stopped to avoid a collision.

It took a second for me to regain my senses before I accelerated and tried to catch back up to the Mustang. I could see it way off in the distance, I had the accelerator on the floor, but when I rounded a small curve, the Mustang was nowhere in sight. I was at an intersection with numerous buildings on both sides of the road. With no clue if my suspects were hiding or driving, I opted to systematically search behind buildings. When I wasn't able to locate the Mustang in the area, my adrenaline soon faded, and I knew this one had gotten away.

The adage "God looks after fools and babies" came into play once again. I was lucky that I didn't have a high speed impact when I got off the interstate, and I was probably luckier that I didn't catch the Mustang. I learned later that evening there were two armed occupants in the Mustang, and together they had shot five people, killing one. As I grew older and wiser, I realized that it wasn't worth my life to engage in pursuit over what I thought was a simple traffic violation.

## Not As Smart As A Fifth Grader?

Late one night I received a call for service in reference to a semi-truck trailer stuck under an overpass. The driver either ignored or didn't see the low clearance/height warning sign and drove his rig a few feet under the overpass until it became tightly wedged. The driver told me he had already called a towing company to pull him out. When the tow-truck arrived, the operator made a suggestion that made me feel like a dullard. "Just let a little air out of the tires, and it will lower the height of the truck so he can back it out."

Several years later, I received a call about a lowboy trailer that was stuck in the driveway of a motel. The motel driveway dropped sharply below the level of the main highway, and the trailer became stuck when its bottom drug the pavement. When I arrived I was approached by a man who grinned and said, "Do you remember me?" I thought I recognized him, but I knew for sure when he said, "I already let a little air out of my tires." It was the same driver who ignored low clearance/height warning signs and wedged his semi-truck under the overpass years earlier. Of course the deflated tires exacerbated the problem by lowering the trailer even more. I came to the conclusion that this guy was so daft that he could jump out of a window and miss the ground.

## What's in Your Food?

A fast food restaurant that offered inexpensive hotdogs, hamburgers and fries was convenient, so many of our officers frequently stopped in for lunch or dinner. On one occasion my partner and I went in and walked up to the cash register and placed our order. I noticed the cook was taking already cooked hamburger patties out of what looked like a pan of water and placing them on the grill. During the process of waiting for my change, I noticed a roach crawling across the counter near the grill. The cook quickly reached toward the roach and smashed it with her finger, wiped her finger on her apron, and then inserted her hand into the pan of water to retrieve another hamburger patty. We asked for a refund and never went back.

There was another fast food restaurant near police headquarters that I could walk to easily. One day I went inside and ordered some chicken, a side of green beans, and a biscuit. I got my order then sat down, but before I could pick up my fork, I noticed a large dead caterpillar in my green beans. I took the tray back to the cash register and handed it to a manager standing nearby. I pointed out the caterpillar and stated that I had lost my appetite. The manager took the tray and said, "Eek eek," then turned away. I didn't ask for nor was I offered a refund or another meal. It was about a year before I could eat green beans again, and I haven't been back to that restaurant chain since.

## Firetrucks and Firefighting

Our fire department had transitioned away from using volunteers, but training had taken a back seat to hiring, purchasing equipment, and generally getting the department up and properly running. The alarm sounded. Then the voice of the radio operator came across the speaker in the fire department bay announcing a grass fire on the edge of town.

The pumper rolled out carrying the fire chief and three firemen. As the story goes, on arrival to the area, the firemen realized the water hose would not reach the fire from the road, so they pulled the pumper over the curb and out into a field. The three firemen pulled an inch and a half booster line to the fire, and the fire chief stayed with the pumper to make sure it functioned properly. Eventually, either the fire chief got bored, or he thought his firemen needed his expertise because he left the pumper unattended and headed to the fire.

Shortly thereafter, I heard one of our police officers key up the radio and say, "Somebody ought to tell the fire department their truck is on fire." The catalytic converter under the truck had set the tall grass on fire. The fire burned the electrical wiring to the booster hose reel, and the reel automatically started turning in reverse. I was already on my way to see what was going on, and I arrived just in time to see the fire chief and three firemen chasing the water-spewing booster hose back to the pumper. After the nozzle reached the reel, it slammed the top of the pumper each time the reel turned. With no booster line and no water to extinguish the fire, the firemen broke branches from pine trees and started slapping the burning grass. The fire chief turned off the motor, but the damage to the pumper had already been done. The amount of damage was probably less than the damage to the firemen's ego, but the laughs for the police department were huge.

## Another Gift

The chief asked me to attend a Lion's Club meeting because they wanted to donate some reflective vests to our police department. I attended and found their agenda boring because it wasn't about police work, cars, boats or motorcycles. My turn to speak came soon enough, and I approached the podium to accept the gifts and say thank you. I started explaining the appropriateness of the reflective vests for police officers working at night because they were hard to see in their dark-colored uniforms. I wanted to make it clear how large the problem was so I said, "The problem is so, it is so, it is so," but I couldn't express myself without using profanity. I finally uttered the word *big* to describe the size of the problem.

I had fallen into a really bad habit indicative of many young police officers using profanity as a routine part of my vocabulary. This was a lesson that I would use throughout my career and a story that I would share with many young police officers. Every time I told my story, it made me think of a quote by Aristotle. "We are what we repeatedly do. Excellence, then, is not an act, but a habit." I had repeatedly used profanity and my vocabulary wasn't an act, but a bad habit.

## Just How Fast Was It?

Lane, a fellow officer, was watching traffic when he suddenly heard the roar of a car engine. Before he could turn his head in the direction of the sound, a Mustang appeared and flashed by. Lane pulled onto the road, and accelerated his police car in pursuit of the Mustang. He didn't think that he would be able to catch up to the Mustang, so he picked up the police microphone to notify other police units in the event an officer was further down the road.

I had already learned that the way we talk in everyday life is the way we will talk in a crisis, and this was a great case to support my theory. What Lane wanted to say was "A car just blew past me and he was hauling ass." What he did say was, "A car just blew past me and he was hauling, well he was hauling, (short pause) Ur uh, he was hauling fanny." Six blocks down the road I clocked the Mustang with radar then effected a traffic stop. As I was walking back to my car to write the driver a traffic citation for traveling fifty-five mph in a thirty-five mph zone, Lane drove up. I said to him, "He has a passenger in the car with him, so he was hauling two fannies." That was the only time I ever saw Lane turn red.

## The Deadly Riot

It was a chilling sound when the radio cracked the quiet as the radio operator activated the radio frequency and broadcasted, "All cars, all stations, signal sixty-three at the county jail." My partner at the time, Rick Jackson, and I activated blue lights and sirens, and two police cars headed out of town toward the county jail. Signal sixty-three was a code for officer needs help. Rick and I arrived at the jail at the same time and entered though the back door. Just inside the door stood a deputy who took my weapon and another who took my eyeglasses and handed me a baton. I wasn't sure what I was going to do with the baton because without my eyeglasses, I couldn't see well enough to strike a tree in a thick forest.

The two of us and five county officers were herded onto an elevator, and we headed to the top floor where the male inmates were housed. Deputy Barry Vaughn had previously entered a cell to check on an inmate who feigned being ill. The inmate removed one of his four-inch platform shoes and beat the unarmed deputy to a pulp. The fight incited other inmates to riot. As the elevator climbed, I became alarmed thinking about the door opening to expose fifty stark raving mad inmates with homemade knives. I was as nervous as a mouse in a pit of pythons. The elevator stopped, the door opened, and all I could see were brown shirts. The deputies had already gotten the riot under control.

A group of police officers picked up the inmate by his clothing and tossed him into the elevator. His head slammed the wall hard. Rick and I joined other officers on the elevator with the inmate, and when the door shut, I was appalled by what happened. There were no cameras inside the elevator, and the police officers began retaliating against the inmate by kicking him in the head, chest, and groin. Rick and I tried to get them to stop by pulling them back, but it was like trying to stop raging bulls. When the elevator reached the ground floor and the door opened, the physical abuse stopped. The officers again picked up the inmate and threw him out of the elevator. He slid across the polished tile floor, and his head careened against the concrete wall; he didn't move. One of the officers said, "I think he's dead." Medical personnel who had been waiting outside were called in and immediately began CPR.

The inmate was resuscitated and later tried and convicted for his assault on Deputy Vaughn. Deputy Vaughn never returned to work as a deputy sheriff, and I never forgot that I had firsthand experience with mob mentality.

## Chapter 24

## Happy Happy Birthday

P am and I went out to dinner with friends, and about the time we finished eating, the restaurant owner approached and asked if it was my birthday. When I told him no, he asked if it was anyone's birthday at the table. When everybody said no, he told us he received a telephone call from a woman who told him it was my birthday, but he wanted to make sure before he had his employees come over and sing.

It was puzzling for a minute until I remembered Pam and I visited a family earlier in the day, and I mentioned where we were going for dinner. I had never been one for revenge, but returning the favor for a good practical joke was right up my alley. The next day I placed an ad in the local newspaper listing the woman's new minivan for sale at half the price they paid for it a month earlier. As one could imagine, they started getting lots of inquiring telephone calls. The woman thought it was funny, but her husband was furious. One of the callers threatened to sue him for false advertising when he said the car wasn't for sale. The next time I talked to the woman, I told her I was a chip off the ole block. I learned not to mess with Dad, and she should learn not to mess with me.

## Another Payback

Dad told me many times that I could pay for my raising by raising children of my own. I repaid Dad in 1982 for crashing his Oldsmobile into the oak tree in 1959. My daughter, Jennifer, at age three was with her pregnant mother, Pam, visiting a neighbor. Jennifer took the car keys from Pam's pocket book, slipped out of the house, unlocked our car, put the key in the ignition, and pulled the gear shift into neutral. I have no way of knowing if she ever turned the steering wheel, but the car rolled out of the driveway, across the street, into the driveway of another neighbor, and crashed into the pillar of their carport. I am thankful I had good insurance, but I am more thankful my toddler didn't get hurt.

A few weeks later Mother Nature told us it was time once again, so we hurried off to the hospital. About ten hours later, with the doctor by my side, I delivered our second bouncing little baby girl. We named her Erin Michelle. We nicknamed her Shelly, and I called her that many times over the years, but it never really stuck.

## The Bridge from Hell

Camping sounded like good fun, and it was an inexpensive way for my young family to spend weekends together. My Uncle Mo had a truck with a slide in camper for sale, and I thought that was the perfect solution for camping. In March, I decided to fly to his home in Huntsville and make the purchase.

Flying from Atlanta to Huntsville in a twin engine Martin 404 propeller driven airplane in turbulent weather wasn't a great way to start a weekend. To me, the flight might've been much quicker if we had flown straight to Huntsville. With the pilot avoiding bad weather by zigzagging in one direction, then another, and the airplane bouncing up and down, it seemed like the flight took twice as long as it should. I would have preferred if the pilot had kept the airplane on the ground and taken the interstate.

Uncle Mo and Aunt Dot met me at the airport and took me out for a fine dinner. The next day I was on my way home with our new truck and camper, but I hadn't thought about the slide-in camper being wider than the truck. The side-view mirrors protruded even further. It felt like it was so wide that it took up two full lanes.

Leaving Huntsville heading toward Scottsboro, I was so thankful that I didn't have to drive over the narrow steel, super structure, B.B. Comer Bridge that was built in 1930. I drove Mom's 1965 Chevrolet Corvair across it years earlier, and I remembered thinking that the lanes were barely wide enough to hold a pencil. There was a slight rise in the road, and traffic was light when the bridge I dreaded the most came into view. With my stomach in my throat and panting rapidly, I quickly found a small place to pull over.

I was upset that I calculated my route wrong and hadn't realized it was the same route I took years earlier. After a few minutes, I started to breathe normally and concluded I could go many miles out of my way or cross the bridge. Logic won, and I knew what I needed to do. When I could no longer see traffic in either direction, I slowly pulled out onto the roadway driving perhaps fifteen mph. No sooner than the truck pulled onto the bridge, I started panting again. When I tried to drive on the right side of the yellow center line, I thought the mirrors were going to strike the bridge rails, so I made sure to ride just to the left of center.

While driving over the first half of the bridge I was very agitated, my breathing was rapid, and I thought I would not be able to cross the bridge safely. About the time I reached the halfway point, I realized I had a chance to make it all the way across, and I started to breathe easier. I started feeling like I was going to conquer the world. The physical and emotional punishment was about gone when I looked ahead to see a semi-trailer truck barreling down on me at warp speed. I gasped so hard that I think I sucked up all the cigarette butts from the ash tray. The two-lane bridge was narrow, and I knew it would take three lanes to accommodate the wide semi and my wide truck. When the semi was about a car length in front of me, I closed my eyes tight, held my breath, and braced for impact. I don't have a clue how the semi passed without hitting me, but my truck swayed like an accordion, and I was still in one piece. I got across the bridge then found the first possible place to pull off the road to gather my wits. I sat right there for a few minutes, but it felt like three weeks.

## The Catamaran

In June, we went to visit Aunt Dot and Uncle Mo at their cabin in Guntersville on the Tennessee River. Their son Ben was already there when we arrived. That afternoon, Ben and I decided to go on a short ride on his Dad's Catamaran. We forgot to get paddles, but we did remember to strap a cooler of beer to the base of the mast before we shoved off. As we managed to get to the channel in the middle of the river, the daggerboard got caught in milfoil, and shortly after, the catamaran virtually stopped. Milfoil is a highly invasive aquatic plant with curls of submerged leaves and flowers. We sat there for a few minutes, and when it didn't look like we were going to move, Ben lifted the daggerboard through the keel of the catamaran and freed it from the milfoil. When the daggerboard was no longer stuck, the wind and current started pushing us down river. Neither of us knew very much about sailing, but it was easy to see we were getting farther and farther away from his dad's boathouse.

About a half mile down river, Ben slid the daggerboard back in the water, and again the daggerboard got caught in the milfoil; we stopped. Since we were stuck, and we had nothing else to do, it made perfect sense to have a couple of beers. It worked out so well that we had another. Afterward, Ben lifted the daggerboard, and the catamaran started down river once again. We kept thinking we would run out of the milfoil if we waited long enough, so we kept going. We tried to sail out of the milfoil, but without the daggerboard we couldn't get the catamaran to mind. We could see that both sides of the main channel were free of milfoil, but nothing we did helped us to get unstuck. We were probably another mile down the river when Ben said, "We have to do something, Charlie," so he inserted the daggerboard, we stopped, and we drank more beer. We laughed at our predicament and even joked that since we were marooned sailors, we would each have to get a tattoo.

We had been gone for a couple of hours and were starting to be concerned. I spotted a motorboat not too far away, so we both jumped up and started waving our life jackets. The driver recognized that we were in distress and headed our way. He came at us with pretty good speed and shut off his motor and lifted it out of the water before he hit the milfoil. His momentum brought him close enough so we could talk. We told him our dilemma and asked him if he would help us get unstuck. He quickly pitched us a rope and let the slack out as he and his son paddled out of the milfoil. Once he was clear, he put his motor back in the water, cranked it, and pulled us out of our predicament.

Free at last, we thanked the man and set sail for home. There was just one little problem that we had not counted on, the wind was now in our face. By the time we figured out how to tack sail, we were even farther down the river. More time had been lost, and after a considerable amount of time, we started to recognize some landmarks. We began to feel a little more comfortable thinking we might make it back. It was late in the day when we spotted our starting point which was on the opposite side of the river channel. When we tried to cross the channel, we got stuck in the milfoil again. There just wasn't anything else in the world we could do except drink a beer. About fifteen minutes later, someone on the dock spotted us and sent Uncle Mo out for the final rescue. We were exhausted and sunburned and glad to be on dry land. Pam told me that if we hadn't gotten back pretty soon, they had planned to call out the marine patrol. I told her my sailing days were over, and she needn't worry because I was too afraid of needles to get a tattoo.

## No Way To End A Vacation

We were leaving Guntersville Lake heading south on four-lane highway 431 toward Albertville, Alabama, when it happened. The road was wet, and there was a pretty strong wind as we started up a small mountain. I was driving in the inside lane, and a small pickup truck started passing us very slowly on our right. The truck was about half a car length past our car when it started turning sideways. It seemed like it was happening in slow motion as I took my foot off my accelerator and watched the truck slide sideways in front of our car. The truck was so close I could very easily count the freckles on the driver's nose. I don't know if it was a wind shear or perhaps slick tires, but the little truck hydroplaned past us into the oncoming lane and was t-boned by a northbound car traveling at least sixty miles per hour.

It gave us all such a scare that I drove to the nearest pull-off on the side of the road. By the time we stopped, there were already seven or eight other cars stopped at the accident, so we didn't go back. We were too stunned to say very much, and even our little daughters were unusually quiet. We waited on the side of the road for several minutes until we got our composure and felt like moving on.

After we got home I called my uncle to let him know we arrived safely, and he told me about an accident on highway 431 that killed two people. It was déjà vu. I started reliving the accident, but I didn't tell him we witnessed it. I started imagining the faces of the two people who were killed, yet I only saw the collision in my side view mirror. *This can't be happening*, I thought, and then I saw a pair of deep blue eyes, but I couldn't make out the rest of the face. I wondered if I was losing it. I must have been quiet, or possibly even mumbling because Uncle Mo asked me if anything was wrong. Since I really didn't know, I simply said, "No." He told me a few more details about the accident and how much they had enjoyed our company. After we said our goodbyes, I started thinking about the accident, and I was dumbfounded how the truck had come that close to us without colliding. That was as close a miss as I've ever had.

## Church Camp

Several members of our Methodist Sunday School Class decided on a class-wide camping trip. Pam and I had not been members of the class very long, and we thought since we enjoyed camping, it would be a great way to get to know some of our class members.

We had sold the camper we bought from Uncle Mo and replaced it with a nice pop-up camper. The first night around the camp fire, I noticed one of the men walk away with his solo cup and return a short time later. When he returned, a different man walked away with his solo cup and returned a short time later. It really got my attention when two more men did the same thing. When the first man who got up and walked away headed out again, I didn't think he was going to the bathroom. I became suspicious, and I followed him until he got to his camper. He reached inside the camper door and pulled out a bottle of Scotch and poured a little in his cup. I must have made a sound because he turned around, saw me, and just grinned. He asked me if I wanted a sip, and I said "Hell no, I don't want a sip, but if I could have a couple of sips I would be grateful." I slept well that night.

It really was embarrassing that I didn't know it would have been okay to bring some beer along, so the next day I took care of that matter. That night when we were sitting around the camp fire, we started hearing music coming from another part of the camp ground. Someone commented, "Those people sure do have their radio turned up loud." A couple of the ladies walked away and came back about ten minutes later. They told us we wouldn't believe what they found. We followed the two women to the other side of the camp ground where we saw four old men sitting in recliners around a camp fire. They had two guitars, one fiddle, and one banjo, and they told us they had to come out here to pick because their wives wouldn't let them do it at home. We must've listened for forty-five minutes because they were quite entertaining.

## Porta-Potty Phobia

For the next several years, we continued to camp with our Sunday School Class, neighbors, and other friends. On a nice spring weekend we decided to meet some friends from Alabama at Roosevelt State Park and camp. Bonny and Keith Payne were avid campers, but Bonny had a strong aversion to things like bathhouses and porta-pottys. For the lack of anything else to call it, I will say she had portablepottyphobia. The Payne's were on vacation that week so they came in a day early and set up camp. They had a divided four-person tent that they used one half for Bonny's folding portable toilet seat. We arrived about 6:30 p.m. that Friday, set up our camper, and enjoyed a nice meal and great fellowship. Saturday was a typical day. Keith and I sat around the camp whittling and skipping rocks across the lake, and the girls went antiquing. Saturday night was uneventful, and we had lights out about 10:30 p.m.

Around 2:30 in the morning we heard Bonny screaming uncontrollably. Thinking it might be a snake in their tent, or worse a bear, I grabbed my service revolver and flashlight and headed to their camp site. When I got there Keith was standing just outside the tent. He told me everything was alright. I guess my hesitation in immediately turning around to leave prompted him to say, "She went to use the bathroom but didn't take a flashlight. She tripped over the folding toilet, knocked it over and spilled the contents." I wasn't about to ask if there was anything I could do, so I said I was sorry and headed back to my camper. Although we remained friends, we never had the opportunity to camp with them again. Keith later told me that he replaced his tent the next week.

The following September, Bonny and Keith came to visit us for the weekend. We were not the types to sit around the house and do nothing, so we all loaded up in my van and went to the Yellow Daisy Festival at Stone Mountain Park. We had lunch, and we enjoyed the fresh air and sunshine as we walked around all the various booths where people were selling their arts and crafts. Around 2:00 p.m., Bonny said that she had had enough, and it was time to go. Everyone else said, almost in unison, that we weren't ready to go. I saw Bonny lean over and whisper something to Pam. They both stepped to the side, turned their back to us, and engaged in a soft conversation. Pam would tell me later that Bonny only wanted to leave because she needed to use the bathroom, and that she convinced Bonny the porta-potty wasn't the best place in the world, but it beat the alternative. Bonny walked over to one of the porta-pottys and opened the door then closed it quickly. She went to the next one, opened the door, and after a brief look inside she went in. Keith turned to me and said, "Miracles happen every day." When Bonny came out she walked over to where Pam, Keith and I were standing and said, "You know, that wasn't near as bad as I thought it was going to be. They even had a little pouch (Urinal) on the wall for my pocketbook." Keith busted out laughing, it was all I could do not to, and Pam said, "No you didn't." We finished looking at all the arts and crafts then went home. I never asked if it was Keith or Pam who told Bonny about the urinal, but she was rather subdued for the rest of the day.

## Dodge Ball

We bought a brand new sport utility vehicle and quickly started having problems with the rear wheels bouncing every time we accelerated from a stop. I took it to the dealer where I made the purchase, and two days later they called to say it had been repaired. When I drove it off the lot, the rear wheels started bouncing, so I took it back to the shop. The next day I went back to get the vehicle and was relieved when it drove normally. Within ten minutes, however, the wheel bounce started again. Over the course of a couple of months, I took the vehicle to the same dealership a total of twenty-six times, and they were never able to solve the problem.

At the time, this particular manufacturing company had an appeals committee where unsatisfied customers could air their grievance. I filled out the paperwork, explained the problem, and mentioned that I had unsuccessfully taken my vehicle to the dealership twenty-six times for repairs. I mailed my grievance to the company, and I got a reply back in the mail in about three weeks. Words can't explain my feelings when I opened the envelope and read that the committee had dodged the ball. They ruled that I should take my vehicle to the dealership for repairs. The vehicle was a lemon, but I didn't want to fool with the Lemon Law. I traded the vehicle and haven't owned another one of that make since.

## How Silly?

When Erin was in first grade, she invited me to join her at her school cafeteria for lunch. When I had a day off I took the opportunity and did just that. We got our tray of food, sat down at a table, and she started introducing me to several of her little girlfriends. She said, "Everybody, this is my daddy. He is silly." I knew instantly that I resembled her remark, and when Pam got home that evening I told her the story. As a police officer, being silly was a trait I rarely shared with people I worked with, but around friends, well, that was another story. From time to time, and now and again, Pam doesn't necessarily remind me of that story, but she doesn't let me forget I can be silly. Incidentally, I get my silliness from my mother.

## Chapter 25

## The Bobwhite Caper

On patrol one night in an area with several car dealerships, I noticed a car tire roll down the middle of the road. None of the businesses were open, so I knew something wasn't right. I contacted partner Rick Jackson by radio, told him what I had observed, and asked him to come to the area.

We couldn't locate anything out of the ordinary, so I decided to get out of the police car and walk around. There was a wooded area about a block square, and I parked my police car in the woods out of sight. As I walked to one corner of the woods, I spotted the figure of a person, illuminated by moon light, walking along the tree line. I stepped behind a tree and waited. A couple of minutes later, the figure came near, and I heard a whistle that sounded like a bobwhite. I returned the bobwhite whistle, and then I heard another, so I whistled once again. "Is that you, Dan?" a man's voice said. I stepped from behind the tree and startled a man who we would find out later had been stealing car parts with his partner Dan.

Rick located Dan and told him he knew that he had been stealing from dealerships. Dan asked Rick how he knew, and Rick said, "A little birdie told me." Afterward, Dan confessed. We located the dealership from where the tire had been taken, and I started transporting both suspects to the county jail. Before I reached the jail, Rick called me on the radio to tell me he had located the suspect's car, and it was loaded with car parts from three different car dealers. The lesson I learned was, "A bird by the woods is worth two in a police car."

## Quotas

My police chief asked me to accompany him on a speaking engagement because I had been with the department longer, and he knew I had historical knowledge of the city that he might need. A citizen asked the chief if his police department had quotas. The chief replied, "No" and turned to me and said, "Do we?" My response was quick as a wink. "No sir," I replied, "But remember you promised I would get a free microwave oven if I write three more tickets this week." The audience laughed heartily, and I hoped they knew I was only joking. It only took a millisecond, however, to read the chief's body language and realize, quick as a wink, that I had made a CLM (career limiting move). I assumed he was embarrassed because I got a laugh and stole his show.

The following month I was invited to speak to the same civic group. At first I thought perhaps they invited me because I was funny, then it dawned on me perhaps speakers were in short supply and they couldn't find anyone else. The day of my speaking engagement came, and I was well prepared. When I arrived and started speaking, a man in the back of the room raised his hand and asked me the same question about quotas. I told him that a quota was the least number of traffic citations a police officer was required to issue in a set period of time, but we allowed our officers to write as many citations as they wanted. The audience roared. A lady asked me why I thought so many people think nothing about flying down the road. She said she knew of a guy who received three citations but still exceeds the speed limit. I told her not to worry about it because when he gets a couple more he will have to get a bicycle. My time went quickly, I really enjoyed myself, and the audience must have too. After I wrapped up my presentation, I received my very first standing ovation.

# I Took It Personally

Most people disliked handing out discipline, and I was no different. The first time I was involved in terminating the employment of a police officer, I was asked by the chief to come to his office to be a witness. When the officer left, I told the chief that he made it look easy. He replied, "It is not easy, but it is much easier when you have *right* on your side."

It was a lesson I remembered months later when the chief was out of town, and it fell on me to terminate one of our police officers. It was a week before Christmas, and dealing with this situation made a cheerful holiday less cheerful. The officer was observed taking coins out of cars parked at a local car dealership. This was long before we instituted internal affairs investigations, and I had a good witness, so I consulted with the chief by telephone then called the officer to my office. After hearing him ramble about it not being a bid deal because it was just pocket change, I told him he was being terminated. The officer said, "I just hope you are damn happy because you just ruined my Christmas."

I had always been good at taking criticism, but his comment really ticked me off. I had right on my side and he didn't. I told him he did this to himself, and if he didn't want to make matters worse he should get out of my office quickly, or I would have his ass thrown out. This was a learning curve for me, and the next time I had to tackle this unpleasant responsibility, I was much more composed.

## Chapter 26

## Something About Canoeing

C anoeing in the Okefenokee Swamp was an experience that I will remember for a lifetime. The swamp is home to 200 varieties of birds
and sixty kinds of reptiles. I saw alligators swimming through tea-colored
water, and when the Great Blue Herons flapped their wings it sounded like
helicopters taking off. I saw egrets wading through tall grass, strange looking cypress trees, insect-eating plants, and other things that can't be seen
anywhere else. Bob Welborn, his sons Justin and Aaron, two of their friends,
and I had several memorable canoe trips in the swamp, and I learned that
traveling and camping in the swamp was not without challenges.

My first trip with the experienced swamp rats was in 1992. It was a
twelve-mile trip in December on a trail called Canal Run. A private company dug Canal Run between 1891 and 1893 in an attempt to drain the
swamp to harvest the cypress timber. The trail was easy to follow because
it was straight. There were sandy banks on each side of the trail created
by the 1800s dredging process, but erosion made an occasional opening to
beautiful flower-studded and water filled wilderness prairies.

Being a novice, I wasn't sure what to bring, but being a former Boy
Scout, I wanted to be prepared. I strapped on a leather sheath with a twelve
inch bowie knife to the side of my right shin. This brought laughs from the
younger men. One even commented, "So what are you going to do with
that, Charlie, kill an alligator?" Several miles down the trail, Bob spotted

an opening to a prairie and suggested we check it out. With a twenty-one-year-old man named Bill in the front of my canoe, I steered through the opening. About ten feet in, we spotted a tiny patch of land covered in tall brown grass. About the time the front of our canoe reached the patch of land, I spotted an eight foot alligator lying with its snout near the water. As I started back paddling, I loudly announced "Alligator" to everyone. Bill was close enough to touch the alligator's snout with his paddle, so when he spotted the alligator, he started scooting backwards. I thought he was going to climb into the back of the canoe with me. If you know anything about canoes, you know that would have dumped us both in the water.

One of the young men shouted, "Get out your knife, Charlie." The cold-blooded alligator was simply soaking up the sun and really wasn't interested in us. When we put a little distance between us and the alligator, we snapped some pictures, went on our way, and I didn't get any more ribbing about my knife.

We arrived at our evening camp location at a wooden platform called a chickie. Bob's son Aaron and his canoe partner Jason were the last to arrive. Their canoe slid onto the bank, and Aaron quickly jumped to shore. His sudden movement caused the canoe to flip sending Jason into the water. The air temperature was around fifty degrees, but without a change of clothing the December evening temperatures would prove challenging for Jason. He was an incredibly good sport and didn't utter one word of complaint. We all spread our sleeping bags out on the chickie which was built on a small parcel of ground and slightly cantilevered over the water. We built a camp fire, and Jason started drying out his clothes. We all had lots of stories to tell about our fun day, but soon it was time for lights out.

Bob climbed into his sleeping bag, let out a blood curdling scream, then shot out like a shooting star. I knew he had been bitten by a Water Moccasin, but with flashlight in hand, he found that his sleep-mate was a small lizard. Our sleeping bags all lined the small chickie like sardines in a can, and our heads were at water's edge. Bob's reptile experience had done nothing to help me go to sleep, and as I lay still in my sleeping bag, I started hearing occasional bubbles in the water. We were miles and miles in the wilderness, and the only sounds to be heard were those of nature. I had previously watched numerous nature shows on television where large alligators gobbled up prey. In retrospect, I am pretty sure the bubbles were caused by gas from decaying vegetation, but at the time I couldn't get past the notion that I was prey.

Cozy and still, I started to relax. It was a curious quietness, save the frogs like a choir with their melodious tune; the sounds of the night were rhythmic and few. The stars had popped brilliant and proud, reminiscent of my childhood when gazing the sky. I was one with the world, the night was at piece, and before I knew it, I was deep into sleep.

The trip back to our van the next day was uneventful, but the entire experience had been exhilarating, and I would yearn for more. I learned a valuable lesson on that trip which was wait to unroll my sleeping bag until it was time to use it.

The following year Bob planned another trip to the swamp on a different trail. A week before we left, I stopped by a sporting goods store and picked up a new sleeping bag that was rated to keep me warm down to twenty degrees. We were scheduled to camp both nights on a chickie that was built on stilts, and surrounded by water. Since chickies were wooden, we weren't supposed to have a fire except for a camp-type gas stove. Being creative and having experience with a cold night in the swamp, I devised what I thought was an ingenious way to have a tiny camp fire. I owned a small upright smoker that came with two metal pans; one was for charcoal and the other was for water. Just before we launched, I handed Aaron two plastic grocery bags and asked him to fill each one half full of sand.

It was a clear and calm day, and we enjoyed the sights, sounds, and camaraderie as we paddled for miles. We reached our platform, set up our gear, and started talking about our trip. By nightfall the December evening was starting to get cold, so I set out one of the metal pans, filled it with sand from one of the bags, and put the second pan on top of the sand. Using some small pieces of firewood I brought from home, I started a fire in the top pan. The fire wasn't very large, but the dancing flame was alluring and a welcome addition to the cold night.

The next day the sky was overcast, and canoeing wasn't as much fun. The wind had picked up and for every two strokes of paddling, the wind pushed us one stroke back. It was an arduous trip, but we finally made it to our chickie where we would camp for the night. Feeling fortunate that this chickie had a roof, and because the wind was getting stronger, we used several large polyurethane tarps to drape the sides to make a wind break. When we finished unloading our duffle bags, a couple of the guys asked me to start another fire. Using the two metal pans and the second bag of sand, we were soon back in business. The fire helped, but not nearly as much as it had the night before because we still had wind whipping in and out of small gaps between the tarps.

At bedtime I extinguished the fire with some swamp water, and then crawled into my new sleeping bag. It was around thirty-six degrees. The wind was incessant, and at times the gusts reached twenty mph. It cut through my sleeping bag causing lots of discomfort and a long chilly night. The next day when we started packing up, I picked up the pans and realized the heavy wind had caused the fire to burn hotter. The intense heat had permeated the sand and burned an outline of the pan on the wooden chickie. It made me feel really bad, but there wasn't anything I could do at that point.

On our way back, we decided to have a last look at one of the prairies. The sun was out, the sky was blue, and it was a perfect day to enjoy nature.

We were paddling slowly through a prairie looking at carnivorous plants, watching the rough brown grass gently swaying in the breeze, and watching some egrets off in the distance. Suddenly, I started smelling a foul odor. I thought Bill on the front of my canoe had farted, but the smell lingered as we paddled along. Thinking no person could fart that long, I simply said, "Phew." Bob spoke up and explained the smell was methane gas from decaying vegetation. Everyone except Bob had suspected their canoe mate for the odor, and we all had a good laugh.

The following year we canoed a different route that took us through a very narrow canal lined with low tree branches that hung over the water. Our trail went from the Suwanee Canal side of the swamp to the Stephen Foster side; we were traveling east to west. Bob was in the front of my canoe, and when he encountered a branch in his path, he moved it aside until he floated by. When he released each branch it flew back at me like a large switch. Luckily, each time I managed to block the swinging branch with my paddle.

It was a shock when an eighteen inch thin Chain Pickerel fish with a sharp nose and teeth flopped in our canoe. It was sort of weird looking, and I didn't want to touch it. It was right at my feet, so I didn't have a choice. I bent down to grab it just as Bob pulled back a large branch. The fish was slippery, and it took me a second to get a grip. When Bob released the branch, I heard it swoosh over my head and swoosh back. Because I wasn't there to intercept the swinging branch, it swung back and hit Bob in the back of the head. The impact knocked his eyeglasses off, and they disappeared. We both thought they might have fallen into the water which made him a little anxious because like me, he couldn't see diddly-squat without eyeglasses. I was able to grip the fish and toss it out of the canoe, and then I spotted Bob's glasses in a box of food.

In 2000 the Okefenokee Swamp was suffering from a drought, and the park was closed due to a lack of water. Bob decided that we needed another canoe trip, so he mapped out a trip down the Suwannee River in Florida.

Most of my life I had heard the song, "Old Folks at Home," with the opening lyrics as Stephen Foster wrote, "Way down upon the Swanee Ribber." A few times I had driven across the interstate bridge spanning the Suwannee River and saw a sign with the name of the river and the musical notes of the opening lyrics, and each time I would mentally sing the song. Depending on who was in the car, we might've even sung the song out loud. This day was no different when we passed the sign and crossed the river, except now I was going to be able to feel firsthand the aura of the 149 year old song. I was excited.

We had lovely weather our first day paddling down the river; it was scenic and a lot of fun until Bob had an allergy attack. I guess he didn't have medicine or tissue to handle his runny nose, so when he needed to blow his nose, he tilted his head to one side of the canoe, closed one nostril with his finger and discharged the other. The unfortunate side of this was that I sat in the back of the canoe right in his line of fire. With a little wind from the movement of the canoe and the sun shining brightly, I could see and feel the spray. I yelled out to him and explained what happened. A few minutes later he discharged his other nostril except he used the other side of the canoe. I guess he thought he was doing something different, but the results were the same. I yelled out again. He apologized, but soon his nostril Niagara Falls started to run once again. When he started to lean to one side, I picked up his jacket and shielded my face. This was going to be a very long canoe trip, I thought, if one of us doesn't come up with a solution to the snotty problem. I rumbled through our gear until I found a roll of paper towels and gave it to him. Thankfully, by night fall his rushing-waters nose turned into a dry-river-bed-head.

The evening was as lovely as the day, there were no predictions for rain, and it was to be our only night on the river. Bob's sons and their two friends pitched a couple of tents, but I came up with the bright idea that Bob and I could sleep under one of our large tarps. We had a nice evening of fun and fellowship then called it a night. We were camped on a sandy bank in the bend of the river, and the water vapor condensed on the underside of our open tarp. In the morning when we woke up, our sleeping bags were soaked from dripping condensed water. I learned another valuable lesson about Mother Nature.

The return trip was electrifying. The dark waters, sometimes coffee-colored, and tall, white limestone banks were beautiful. The water was deep, and then it was shallow. In places, we saw submerged vegetation that was so bright red, it looked like a heat lamp under the water. There was an occasional small section of rapids, which for us was exciting like the Colorado River is for others.

We had a splendid time on the Suwannee River. We did swamp hollers, told tall tales and maybe even howled at the moon, but not once did we break out in song.

## Chapter 27

## The Longest Weekend

As assistant chief, one of my responsibilities in the police department was handling vehicle maintenance and department property. The chief upgraded our radio equipment, and he told me to eliminate the old radio equipment. At the chief's command, I advertised the surplus equipment and received interest from several businesses. The chief said cash only, and that sounded a little strange to me, but he was the boss. We sold a couple of mobile and portable radios, and I turned the cash over to the chief. I was uneasy about selling equipment in this manner, so I had been using a receipt book to make sure I had good documentation of the transactions.

One afternoon I was in the breakroom when the finance department manager came in. We made some small talk, and eventually I started talking about selling surplus radio equipment. The finance department manager said she had no idea what I was talking about. This made me super uneasy, so I changed the subject. We sold surplus radio equipment to three more businesses over the next several weeks, and after the last transaction my curiosity got the best of me.

Wednesday morning I went to see the finance department manager. I point-blank asked if her department had received any cash from the chief, and when she said no, I went to see the city manager. After I told him the story of the cash sales, he excused me, and then he called the finance department manager to his office. On Friday afternoon, the city manager called me to his office for what I thought would be a consultation about the ongoing investigation. I was speechless when he told me that the chief claimed he had not received any cash from me. The city manager said he had no option except to place me and the chief on leave with pay. "Be in my office Monday morning at 9:00 a.m." he said. He told me he would take both of us to the county police department for a polygraph test.

On my way home I had no idea what I would tell Pam, and I worried what she would think about me. When I told her what happened, she said she loved me, she knew that I had done nothing wrong, and she knew things would work out for the best. I was thrust into a time machine that seemed to be broken. No matter how much love and support Pam gave me, it was undoubtedly the longest weekend of my life. My career was over, my family would be ashamed, and I didn't know if I could face the members of my department when I went to clear out my office. I knew I hadn't taken any money, but it would be hard to dispute the chief.

Monday finally came, and as we were all getting ready for work and school, I thought more about the chief's allegations. I thought I was going to need a miracle, then I realized that I already had one, her name was Pam. With her support all weekend, and her encouraging words that morning, I lifted my head and went to see the city manager as directed. As I walked in his office, he smiled, but I didn't think there was anything to smile about. He told me that the chief had resigned because he didn't want to take a polygraph test, and now it wouldn't be necessary for me to take one. This was good news, but I still felt accused of theft, so I told the city manager I was ready to take my polygraph test. He replied, "I told you that you don't have to take one." With great conviction, I told him I still wanted the polygraph test because I had been accused, and I wanted to make sure I was cleared of any wrong doing. I didn't want any lingering thoughts by anyone that I had anything to do with breaking the law. Arrangements were made, I took the polygraph test, and of course, I passed with no deception. With the chief gone, the job of interim chief fell on me.

## The New Chief

The city advertised for a new chief, I submitted an application, and I was selected for an interview. The morale in our department was low, and there were several different cliques with each one pinned against the other. We needed a superhero, but we didn't know it.

When I walked into the board room to interview with the city council, I was cordially greeted. After I answered a few predictable questions, the mayor asked me if I thought I had what it takes to fix the problems in the police department. I felt pretty good about my answer because it was logical, and thorough, and most of the councilmen nodded several times while I was talking. One of the councilmen said, "Well I don't know, Charlie, there's still the issue of the missing money." His statement floored me. I thought that issue was long over. I had demanded a polygraph test, passed the test, and proved my innocence to the world. I stood up and said, "My apologies, I thought this was supposed to be an interview. I can see I am wasting my time and yours." Then I left the room. I was overly disconcerted, angrily defeated, visibly despondent, and determined never to be caught in that situation again.

The council hired a man who had great credentials but had never been a police chief. It wouldn't take long before the entire department realized that the character of our new chief matched his credentials. We had our superhero. He was a workhorse, and he expected no less from each of us. Under his leadership, the department healed. Our professionalism grew efficiently, expeditiously, and exponentially, and I was proud to give him applause.

Our new chief taught us many things, but one specific thing I learned would help shape my future as a leader. "I won't beat you up if you are close to being right," he said. In essence, he said if our decision was only slightly wrong, but we made that decision for the right reason, if he punished us we would never make decisions again.

We owned snow chains for the police cars, but I intentionally locked them in a cage with a pad lock. Past experience taught me the chains had a tendency to come loose and damage car fenders. It snowed one weekend when I was out of town, and one of my sergeants used a crowbar to break into the cage and retrieve a set of chains. Predictably, the chains were installed on one car, then came loose, and flapped against the outside fenders causing a significant amount of damage. When I got to work Monday morning and saw the damage to the car, I was livid. When I saw the busted cage, I was out for blood. I stormed into the chief's office to tell him I was going to "write up" the sergeant. He calmly looked at me and said, "Why did he do that?" I answered by saying, "He probably wanted to make sure he could drive in the snow, but I knew this would happen." The chief asked me if I told the sergeant why the chains were locked up, and I told him, "No." The chief said, "So you are telling me you never communicated your feelings to the sergeant, and now you want to punish him for doing something for the right reason. If you punish him, do you think he will ever make a decision again?" I knew he was right, but it was a hard pill to swallow because I didn't want to be wrong.

## Chapter 28

## Pagers In Church

Pagers had come into vogue, and all our department supervisors were is-sued one for department use. That first Sunday I wore mine to church. I forgot to turn off the sound and place it on vibrate. As sure as could be expected, my pager sounded loudly in the middle of the preacher's sermon. I quickly grabbed the pager and silenced it, but not before I received grins, giggles, and glares from the entire congregation. It was a valuable lesson that I would not repeat.

The following Sunday I wore my pager to church again, but this time I remembered to place it on vibrate. About the same time in the preacher's sermon my pager started to vibrate. I had never experienced a vibrating pager, and it startled me so badly that I jerked backwards, struck my elbows hard on the back of the pew and created a loud boom that echoed across the sanctuary. This time the preacher said, "Charlie Sewell, if you need attention, just raise your hand." The congregation laughed, and my face turned red. I stopped carrying the pager to church.

## What is Lunch Without A Napkin?

Jennifer was in middle school, Erin was in elementary school, and I pre-pared their lunch each morning. I always included a hand-drawn napkin with some type of silly cartoon. After a year of drawing napkins, I picked up Erin after school one day and asked how her day had gone. She instantly started crying. She said she didn't get a napkin that day. I humbly apologized. That was the first indication I had that any of the hand-drawn napkins were appreciated.

A year later, my mom, Grannie to my daughters, secretly asked Erin to save her some of the napkins. Mom had developed lung cancer which had metastasized from another location in her body. Unselfishly, and with difficulty in breathing, Mom took delivery of the saved napkins and used a toy to trace the images onto quilting squares. She added a little color to the drawings, and planned to use them to make a quilt. Mom finished all the squares, and she wanted badly to finish the quilt before she died, but she became too sick to continue. Some of Mom's friends, and her older sister, Billie Foutch Smith Breedlove, quilted the squares. Aunt Billie then took the quilt to her home, and bound the edges.

Mom was hospitalized and placed on a morphine drip because her lungs had deteriorated to the point she could only take tiny sips of air every few seconds. She was in a two room suite at DeKalb General Hospital. One room was a typical hospital room, and the other was a living area with kitchenette where my dad stayed at night. My sister Gail was in the living area, and Mom overheard her crying. Mom said to me, "What is the matter with Gail?" Gail was upset because she knew the end of our mother's life could be counted in hours. Mom also knew the end of her life was imminent, but she was more upset and worried about Gail. Like her mother before her, our mother was one of the sweetest women on the face of the earth. She never cussed, smoked, drank alcohol, and I never heard her say an unkind word about anyone. As a matter of fact, many people who knew her called her Grannie.

Mom so wanted to see the completed quilt, and she got her dying wish when Aunt Billie gave it to her on Sunday, January 17, 1993. That same day, Mom hosted over 100 visitors from her hospital bed. By the following Thursday, she was in such great pain that she said goodbye to her family. After the emotional goodbye, she asked her doctor to increase her medication so she could go into an induced coma and pass without pain. Her breaths had become so brief that we were all surprised that she was able stay alive. Mom's younger sister, Bettye Foutch Benson, along with Dad and my baby brother Jim, kept a vigil at the hospital. The next night, Aunt Bettye, who was a nurse, pointed out the stages of Mom's death as they were happening. Mom fought and fought until she had no lungs left with which to fight. Jim was holding Mom's hand when she stopped suffering around daybreak on Saturday, January 23, 1993. We all knew she was rejoicing because she was able to join her parents, and our Heavenly Father. Mom was only sixty-one years old.

My dad gave Erin the quilt a short time later. Erin told me recently the quilt has always been special, but it means much more to her as an adult than she ever could have imagined when she was eleven.

## Behind Every Good Man

Dad had a very successful career as a military leader and retired from the National Guard with the rank of Colonel. He was also extremely successful as a school principal and diligently worked through the mind-numbing and degrading influence of political bureaucracy to bring six troubled schools and one new school to the peak of performance.

When Mom was buried, it seemed like Dad's heart and soul went into the grave with her. He had always been a huge television junkie, but after Mom was gone, he just sat in his house with curtains closed and stared at the dark walls. The messages in his eyes were gone, and his blank stare made me think he wasn't thinking, but I know he was thinking deeply. Gail cleaned his house and put food in his freezer twice a week, and I called him at least once every day. He loved to fish, and he loved his eighty-five-foot houseboat, but his fishing lures remained dry, and his boat never moved. It was hard for me to put things in perspective. Had Mom always been the thrust behind Dad's success, or was he so torn by his loss that he had no will to live?

Dad didn't see the light at the end of the tunnel until one day later that year it shined. He met another woman, and on Thanksgiving Day that same year, they married. It was a sad day for me and my siblings, and it remains said to this day. They would stay married for nearly nineteen years, but I often heard him cry for my mother. He was never the same person, and I often wondered if he was just biding his time to join Mom. It is still a mystery to me if Mom was Dad's backbone, or if Dad put his own backbone in Mom's grave.

## The Bbq Team

Right after Mom died, I hooked up with some friends who enjoyed competition barbecuing. On my first trip with the Cooking Crew, we headed out on a Thursday to go to Charleston, South Carolina. We left Atlanta late in the day in an older class B motorhome pulling a trailer carrying a large smoker. It started getting dark within an hour, and we realized that of all the lights on the motorhome and on the trailer, only one headlight was working. We stopped and tinkered with the wiring, and when we couldn't get any other lights to work, we continued on our way. Three hours and forty-five minutes later, we reached Marion Square and set up our awning and smoker. With only one headlight and no taillights, I thought it was short of a miracle that we hadn't been stopped by the police or smashed in the rear by another vehicle.

The next day we enjoyed visiting with other teams and hanging out until it was time to light the fire in the smoker. With a whole hog on the grate, we took turns manning the fire all through the night. The next morning, one of the other team members stopped by, and we learned that this area of South Carolina preferred a mustard-based barbecue sauce rather than the ketchup-based sauce we normally made. We scrambled to the grocery store for supplies and quickly whipped together a new sauce recipe for the judges. We entered a whole hog, a pork shoulder and baby back ribs in the competition, but we won nothing and went home empty handed.

Heading back to Atlanta late Saturday with one headlight and memories of a fun trip, we were stopped by the South Carolina Highway Patrol. The officer was nice, but he told us we couldn't continue our journey unless we had taillights. The resourceful owner of the motorhome retrieved a twelve-volt battery that was attached to the motorhome's generator and strapped it on the trailer. Using his pocket knife to strip a couple of wires, he connected them to the battery and presto chango we had taillights.

## Chapter 29

## FBI National Academy

My police chief suggested that I apply to the FBI National Academy (FBINA), and I thought a school can't be all that bad, so I sent in an application. A few months later, I was standing in the parking lot of police headquarters and spotted the chief running in my direction. This was really out of character, and I wondered if there was a bomb or fire in the police department. He approached, and with a big grin, told me I had been accepted to the FBINA. He had attended years earlier, so he gave me some tips about getting into better physical shape and things I could expect.

In July of 1994, after a physical and a federal background check, I was on my way to Quantico, Virginia. It was hot like a frying pan when I stepped out of my van in front of the building where I was supposed to register. My shoes literally sank down into the melted tar on the parking lot, and I thought to myself, *and I am supposed to run on this.*

The academy was located in the same compound where new FBI agents were being trained. One building had a bank, post office, bar, and a cafeteria. The building next door had a gymnasium, swimming pool, and classrooms. My dorm was the third building. Each building was connected by glass enclosed walkways.

I didn't have to worry about the police department, yard work, taking care of children, or taking care of a house. For three months, all I had to do was study, go to class, do my own laundry and enjoy the experience. Life was great. This, however, was only possible because of my supportive and loving wife at home who took up my slack.

The academy offered many classes including legal issues, community policing and effective communication. All students were required to take a physical fitness class consisting mostly of lessons in the classroom. In addition, students could voluntarily accept a fitness challenge which included running in groups with the goal of winning a yellow brick.

There were fifty students in my running group, and we were fortunate to have a few former soldiers who could call cadence. One of the soldiers was a Marine who wore a prosthesis because he had one leg amputated just below his knee. Running wasn't really my forte, but the cadence helped take away the drudgery, and I ran pretty well with my group. One day we were running a particularly long run through the woods and on pavement. It was a hot and sticky August day, and the run became arduous. On our run out, we passed a Marine post that we would pass again on our return. The Marines inside the post must have spotted us as we ran out and noticed the guy with the prosthetic leg. I suspect someone in our group stopped and told them he was a Marine because as we passed back by the post, all the Marines, wearing full uniform, came out to the road with a United States Flag and ran the remaining mile back to our starting point with him. When we stopped running, the Marine removed his prosthetic leg to reveal that the friction of his prosthesis had rubbed his stub raw, and he was bleeding. Everyone was amazed at his determination, especially because he had been in such pain.

One design of the academy was networking, and our session had two hundred sixty students from twenty-six different countries around the world. One benefit of graduating from the academy was becoming part of that network for the remainder of your life. I knew I would always be able to go almost anywhere and be able to call a local graduate from any session and get help if needed.

My time at Quantico was wonderful, but after two months I was really missing my family. I didn't have classes until mid-afternoon on Monday, so Friday afternoon I flew home. Pam and the girls picked me up at the Atlanta Airport at 6:00 p.m. On our way home we stopped at our favorite restaurant for dinner. During dinner, Pam told me she was proud of herself, and she explained several issues she handled while taking care of the house. The one thing that she couldn't handle, however, was a ceiling fan that wasn't working.

The next morning I tried unsuccessfully to get the ceiling fan to work, so I drove to the hardware store to get a replacement. On the way home I got about a half mile from the store, and I noticed blue lights in my rear view mirror. I slowed down and pulled toward the side of the road, and I was surprised when the police car didn't pass. It looked like one of my police cars, but I couldn't tell for sure. I didn't think I had violated a traffic law, but I patiently waited for the officer to approach. A strapping young police officer approached and asked me for my driver's license and proof of insurance. This was uncanny because he was wearing one of my department's uniforms, and I didn't know him. I handed him my driver's license and insurance card and asked what I had done. He said, "Nothing sir, I am just practicing my pullovers." My words wouldn't come out, but I wanted to ask him if he was crazy. He handed me back my documents and said, "Have a nice day."

I stopped at the closest telephone booth and called the chief. I gave him the name that I read on the officers name plate and asked who he was. The chief explained that they hired two experienced police officers the week I left for the academy, and this officer had just been released from the Field Training Officer (FTO) program. I told the chief about the practice pullover, and he asked me if I was kidding. I responded, "No offense sir, I have a ceiling fan to install, and I certainly wouldn't waste what little time I have with my family to call and joke with you." He told me to go on home and be with my family, and he would take care of the matter.

The ceiling fan went up easily, and we had a great family visit. My flight out of Atlanta was early Monday morning, and I arrived at National Airport in Washington, D.C., before lunch. When I got to my dorm room, there was a message from the chief asking me to call the office. When I got the chief on the telephone, he told me the officer who had stopped me was no longer with the department.

We had been at Quantico for more than two and a half months, and I was becoming physically fit, probably for the first time in my adult life. It was just over a week away from graduation and time to earn the treasured yellow brick. The "Yellow Brick Road" was a six plus mile course made up of gravel road, dirt paths through the woods and a lengthy obstacle course. Three classmates that I spent a lot of time with came up with the idea that we should run the three miles out to the beginning of the "Yellow Brick Road." This would make the entire run that day nearly ten miles. I had never run that distance, but I didn't want to be hard to get along with, so I said okay.

The first leg of the run out to the normal starting point was an easy run on pavement, but I wasn't expecting what lay ahead. Up a steep hill through the woods we came across rock after rock that was partially exposed by years of rain and spray painted yellow, thus the name "Yellow Brick Road." It was the same yellow rocks that had been featured in the 1991 movie "Silence of the Lambs."

It was fairly easy up, down, around, and about until we came to the obstacle course. We ran through swampy water, used ropes to climb steep embankments, crawled in the dirt under low hung barbed wire, and jumped from one elevated log to another. This portion of the run seemed to last forever, and at the time, I thought I was experiencing the most excruciating part of the "Yellow Brick Road." I could not have been more wrong. We finished the obstacle course and started running downhill, but we kept going down until we reached the belly of the beast.

It was about two miles to the finish line, and I was wearing down fast. There didn't seem to be any air moving, and I wasn't sure I would be able to finish, but I kept thinking about the Marine with one leg and knew that I couldn't stop. We started running up the hill, and it got harder and harder. My buddies kept giving me words of encouragement, but the hill kept getting steeper and steeper. By that time my gait may have looked more like an elderly man with a cane trying to walk fast, but I was still moving. We finally reached the top of what seemed like a hundred-mile hill, and the finish line was in sight.

I finished the run and proudly received my yellow brick, then I sat down on a picnic table to enjoy an ice cold cup of draft beer provided by the academy. In about ten minutes, I finished my beer, exchanged some high fives with friends, thanked my buddies for their support, and then got up from the picnic table to go to the shower. It was like walking on cooked noodles. My legs were so weak I had a hard time making it back to the dorm.

A fellow student, Jack Watts, was not able to run with the class because his wife had been hurt in a car accident, and he had gone home for a few days to tend to her. When he returned, he asked a number of people to run the "Yellow Brick Road" with him so he could earn his yellow brick. The yellow brick, by the way, was simply a solid standard brick spray painted yellow with plastic stick-on-letters bearing the name of the academy and our session number. It might as well have been solid gold with letters made out of silver. It is a wonderful trophy that I proudly display in my home today.

Jack wasn't having any luck, and I felt sorry for him. I agreed to run the "Yellow Brick Road" a second time only if we could start at the starting point rather than run the extra three miles. It was a slightly more leisure run stopping along the way for Jack to snap quick pictures of some of the obstacles. When we graduated a few days later, he said he hadn't had an opportunity to get the pictures developed, but he promised to send me copies when he did. I knew he would send them in a week or two because we belonged to the same network.

For Labor Day, one of my fellow academy students invited me and his roommate to spend the three day holiday with his family in Suffolk County, New York. One of the places he wanted us to see was the World Trade Center (WTC). The WTC was under the control of the Port Authority Police Department, and my host's brother-in-law was a Port Authority Police Officer. The wait to ride the passenger elevator to the observation deck was about ninety minutes, but the brother-in-law pulled some strings and got us on the freight elevator right away.

The elevator was extremely fast until it wasn't. It stopped abruptly, so I asked the operator what happened. He said the building hit the elevator. I tried to correct him by saying, "Don't you mean the elevator hit the building." "No," he explained, "The building sways in the wind and it hit the elevator." That was something I didn't want to hear.

We reached the observation deck in no time, and the view was spectacular. I could see the Statue of Liberty, the day was clear and everything was great. There were two steps down from the floor to the bottom of the glass window, so I sat on the floor and put my feet down a step to enjoy the view. It was like being hit by a freight train when I made the incredible mistake of looking down. I suspect I looked like an accomplished gymnast when I made three head-over-heel flips backward then bolted toward the closest elevator. I don't remember anything specific except that I knocked down several people getting them out of my way so I could be the first person onboard when the elevator doors opened.

In the years to come, many people would learn about my acrophobia and most seemed to misunderstand. If I was driving and told anyone that I was going to alter our route because of a very tall and narrow bridge ahead, many would offer to drive. I would explain that I wasn't afraid of bridges, just afraid of height. Even if someone else was driving, I would still be up very high. It seemed to me that most people would add two and two together and get five because many folks still tease me anytime we approached even the lowest bridge.

Later that day, the brother-in-law took us to meet his mother. She was sweet and charming lady. We chatted for a few minutes and she asked me where I lived. When I told her I lived in Georgia, she let out a bellow and said, "God Damn, I hate Georgia. In 1957, my husband and I were traveling through Georgia, and he got a speeding ticket from a Georgia State Trooper that he didn't deserve." I tried to rationalize with her by saying the trooper is probably dead now, and law enforcement has changed a lot since then, but it didn't make any difference to her. She still made it emphatically clear her displeasure with the State of Georgia.

Pam, Erin, Dad and my stepmother came up for my graduation from the FBINA. There were so many people in attendance, the academy staff had to sit a number of people in a separate room where they could watch the graduation exercise on a large television monitor. When they called our names one by one, we each walked across the stage to get our diploma. The Marine with one leg, who also ran the "Yellow Brick Road," received a standing ovation when his name was called. Less than two percent of police officers in the world are selected to attend the prestigious FBINA, and I will always be grateful for the opportunity to train with the finest.

## Chapter 30

## We Finally Won

When I returned home, I resumed traveling with the barbecue team. For several months, we traveled to various places in Alabama and Georgia to compete in sanctioned barbecue contests, but we couldn't seem to do much better than third or fourth place in ribs. On one of the trips, a couple of wives joined the crew. On the trip home with a third place trophy for our entry of baby back ribs, the discussion of barbecue sauce came up.

Nearly a month later, we entered another competition armed with a new barbecue sauce that two of the crew members created in their kitchen. On the second day when all the entries had been judged, everyone congregated near a stage, and the emcee started calling out the winners. After he announced the third place winner, we were a little deflated, and after the second place winner was called, we turned to leave. Before we could get halfway through the crowd, the emcee announced we were the first place winner in the rib category. Naturally, we all scurried onto the stage to receive our trophy, a nice check, and have our picture taken by the local newspaper reporter. As we were leaving the stage, the emcee asked us to wait. He then announced us as grand champions. That meant another check, another trophy, and more pictures for the newspaper.

## The Bbq Team—The Champs

After our grand championship win, the team recognized our competition strength was cooking ribs, so we gave up cooking whole hog and pork shoulder. Cooking only ribs, over the next few years, the team traveled a sanctioned circuit and would go on to win several first-place trophies, many grand champion trophies, and we were crowned the state champions in seven states. As a matter of fact, we won so many trophies that I always took my van as a second vehicle so we had room to bring all the trophies to display.

# I Got The Point

Sweet sixteen wasn't so sweet in 1995 when I walked into our game room. The birthday party was supposed to be a rite of passage, and Jennifer's first male/female social since first grade. Her toys had been replaced with electronic devices, and the psychological, moral, and physical changes were evident. Teen idol posters replaced her lovable kitten posters, and everything pointed toward responsibility. To that end, we decided to be mellow.

I had known for years that children under the age of twenty thought their parents were categorically stupid. But waiting too long to show my presence in the party room transformed my visions of grandeur to visions of dismay, and the subject of parental naivety was indelibly clear.

Playing darts must have been too easy because the teens started throwing them from twenty feet back. This required a high arch to reach the dart board, and after six or seven ripping dart holes in the suspended ceiling tiles, boredom must have set in. Snacks were plentiful and things were good except for the imagination of fifteen not fully developed teenage brains. I might have pictured a pillow fight, but dodge ball with Pigs in a Blanket was not on my radar. The game room looked like an explosion at the Oscar Mayer Weiner factory.

After removing one dart from the game room ceiling, I got the point. I learned that decreasing parental supervision can increase harmful behavior.

I also learned that one essential part of being a good parent is love and respect. Yet another is being a good teacher and setting strong boundaries to assist children in becoming successful adults.

# The B.R.A.G.

In 1996, my brother-in-law, Chris, and I joined 2000 other bicyclists to ride the Bicycle Ride Across Georgia (B.R.A.G.). The B.R.A.G. was a 440 mile ride from Atlanta to Savannah. It was a journey to discover forgotten Georgia by bicycle. It wasn't a race, but a recreational and social event that was loads of fun. It was a challenging trip. The riders were from all ages, from all walks of life and in various stages of fitness.

I had prepared for the big ride with a couple of ten mile rides, but I was ill-prepared for what was to come. The first day was a fifty-mile ride, and I was using Chris' wife's bicycle that was too small for me. About twenty-five miles into the ride, the weight of my body started to hurt my bent wrist. About thirty miles into the ride, my tailbone started to hurt. About forty miles into the ride, I hurt all over, and I stopped to lie under a shade tree. A couple of minutes later, a man who might have been in his late seventies, rode up to me and said, "Get up boy. If I can do it, so can you." Humiliated, I got back on the two-wheel-torture machine and continued the journey. It seemed like an eternity, but we finally made it to our day's destination.

We stopped by the SAG wagon which was a semi-trailer that hauled our supplies and gear from place to place as we biked. We picked up our gear, pitched a tent, and then headed to the showers provided by our college host. It was a hot June day, and after we washed off sweat and grime, we climbed in the tent for a well-deserved rest. We hadn't counted, however, on the high temperature inside the tent, and we started to sweat again. With the lack of shade and the direct sun, we abandoned the tent until nightfall, and retreated to an air conditioned bar.

Up before the crack of dawn, we headed out for our day's sixty-five-mile ride. It was just as difficult as the last, but I enjoyed the small backroad ride. We experienced sights and smells that we could never have enjoyed riding in a car traveling down the interstate. The entire week turned out great, and the camaraderie helped take my mind off the increasing pain in my rear.

The next to the last day, we arrived at our destination and stopped by the SAG wagon. I told Chris that I had experienced enough hanging out in a hot tent, and I was going to find a motel. He balked at the idea saying we would miss out on all the fun hanging with folks telling jokes, singing, listening to guitar music, and socializing in a variety of ways. Matter not, I was done with camping.

I located a telephone in an office of our military base host. After calling and arranging for a motel room, I packed my gear on my bicycle then pushed it about a half mile to the motel. Chris was reluctant, but he followed suit. No sooner had we gotten our gear and bicycles in the room, the bottom fell out of the sky, and it rained like dumping water out of a number ten wash tubs. The next morning when we reconnected with other bicyclists, we learned that the parade ground where all the tents were pitched had flooded, and everyone's gear was soaked. I didn't have a foreshadowing about the weather, but Chris may have thought I did. He thanked me several times for pushing him to go to the motel.

When we finally arrived in Savannah, we greeted our wives who had driven from Atlanta together to pick us up. After we loaded our bicycles and gear, I checked myself into the local hospital and had my bicycle seat surgically removed.

The following summer my closest buddy, Jim, Pam's cousin Mike, and I decided to ride the B.R.A.G., but Chris had a conflict and couldn't join us. The ride started on Saturday in Lafayette and ended on Saturday in Albany.

Jim was a minister, and before we started out the second morning, he wanted me to attend church with him in Rome. We both were wearing short, skin-tight bicycle pants, t-shirts and tennis shoes, and I didn't want any part of it. He insisted, and I thought if it was okay with the minister, then it should be okay with me. We entered through the front doors of the church and realized there weren't many places to sit. We opted for a back row pew that was occupied by three elderly women. I know our clothing didn't fit the usual image of church goers, and our three pew mates didn't fit the image of sweet elderly women. They must have perceived us as hoodlums because they didn't speak and never looked in our direction. The preacher recognized Jim, and after his sermon, he introduced Jim to the congregation saying Jim and the red-headed man were with the folks riding the B.R.A.G. He then asked Jim to give the benediction. Following Jim's benediction, the preacher dismissed the congregation, a bright star shone through the windows, and a miracle happened. The three elderly ladies greeted us like we were two of the three wise men visiting baby Jesus in the manger. A few of the other congregants who had nothing to do with us earlier, now greeted us warmly.

After the third day's ride, we dincd at a local Mexican restaurant and got marooned by a monsoon. I knew the guy that I helped run the "Yellow Brick Road" lived close by, and I didn't relish the thought of riding my bicycle in the pouring down rain, so I called Jack to see if he would give us a ride. Jack lived only a half mile from the restaurant, and he had a pickup truck, so I figured it wouldn't be a big deal. He answered the phone, and I was astonished to hear him say no to my request. He said his wife had a headache, and he was going to stay with her. I guess there are always exceptions in the FBINA network. Incidentally, I still don't have copies of the pictures he took along the "Yellow Brick Road."

## Johnny Jerk

Did you ever observe someone drive like a maniac and ask yourself how the hell did he or she ever get a driver's license? It seemed to me that most people were somewhat patient when they got behind a slow-moving vehicle that had a sign denoting, "Student Driver." Often, that sign signified a teenage driver. Without the implied protection of that special sign, drivers who didn't meet or exceed the posted speed limit were often game for aggressive drivers.

During the summer of 1997 I was teaching my fifteen-year-old daughter Erin to drive, when suddenly and unexpectedly, we heard a four-second blast from a truck horn directly behind us. She was probably driving thirty-four miles per hour in a thirty-five mph zone, and she noticed the horn-blowing Johnny Jerk in her rear view mirror signal his I.Q. by extending his middle finger.

Trembling and in tears, she said "What did I do wrong Daddy?" Struggling for the perfect answer a father should give his daughter, I could only think to tell her that she had done nothing wrong. What I really wanted to say was, "Slam on your brakes baby."

I wondered if the jerk behind us realized he was offering an obscene gesture to a child. I guessed that he unleashed his temper before he engaged his brain. Erin was well within the law, within her rights, but she wasn't within the distorted driving parameters of the frenzied Johnny Jerk. Perhaps if Erin had maneuvered the car to the side of the road to let him pass, he might have reached his destination a couple of seconds earlier.

I told her that she should be careful about judging people because things are not always what they seem. "It usually isn't instantly clear if the driver of the car at the green light isn't paying attention or if the car stalled. Is the car in front speeding up and slowing down because the driver is fiddling with the radio, or is the driver looking for the correct address to deliver a Meals on Wheels?" I also told her that sometimes things are perfectly clear, and the guy that blew his horn was (DWI) Driving While Ignorant.

## The Albatross

The travel began to be a little much, so I pulled out of the BBQ team and built my own smoker. A local gas company gave me a 325 gallon propane tank, and a friend gave me an old truck axle with wheels that he found in the woods. Using a permanent marker, I drew out the location of the doors and fire box, and had the tank and axle delivered to a welder. Once my new smoker was complete, I hooked it up to my trailer hitch and brought it home. It was about fifteen feet long and more than fifteen feet worth of pride to me. I spray painted it with heat resistant black paint and parked it beside the house. When Pam came out to see it, she said, "What is that Albatross?" It looked a little like a miniature submarine on wheels, so I guess it did look a little unusual sitting in the driveway.

I wanted to only cook for a few friends, but pretty soon I had established my own reputation. A newspaper reporter got wind of my barbecue, and she called to ask if she could come out for an interview. I agreed. On May 24, 2001, the Atlanta Journal-Constitution ran a two page feature story in their food section about me and my "Smokey Pig Barbecue."

The city where I worked planned to sponsor an outdoor festival and provide games, entertainment, and barbecue for their residents. Agreeing to cook the barbecue that would be served starting at noon on a Saturday, I set up my smoker the night before and started cooking Boston Butts. When it was time to serve, there were a couple of people in line, but within a few minutes there were twenty people in line, and then there were forty. All afternoon, with the help of some other city employees, we served each person in line two pieces of white bread, pulled pork, homemade barbecue sauce, chips, slaw and a drink. There really wasn't an official count, but it was estimated that 1500 people came through our serving line that day.

I continued to add onto my smoker, as my reputation as a barbecue cook continued to build. By the time I was finished, my Albatross was equipped with a collapsible roof, an overhead shelf the length of the smoker, a kitchen cabinet with drawers, doors, and a Formica counter top. It had a double stainless steel sink, a hot and cold water system, and two large storage boxes.

A local civic group asked me to cook barbecue to help them with their annual fund raiser. Being civic-minded, always wanting to help, and always enjoying the accolades that came from serving barbecue, I said yes. I packed my smoker and another smoker they rented with Boston Butts, cooked all night, and served nearly 3000 people the next day.

# I Couldn't Believe My Eyes

When Erin was eighteen, I took her and her boyfriend to a theme park because neither one had a driver's license. I was sitting on a bench waiting for them to finish a roller coaster ride, and I noticed a very large man walk up to an exit turnstile, then he turned around and walked away. Now when I say large, I am probably talking 500 pounds or better. About a minute later he reappeared, and it looked like he was giving close scrutiny to the turnstile. No sooner than he appeared, he disappeared.

I turned my attention back to the roller coaster and saw it coming down a steep incline, and then something caught the corner of my eye. I turned just in time to see the man bouncing in place about ten feet from the turnstile. He had his hands firmly planted on his side, and he was holding up his girth. After several bounces he turned sideways and hopped his way toward the turnstile. I wasn't sure what was happening, but when he reached the turnstile I couldn't believe what I was seeing. It was like watching a balloon half full of water squeezing through a belt buckle as his circumference flopped up and down and bounced right through the turnstile. It was only then that I realized he had indeed been sizing the turnstile to make sure he could get through.

# At The Village

During the next festival sponsored by the city, I cooked barbecue once again. All day I had lines of people waiting to be served. I was as busy as could be when the disc jockey (DJ) for the event stopped by for a visit. I figured he thought he would buddy up to me and get ahead of the line for a plate of barbecue. Instead, he asked me to join him at the stage.

When I got to the stage, I saw the city manager, the fire chief, the public works director, and the police chief standing close by. I imagined the DJ was going to introduce us as sponsors of the event and publicly thank me for cooking the barbecue. When he handed me an Indian headdress, my imagination went nuts. One of the other city employees had a Leatherman hat and vest, another had a cowboy hat, the third had a police helmet, and the last employee had a construction helmet, but I still wasn't catching on. We were asked to walk onto the stage, and then the music started. Over the loud speakers I heard the song Y.M.C.A. The other four started dancing, and I stood still like a bump on a log. I heard the lyrics "Young man, there's no need to feel down. I said, young man, pick yourself off the ground." I can tell you for certain that I wanted to put myself off the stage and down on the ground. Being a good sport, however, I tried the best I could to not look any stupider than I felt.

I was familiar with the American disco group called the Village People, but I never paid a lot of attention to their music. When the chorus started, "It's fun to stay at the Y.M.C.A." the other four employees danced the letters, but all I could do was bounce and throw my hands about. I felt so goofy that all I needed to fit the part was long baggy ears. I think the DJ and audience was having so much fun at our expense that when the song ended, the DJ started playing it again. I saw out of the corner of my eye that one of the employees had turned toward the steps, and that was the proverbial music to my ears. We all exited the stage, and the audience gave a huge applause. The lesson I learned was to ask questions first.

I began to realize that I was putting a heck of a lot of effort into cooking for other people, and the charitable donation of my time and effort was costing me more than I realized. When I added everything together, I calculated my food purchase time, my twelve hours of cooking time, the hours of serving time, and the time to cleanup my equipment when I got home to be around forty hours.

Another local civic group invited me to attend one of their meetings to discuss their upcoming fund raiser. I told them I would be happy to cook barbecue, and they would be able to make approximately $4,500.00 to $5,000.00. I explained the forty hours that I would have to invest and asked them to compensate me $500.00. This was only $12.50 per hour which was less than I made as a police officer. I had several thousand dollars tied up in my equipment, I had the skill and ability to handle the job, and I thought my offer was extremely fair. One of the members spoke up and said, "That's robbery." Waiting for a club officer to defend me and my offer, I walked out in disgust when it didn't come.

Feeling more abused than used, I gave up cooking for fund raisers. I went on to cook in a couple of non-sanctioned barbecue competitions and won a couple of first and third-place trophies for my ribs and pulled pork. In time, I would sell my Albatross, regret it, and buy another then another. As I grew older and cooking for large groups got harder, I sold my large smoker and got my first wish. I bought a small electric smoker that I could set the temperature, forget about it, and enjoy my time cooking for family and friends.

## Chapter 31

## Another New Chief

Our superhero chief took a chief's position in another department but left our department much better than he found it. He was a great mentor and remains so to this day. When the city advertised for a new chief I did not apply for the job. I was still feeling the bite of my last interview. I was interim chief again for about three months; then we welcomed another visionary. We started a new community policing initiative, won several awards, and even went to Washington D.C. to receive a plaque at an awards ceremony.

## The Rowdy Prisoner

After I arrested a man for burglary and started transporting him to the county jail, he became very rowdy and belligerent. I knew I didn't want to remove him from the rear of my police car alone, so I contacted the radio operator and asked her to notify the deputies at the county jail that I needed assistance with a rowdy prisoner. When I arrived there were two deputies waiting at the back door.

The man had calmed down, and the transition from my police car to the booking room was relatively easy. The problem began during the booking process. I thought later that the deputy booking my prisoner must have had a huge chip on his shoulder because it was immediately evident that he was not happy with any answer the prisoner gave him or anything he did.

When it came time to relieve the prisoner of his personal property, the deputy walked around the counter and confronted the prisoner rather than the usual method of requiring the prisoner to place the content of his pockets on the counter. He asked the prisoner to spread his legs which was customary before a search. When the prisoner didn't instantly obey the command, the deputy kicked the prisoner's feet out from under him. In the process both the prisoner and the deputy fell to the floor. I don't know if the deputy was angry or if he was embarrassed, but he started wrestling and punching the prisoner. The deputy didn't call out for help and I didn't offer. I really didn't know what it was all about and honestly, I didn't know what to do. In hind sight I know I should have pulled the deputy up and stopped his aggression.

The deputy wrote a scathing letter to my chief complaining that he was appalled that as a sworn law enforcement officer I didn't come to his aid when he was attacked. I could tell the chief was angry when he called me into his office, but he mellowed a lot after I told him my side of the chain of events. If the deputy had ridden his bicycle into a clothes line when he was six years old, he would have known that karma is a bitch.

## Accused

A young woman came to police headquarters one day and filed a formal complaint against one of my officers alleging sexual improprieties. The accused officer denied the allegation, so an internal affairs investigation was launched. A video of the incident could not be found which made the investigation difficult.

The officer stopped by my office on his way to be interviewed about the complaint. Just before he left, I said to him that no matter how this comes out, everything would be okay. He replied to me, "You don't believe me?" Those would be the last words I would hear him say.

Shortly after the officer left from his interview, I heard an alert tone on the county radio frequency. The radio operator dispatched a county officer and an ambulance to a report of a suicide behind a shopping center just outside of our city limits. When the description of the car behind the shopping center was given, I knew in my mind that it belonged to my officer. The county police reported that the officer used his department issued police service weapon to discharged one bullet to the side of his head.

The chief asked me to accompany him to deliver the death message to the officer's family. We arrived at the home, but no one answered the door. I made a few cellphone calls and finally reached his wife. I am sure she didn't fully buy into the lame excuse I gave her why she needed to come home, but she arrived shortly thereafter. Inside her living room the chief gave her the news. That was not the first time I had been present when a death message was delivered because I had done it personally a couple of times before. This, however, was certainly the hardest because he was one of ours. One of his daughters came home about five minutes later and instantly realized the somber atmosphere. She looked confused, and I was the closest to her, so I told her what had happened. She screamed, charged me with both hands in the air and struck my chest with a heavy blow.

There is a book of details about this incident that I have not written about for various and sundry reasons. I didn't pull the trigger, and I didn't contribute to the tragedy, but I did feel a tad of responsibility. My feelings about the situation over the years would be tempestuous in the least, and this would turn out to be another book marker in the story of my life and one that I would never forget.

## Dad is Going to Kill Me

It was a relatively quiet Friday evening until our radio operator dispatched an all-call of a drive-by shooting. We received a lookout for a blue sedan occupied by two white males. The radio operator said it was reported that the passenger of the sedan fired nine rounds at movie-goers waiting in line at the Town Cinema's outdoor ticket window. Within sixty seconds, a patrol officer radioed that he was stopping a blue sedan occupied by two white males. By the time I arrived at the traffic stop, the officer and his back-up, had two suspects in custody. They had already located a 9mm pistol under the front seat of the sedan.

It was customary to separate suspects in custody to prevent them from collaborating on a story. I recognized the passenger who was the alleged shooter because I had previously arrested him. I put him in the back of my police car and headed toward headquarters. His previous arrest was for auto theft, and since he was sixteen years old at the time, he was released to his father's custody even before I finished my arrest report. Before we got to headquarters, he said to me, "My father is going to kill me when I get home tonight." I glanced down at his driver's license and noticed he had a birthday a couple of weeks earlier which meant he was now seventeen. At that time, seventeen-year-olds were considered adults and subject to jail rather than juvenile detention. I responded to him saying, "What makes you think you are going home tonight?" He started crying. He had been in trouble numerous times as a juvenile and his father had always rushed to his rescue. This night the young man had to put on his big boy panties because after he was interviewed, he was booked into the county jail.

## Chapter 32

## Rude Awakening

A round three o'clock one morning, the siren on our home security system sounded. I don't think it would have mattered whether I was asleep or wide awake, the decibels of the sudden sound reverberated in my brain. I jumped from bed, put on my eyeglasses, and headed for the alarm panel. It was a motion detector in zone eight in our basement that activated the alarm. Still wearing my birthday suit, I had a gun in one hand, a flashlight in the other, and I headed toward the basement.

Pam called out to me, "Wait for the police." I know it was frightening for her because it wasn't a picnic for me. I shouted back, "Honey, I am the police." I opened the door to the basement and started down the stairs. The staircase light was on, but the basement was pitch black, and the only light switch was at the bottom of the stairs. I knew I was illuminated and a sitting duck for any burglar in my basement.

Lights on, basement searched, and I found all windows and doors intact. A poster had apparently fallen off the wall and set off the motion detector. When I went back to bed, it took me a while to settle down and go back to sleep. Perhaps twenty or thirty minutes later, Pam put a sharp elbow into my rib cage and whispered, "Charlie, there is someone in our back yard with a flash light."

I headed for the basement again with my gun and flashlight. Throwing open the outside basement door, I stepped into the yard, and I could see a figure with a flashlight dressed in dark clothing. I illuminated the figure with my flashlight and gulped hard when I saw a shiny police badge. I hated that our alarm monitoring company forgot to cancel the police department, but I am certain the officer standing in front of me hated it worse. It's not every day someone is "unfortunate enough" to see a redheaded man wearing only a pair of eyeglasses.

## Poison

Pam was in London with two girlfriends, so I stopped by a fast-food restaurant and picked up dinner. Around two in the morning, I woke up with nausea, abdominal pain, and vomiting. By six that morning I started getting some relief. When Pam got home a few days later, I told her about getting food poisoning and mentioned that at first I thought I was having a heart attack. The word heart attack worried her greatly, and she insisted that I go see a doctor.

Being the dutiful husband I was, I reluctantly took her advice. Before I knew it, the doctor had a Holter monitoring strapped around my shoulder for forty-eight hours, which made sleeping a real challenge. When that turned up nothing I was given an Echo, Ultrasound, EKG, CT, MRI, but a PB&J would have been better because some of the tests lasted through lunch. To add insult to injury, I was poked with more than my fair share of needles. In the end, the doctor told me I was healthier than crabgrass.

## Chapter 33

## Linebacker

Pam and I were shopping at a local membership warehouse when we noticed a man running toward us. Seconds later we saw a uniformed police officer running toward us, and as he passed, he yelled to me, "Shoplifter." I was off-duty and unarmed, so I didn't participate in the foot pursuit.

About thirty seconds later I heard an audible alarm activate near the end of the row of shelves behind me. It took a second to process what I was hearing. Then it struck me. Someone had tried to open an emergency exit door. I bent over to look through the shelves and saw someone running in my direction. Easing around the end of the row of shelves, I jumped into the aisle as the runner approached and timed it perfectly to position my body like a linebacker at knee height. He tripped over me, flew into the air, and hit the concrete floor hard. Before he could get up, the pursuing uniformed police officer was on top of him applying handcuffs.

The uniformed officer told me he had chased the suspect from the shopping center across the street. He said he was running out of steam and probably would not have caught the shoplifter without my help. After he left with his suspect, Pam asked me why I got involved. I told her that I just couldn't help myself; it was sort of a cop impulse thingy.

# Chicken Legs

My chief asked me to team-teach a class in Savannah at a police conference. I had a little experience speaking to groups of fifteen to twenty people, so I readily accepted. We prepared a PowerPoint presentation and jointly rehearsed it several times. When it was our time to present, the chief went first, and I stayed in the back room listening to him through a speaker mounted on the wall. The chief was always good at public speaking, and this day was no different.

I heard him give his closing comments, and I put the final thoughts to my opening comments. The chief walked into the back room and handed me a lapel microphone and told me to knock 'em dead. *Why would I need a microphone to talk to a small group of people*, I thought? His comment was curious, and it didn't mean anything to me until I opened the door and walked into a huge lecture hall. There before me sat around 400 members of the Georgia Association of Chiefs of Police.

When I walked near the podium, the room drew quiet, and I was certain that even the people on the back row could hear my heart beat. I felt like a pipsqueak in a cage full of heavy-weight boxing champions. I said, "Good afternoon," and got a decent response. Focusing on a small group of about fifteen or twenty people, I began to speak. In less than half a minute, I was calm and on a roll. Things rocked on pretty well, I thought, until someone asked a question that I was not prepared to answer. I was showing a picture of my chief of police, my city manager and me all wearing short pants while loading a washing machine into the back of a public works truck during a neighborhood cleanup day. Someone in the back of the room shouted out, "Is that the chief's legs, or is he standing on a chicken?"

The room erupted in laughter and I erupted in shakes. I struggled to find something to say because I knew my chief was listening in the back room. I wanted to retreat, but I knew the end results would be worse. After a stammer and a stance I took the easy road and responded with, "I'll take the fifth." My comment brought a few laughs and giggles but nothing like the previous outbreak. My heart rate returned to normal, the finish to my presentation was unremarkable, my chief patted me on my back, and the day became another notch on my gun belt. From that day forward public speaking was a cinch.

## A Mentor, A Milestone

Our local school system sponsored a mentor program that looked interesting, so I took an orientation class and joined the program. I was assigned a fourth-grade-boy named Michael who didn't have a father in his home. The first time we met, his teacher asked him to show me around his school. There was nothing especially memorable about the tour, but when it was over, I told Michael I would see him the next day.

The following day I went to see him as promised, but when I got there, his classroom was empty. It was close to lunch time, so I thought he might be in the cafeteria. When I couldn't find him in the cafeteria, I spoke to one of the lunchroom workers who suggested he might be on the playground.

I exited a side door of the cafeteria and walked down a couple of steps and happened to see something out of the corner of my eye. I turned to see Michael walking down a sidewalk about twenty-five yards away. He had five volley balls in his arms, and when I called out his name, he looked at me, dropped all the balls, and started running toward me. I saw the balls roll down the sidewalk and out of sight about the time Michael leaped to give me a huge bear hug.

I was told during my orientation class that as a mentor I might never know how much I would mean to a child, but I was fortunate to receive a large and rewarding acknowledgement on my second day. I visited Michael and his class the remainder of the year and through the next year. He was a rising little league star, so I made sure I attended many of his games, and I never missed his birthday or other holidays.

Certain school lunches were better than others, so I was very selective when I chose to eat with Michael's class. I made sure to go twice a week, and I soon started to know most of his classmates. One day we were eating when I mentioned something about being redheaded. One of the girls at our table immediately chimed in that I wasn't red headed. Well, Mom always told me I was redheaded, and plenty of people had called me Red for more than fifty years, so I was floored by the comment. I admit that my hair was much redder when I was younger, but there really wasn't any arguing that I was still a ginger. When I went home that day I told Pam about the girl's comment. She said the girl was thinking about the women in her culture that sprayed or died their hair fluorescent red. I guess by those standards, I wasn't a redhead.

Michael's teacher was more than happy to have me speak to her class. On one occasion I took a set of my dental x-rays, showed them to the class, and asked if anyone could identify the animal. Since x-rays show the entire tooth including the roots, the x-rays made the teeth look much larger than what can be seen in the mouth. I got answers from a dog to a dinosaur until one student guessed correctly. During another class, I took two intact but empty Emu egg shells and showed them to the class to see if they could guess what they were. They gave me answers from Bald Eagles to dinosaurs. I was having more fun than should have been allowed at a school, and then the school year came to a close.

Michael told me he was moving when school was out, but he didn't know his new address. I was kind of lost the following year without Michael in my life. Spring forward seven years, I was standing beside my police car outside a business and I heard screeching tires. Looking toward the street, I noticed a large sedan stopping in the middle of the road. The back door opened, and a large young black man with an Afro started running toward me. He was swinging his hands, his gait was menacing, and I was apprehensive. I didn't know whether to draw my gun or retreat inside the business, but I stood my ground. When the man got close I recognized that it was Michael. He took one leap and jumped, and he hugged me so hard it was uncomfortable.

Michael had been living in South Carolina, was still playing baseball, and he was about to graduate high school. It was a grand reunion that I will never forget. It was the last time I ever saw Michael. Being a mentor was a twofer for me because Michael gave me a large and rewarding acknowledgement on our second day together and another on our last. When I reflect back on those days, I realize that every day with Michael was a reward and a milestone in my life.

## The Unending Collision

As the assistant chief, I rarely had to answer calls for service, but it was an unusual day, and all officers were busy answering call after call. Because I was also the Uniform Division Commander, and no patrol officers were available, the radio operator notified me of a vehicle collision on the interstate at a southbound exit ramp. When I arrived I found two wrecked cars on the side of the road, and it was a routine accident investigation until two more cars traveling more than seventy mph collided in the lane right next to us. The noise was deafening, and the debris flew everywhere. When the second two cars came to rest, the drivers of the first two cars told me they were frightened and were going to walk up and wait for me at the top of the ramp.

Before I could respond to the driver's comments, three more cars collided in a fiery collision in the second lane. It was astounding to me that the traffic didn't appear to be slowing down given my police car blue lights and the mess of cars, smoke and steam blowing all over the roadway. I started into the roadway to make sure everyone was out of the flaming car. Before

I could get to the car, another three car accident happened. Everyone had gotten out of the burning car, but a woman lay on the ground so close to the car that I was concerned she would be further injured as the fire progressed. The woman had a familiar long brown ponytail, and I knew that I had to know her. But when I looked at her face, I knew that I didn't. About the time I grabbed her hands to drag her away, I heard screeching tires. Two cars careened into existing wrecked cars. One car spun out and struck the concrete median wall and bounced so close to me I thought I was going to be crushed. Traffic started stopping quickly because all lanes were now blocked. Again I heard screeching tires, and then the sound of another collision when one car rear ended another about fifteen cars back up the interstate. I was able to pull the woman to safety, and very shortly afterwards, the car was fully involved in flames. Looking back at the woman again, there was something about her ponytail that made me shudder. There was too much commotion and work to be done. I quickly put it out of my mind.

By the time it was all over there were fourteen cars involved with eight injuries and one fatality. I could never have imagined that many cars traveling at super speeds crashing just feet away. In one respect it was like a dozen airplane crashes at arm's length. It was 5:30 p.m. and past the time I normally went home. Five ambulances and a firetruck arrived, and as other officers were available they came to help.

My nerves were shot. When we finally had the interstate cleared I still had more to investigate and hours of reports to complete before I could call it a day. I had many challenging times in my career and many frightening moments, but this ranked up there near the top. I finally made it home around daybreak, and it took me several hours to go to sleep. When I returned to work that afternoon I spent a few more hours finalizing my paperwork.

## Chapter 34

## It Was About Time

I had always been a little embarrassed by my lack of formal education. I thought since Pam was a teacher and had a master's degree, most people assumed I was college-educated as well. My dad insisted that I start college the summer that I graduated from high school, and in doing so, I found out that I was pretty good in junior college. I excelled in ping pong, skipping class, cafeteria, gossip and girls. It was a waste of Dad's money, but I struggled with it for a couple of years until I gave up and went to work full time driving a fork lift.

Years later my chief suggested I attend Columbus State University's (CSU) Command College. By that time I had received an associate's degree from Georgia Military College and had a few credits under my belt from the University of Virginia after attending the FBINA. At the time, Command College was designed primarily for command-level law enforcement officers who had a bachelor's degree. The concept was to graduate from Command College with a Master's Degree in Public Administration.

Because I didn't have a bachelor's degree, I took extra classes in Columbus, Griffin, and Forsyth, but when it was time to graduate from Command College, I was still short a few credits to earn my bachelor's. Because I didn't have a bachelor's degree, I couldn't be awarded a master's degree.

It was very disheartening to know I had taken many more classes than the average person who earns a bachelor's degree, but I didn't have a diploma to show for my effort. I started back to school the following semester and continued until I needed only two classes in Humanities to graduate. Pam encouraged me to take a C.L.E.P. test. I thought that was stupid because what the heck did I know about culture and history-type stuff. Pam was well read and had a lot of class, but I was just Charlie.

I had been communicating with a professor at Columbus State University, Dr. Jerry Fisher, who was very helpful in mapping out plans for me to graduate. He followed Pam's lead and started harping at me to try to C.L.E.P. Humanities, so I finally gave in. I knew it was going to be an effort in futility, but Pam and I drove down to CSU, paid the fee and into the little computer room I went.

Upon completion of the C.L.E.P. test the computer gave me a score, and if I remember it correctly it was in the low fifties. Being accustomed to normal grading scales I knew I had failed. After exiting the room I asked the lady at the desk where I could go to register to take the Humanity classes. She asked me what I scored on the test, and when I told her, she smiled and told me I had passed by a few points.

With great enthusiasm, I told the lady I had just achieved enough credits for my bachelor's degree, and I darted out of the room in a full gallop off to see Professor Fisher. His secretary told me he was out of the office for a while, so I headed in a fast walk toward the car where Pam was waiting. Before I could get to the car, I heard someone calling my name, so I turned around to see the professor chasing after me. He told me he was proud of me, put his arm on my shoulder, and we chatted as we walked to my car. He has always been a terrific supporter and remains a great influence on my life to this day.

I was still a little embarrassed being fifty-two years old and just getting my bachelor's degree, so I didn't participate in the graduation exercise. Two years later I received my Master's Degree in Public Administration and became an adjunct professor at a local college.

## Adjunct Professor

I accepted a job as an adjunct professor teaching criminal justice at the local university. Some students took my classes because they were seeking a law enforcement career; others took my classes just because they needed an elective. Teaching college was one of the highlights of my career. I loved to tell my students war stories that related to the criminal justice curriculum that we were studying. I think most of the students appreciated the fact they were being taught by someone who had real-life experience in the field.

The first day of my second semester teaching CJU101, I was stunned when a female student sat down in the first desk of the middle row directly in front of my podium and spread her legs. My first thought was she had forgotten she was wearing a skirt and didn't realize how she was sitting. Matter not, whatever the reason, I wasn't going to participate by looking. I rarely lectured from behind the podium anyway, so it was easy for me to move about and avoid the situation. Heck, I had daughters her age, and I wasn't going to be accused of being a dirty old man.

That evening I told Pam about the incident and asked her if she thought it could have been intentional. She said she didn't think any woman would do something like that intentionally. I told her it made me think of a job I had at age seventeen working as a full-service gas station attendant. When I washed the front windshield for a female driver, it wasn't terribly rare to get flashed. When it did happen it was easy to tell the difference between intent and an accident. It was usually an accident when the woman was reaching for something in her car. It was usually intentional when the woman made eye contact before she flashed. I always tried to be a gentleman, even at age seventeen, and it wasn't my fault that washing windshields naturally placed me in a front row seat for a peep show.

I still wasn't sure if the female student thought she could influence her grade, had poor sitting posture, or just didn't care, but I didn't want to be in that awkward situation. At the beginning of the next class, I made seating assignments and placed her in the far right corner of the room. I took a good amount of flak from the other students because they said they weren't in grade school, and they were too old for seating assignments. "Flashy skirt" dropped my class the following week, and I followed suit by dropping the seating assignments.

Near the end of that semester, I collected term papers that were supposed to be written about our criminal justice system. As I was grading the papers, I started reading one that surprised me because it was written so well. When I turned to the second page, my eyes focused immediately on the word Slovenia. I searched the internet for a couple of phrases from the paper and confirmed my suspicion. I could only assume the student didn't think I would read her paper, but she had turned in a plagiarized report about the criminal justice system in Slovenia. It was a 100% copied-and-pasted version of what I discovered on the internet, and she was the only student that ever earned a zero in my class. The next class period her father came to see me in a huff. He wanted to know why I had given his daughter a zero. I gave him two answers, "I don't give grades. They are earned," and "I don't deal with parents of adult students."

The following semester I created a special Saturday class for alternative students who couldn't come to class twice a week. The class met every other Saturday, and on the alternate Saturday, the students were assigned online work. On the first day of a new class, I generally asked each student to introduce themselves and tell me why they were taking Introduction to

Criminal Justice. I usually got answers like *interest in law enforcement*, or *I just needed an elective*. On the first day of this new class an older student answered, "I'm a truck driver, and I wanted to learn how to get out of traffic tickets." His comment riled me a little, and it wasn't until a week into class that I realized he had been joking. He turned out to be one of the best students I ever had the pleasure of teaching.

Teaching was fun, and I tried to make learning fun for my students. During one class lecture I said, "Everyone knows what a tort is, right?" Before anyone could answer I said, "A tort is a tiny baked open-top pastry." A female student in the back of the room retorted with a snort, "That's a tart." I told the class she was correct, and that a tort was a civil wrong committed by one person against another. During the first half of that semester, I joked with my students several times about a tort being a civil wrong and not a pastry. When I created the mid-term exam, I added the following question.

*Which of the following is a tort?*

A. *A crime punishable by less than a year in a jail or probation or a fine*
B. *The means and methods by which a crime is committed*
C. *A small open top pastry*
D. *A civil wrong committed by one person against another which entitles a person to compensation*

Another multiple choice question asked students to select the definition of officers who solicited bribes for personal and criminal gain. The choices were:

A. *Meat eaters*
B. *Grass eaters*
C. *Donut eaters*
D. *Vegetarians*

When I graded the exams, I was flabbergasted when I learned two students picked C (*A small open top pastry*) for the first question, and one student picked C (*Donut eaters*) for the second question. All three students were "A" students, so I could only assume each one purposely selected the wrong answer for fun.

At the end of the semester when I created the final exam, I must have forgotten about the mid-term funnies when I crafted the following question. *What is the term for taking or carrying away property belonging to another with the intent to deprive the owner of the property permanently?* The choices were:

A. *Burglary*
B. *Robbery*
C. *Larceny*
D. *Forcible borrowing*

Well, it happened, three students circled the letter D (*Forcible borrowing*). Unlike the humorous "A" students during the mid-term exam, the final exam letter score for these three students was only one letter higher than the letter of their wrong answer. I wanted to ask the trio, "Did someone let some air out of your tires?"

After the class was over, one of the other professors told me that I might want to look on-line at Rate My Professor. He told me that two of my students had left comments. With a little uneasiness, I did just that. One student wrote, "Excellent teacher. I learned a lot. He makes the class exciting and instructive with his personal stories." Another wrote, "Interesting professor, makes you not hate the class, even if you are not interested. Pay attention in class, keep up with reading, and exams are pretty easy." I don't know if this was good or bad, but it made me feel great.

The next semester another adjunct asked me to cover his class because he needed to drive to Florida to check on his mother. It was a criminal justice class, so following his curriculum on search and seizure was easy. About ten minutes into my lecture, I heard a slight commotion. Looking to my left I noticed a male leaning forward chatting with a female student and showing her something on his cellphone. I walked over near the couple and asked if there was something they wanted to share with the class. The male grumbled something unintelligible and sat back in his desk.

I resumed my lecture and about two minutes later, I heard the commotion again. This time the same male student was almost side-by-side on his knees talking to the female student. With a loud voice I said, "Sir, you can sit down and be quiet or leave the room." I guess he didn't need the credits. He walked out.

As soon as the door shut, a different female student spoke up saying, "The same thing happened to my brother, and he hadn't done nuthin' either." I was somewhat confused by her statement, so I asked her what she meant. She said, "He didn't do nuthin' wrong to get kicked out of class just like my brother didn't do nuthin' wrong, and he was illegally arrested." This struck a chord with me, so I asked her to explain the illegal arrest. She said her brother was taking a friend to the store, and they got pulled over by the cops because his tag was expired. "He had been out of work for a few months and didn't have no money for a tag," she said. "The cops asked him if they could search his car, and he didn't want them to, but he said yes. They found a bag of marijuana in the driver's door pocket and arrested him for possession. He tried to tell them the pot wasn't his, but they wouldn't listen. He's a good man, and the cops just wanted an excuse so they could arrest him."

As I was listening to her rant, I contemplated a diplomatic way to respond, but that ended up not being necessary. When she stopped talking, practically the entire class started making loud comments about her brother being just as guilty as the male student that walked out of class. As much as I was enjoying their comments, I had to bring the class back to order.

In another class I started a lecture by saying, "A writ of habeas corpus means to produce the body." Before I could continue a student blurted out, "My daddy had a large pit on his face that was full of corpus until he popped it." There just wasn't any way to make an intelligent response, and it was likely the only time I was ever speechless in front of a class. After I gained my composure, I went on to tell the class that a writ of habeas corpus was a court order to a prison warden or institution that had a person incarcerated to deliver the imprisoned person to the court that issued the order. The student who'd said her father had a large pit on his body dropped out of college about half-way through the semester which was probably a good thing. I won't say her bubbles never reached the surface. They didn't, but I won't say it.

# A Leg Up

Like a lot of people, we kept a lot of our seldom-used belongings in our attic. Pam asked me to get down a bag of clothing, so I climbed the stairs to the storage area and quickly located the bag. Before I grabbed the bag, I heard something that startled me. I looked over my shoulder and saw one tiny set of eyes shining through the darkness. Then there were two sets. As I turned around to hurry out, I accidentally stepped off the plywood flooring and smashed my right leg through the sheetrock ceiling. When I tried lifting my leg up, it was stuck because of a large fragment of dangling sheetrock. I could push down a little, but when I tried to pull up, the piece of sheetrock pushed into my thigh.

I thought the two sets of eyes might belong to squirrels. Then I thought of the squirrels being rabid. I couldn't move, and the rabid squirrels could soon attack. I yelled for Pam to help, and she came up the stairs quickly. With a flashlight she was able to see the problem. She went downstairs and used a broom handle to push the fragment of sheetrock to one side long enough for me to lift my leg up. Once I was free, I retreated downstairs without being attacked.

I had busted a hole in our master bathroom ceiling the size of a folded newspaper next to the vent fan. I had no idea what it was going to cost to get it repaired, but I wasn't sure which was going to be worse, paying the repair bill or admitting that I freaked out and did something foolish. In a rare moment of brilliance, I found a large return air duct grill and screwed it to the ceiling. It covered the vent fan and hole, and I never had to tell anyone what I had done. I successfully got rid of the squirrels and sealed off their entry point, but that is another story.

## It Was in The Gut

Pam and I had a 1999 Miata MX5, and one weekend we went on an overnight Miata trip. About half way to our destination, I started feeling sick and developed an ache in my gut. We checked into our hotel and then had dinner and a cocktail in the hotel restaurant. I was hoping that dinner would perk me up, but nothing I did gave me any relief, so I went to bed early.

The next morning when I got up I felt worse than the night before, and I had a small fever. We had a short breakfast and headed home. We only had a three-hour trip, but driving quickly got difficult. Pam wanted to relieve me of the driving, but she couldn't because she couldn't drive a stick shift. When we got home my fever was a little higher, so I loaded up on a shovel full of stuff from our medicine cabinet and spent the rest of the day on the couch. The next morning my gut hurt even worse. It was Monday and Pam was getting ready to go to work. She offered to stay with me and take me to the doctor, but I foolishly said no. After she left, I called my doctor's office for an appointment, and the soonest he could see me was 2:30 p.m. that day. I felt like someone was slowly slicing my gut with a razor blade. Nothing I could do would ease the severe pain and I lay on the floor in agony most of the day. My fever was 105°, and I wished over and over I had asked Pam to stay. I thought about calling an ambulance to take me to the hospital. I hurt so much I didn't even want to move to get the phone and call 911. Every second of the day seemed like a minute, every minute of the day seemed like an hour, and the wait for me to go to the doctor seemed like a lifetime.

At 2:00 p.m. I forced myself to go to my car and start driving to the doctor. I am not certain how I managed, and I am sure I was an extreme risk to myself and other motorists. Every traffic light seemed to stay red for weeks, and it seemed that each motorist stopped in the roadway forever before making a turn. I made it to the doctor's office, checked in at the nurses' station, and lay flat on the floor.

About ten minutes later, a nurse came to get me and took me to a treatment room that contained a large machine. She asked me to sign some papers authorizing the doctor to treat me, and that I understood that I could die from the test I was about to take. I became very afraid and felt very alone. I wanted Pam with me and I couldn't think of anything else. The nurse put an IV in my arm, and then I was placed into the machine.

After the test was over, my doctor came in to tell me I had diverticulitis. He said he wanted me to go to the hospital right then because diverticulitis could abscess and obstruct my colon or perforate my intestinal wall. He wanted me to have surgery the next morning because he was worried that I could develop deadly peritonitis or an even deadlier sepsis. Diverticulitis is when pouches (Diverticula) bulge in the digestive tract and get infected. I told the doctor that I needed to drop some things off at the house and get a change of clothing. He said, "No sir, I need you to go to the hospital this minute."

I left his office and drove to the police department and asked a detective to drive me into Atlanta to the hospital. I barely remember the ride, but when we arrived, I was rushed in for a battery of tests which included what seemed like several dozen hypodermic needles. It was about dark when I was admitted to a hospital room, and the first thing I did was call

Pam. It was not uncommon for me to come home late in the evening, but for some reason Pam was already worried when she answered the telephone. When I told her where I was, she freaked out. She said she was calling a friend to bring her to the hospital because she couldn't see well enough to drive after dark. I assured her there was no need for her to come that night because the surgery wasn't planned until mid-morning, and she would have plenty of time to get there before then.

My pain started to subside because of intravenous medication, and I had a good night's sleep except for being roused every two hours to have my blood pressure checked, my temperature taken, or to get a sleeping pill. The next morning I was feeling much better until I saw the surgeon walk in my room. I was afraid he was going to take me for surgery before Pam arrived, and I wanted to see her one last time because I feared I might not survive. The surgeon told me he had reviewed my hospital test results, and he felt my doctor and his technician had over-reacted to my first test results. He said the infected pouches weren't as big as he was led to believe, and he believed what I had could be treated by medicine. It was music to my ears. I was so thrilled I felt like he had just given me a winning lottery ticket. Pam came in a few minutes later looking anxious until I told her she could take me home.

A side effect of the experience was I no longer had the incapacitating sense of impending doom cold sweats and feeling of passing out when a needle entered my body. I still don't particularly like getting an injection, but today when I see a needle, I just think, *bring it on baby*.

## Chapter 35

## Into The Pit of Hell

After nine years of service, our chief resigned to take another job, and the city council advertised the position. This time I applied. The city narrowed down their selections then advertised a closed-door meeting for the council to discuss their selection for the new police chief. I was granted an interview.

About nine months earlier, I started wearing a coat and tie to work rather than khaki pants and golf shirt with embroidered badge. When people found out that I had applied to be chief, a few told me they thought I would make a great chief because I had changed. No one said how they thought I had changed, but I thought it all rather humorous because the only thing I changed was my wardrobe.

It was about a week after my interview, near the end of a college class I was teaching, and as I was wrapping up a lecture my cellphone rang. Since I was on call twenty-four hours a day, seven days a week, it was necessary for me to carry a cellphone everywhere. I stepped out of the room to answer and was excited to hear the mayor ask me to come to the city boardroom. I previously told my class that I had applied for the chief's position, so when I told them my call was from the mayor summoning me to the city board-room, they erupted in applause.

Preparing for the position of chief of police had taken years, so when the offer finally came that evening, I was naturally elated. I was also worried because I knew I was going to butt heads with my new boss. Because of that, and in the event the new job didn't work out, I updated my resume. I started searching the internet for cities advertising for a chief of police, city manager, or colleges looking for a full time criminal justice teacher. But there was something besides my new boss that was bothering me, and I couldn't figure it out. I was sure it had something to do with a brown ponytail, and maybe blue eyes. But it remained a dark cloud over my head. I shared this with Pam and she told me that she thought it had to be job stress. I told her that I had some concerns about the new job, but I was not stressed. I wasn't always able to recall things instantly, but usually if I thought about something long enough, I could unstop things that were clogged in my mind. This time, I thought I was going to need Drano.

Many people asked me why I took the job as chief if I knew I couldn't get along with the city manager. My response was simple. My diploma was on the wall, but I needed the title of chief of police to put on my resume to make it easier to get another chief's job. I was eager to be the chief because I had lots of ideas and experience that I wanted to share with my department and the city. The timing, however, wasn't conducive to my success because I had an enormously different working philosophy from the city manager.

Within eighteen months of taking the job of chief of police, it looked like my law enforcement career was coming to a close. It was a helpless feeling that I was not allowed to do my job. With over thirty years of experience, I was quite good at what I did, and working for my previous two chiefs had well prepared me for the position. I felt that the powers that be thought they knew how to better manage a police department, even though they had no supervisory or law enforcement experience. My career was being tossed like yesterday's newspaper. I gave the city 110%, and perhaps I was foolish, but I was always idealistic in thinking that if I took care of the city, the city would take care of me. The adage *No good deed goes unpunished* became reality. Ethically, I disagreed with everything the city manager was doing. I could not do his bidding, and eventually, the situation became intolerable. At the end of 2005, I turned in my badge.

The city manager was later indicted by a special purpose grand jury and re-indicted by a regular grand jury on charges related to his job. As of this writing the case has not gone to trial.

## Shangri-La and The Bootlegger

Retirement was great, and I truly enjoyed a new way of life. I grew a beard and had no responsibility outside of our home. We were empty nesters, and for the first time in our thirty-one years together, finances were not a worry. Pam was still working, so I had full run of the house during the day. I loved to piddle, so this made a very good arrangement. I prepared her breakfast and packed her lunch, which always included an affectionate note or cartoon on a napkin. My day was filled with trips to my workshop, preparing dinner, washing clothes, ironing clothes, cleaning house and an occasional golf game or a beer with a buddy. Life was good.

Utopia came to a screeching stop in June 2006, when Pam retired and gave me a housemate each and every day. My routine was no longer mine, and I no longer felt the responsibility to keep house. As a matter of fact, neither of us felt so inclined, and our new entertainment was to go shopping and spend money. The writing was on the wall, so I started looking for a job.

A job interview is traditionally set before a CEO or committee, but a month later I found myself seated for a job interview at the end of a table surrounded by elected officials, the local media, a police patrol captain, and citizens.

It had not occurred to me that I was interviewing for a police chief job in a Tennessee town rich with my family history. I had driven through and conducted business in the town twenty-five years earlier, but I hadn't thought of the first visit until earlier that day.

Before my interview, I met with the patrol captain who was kind enough to drive me around town. My mind had often played tricks on me, but it was an eerie feeling when we started across an old steel truss bridge. I suddenly had the sensation that I had been there before. My mind churned and I became suspicious, so I asked the patrol captain if there had ever been any bootleggers in his town. With a snicker he started telling me about two women with a history of purchasing tax-paid liquor in adjoining counties and reselling it in their dry county. He said, "As a matter of fact, one of them lived on the street right at the end of this bridge."

In 1982, my maternal grandmother (Grannie) died, and the funeral was scheduled for a rural county in Tennessee. The night before the funeral, my family stayed in the only motel in the town, and my uncle and I decided we wanted an adult beverage for after dinner. He said the county where we were staying was a dry county, so we went to the bigger city in the adjoining county. We looked for an ABC store or some signs about liquor sales to no avail. As we were about to cross an old steel truss bridge I noticed an older man walking along the sidewalk. I rolled down my window and asked him where I could find a liquor store. Looking over the top of his eyeglasses, he chuckled, "Boy, you're in a dry county, but if you go to the first street at the end of this bridge and turn to the right, you can buy whiskey from Miss Lorie who lives in the first house on the right."

I knocked on the front door, and a frail older woman answered and said, "Can I help you?" I told her that I wanted to buy some whiskey, and she invited me in. Once inside, she asked me if I was a police officer. I told her that indeed I was, but I was from the Atlanta area and had come to Tennessee to bury my grandmother. Miss Lorie's living room had almost no furniture, but the walls were covered with felt Jesus and Elvis pictures. She asked what I wanted then disappeared out of the room returning quickly with a half pint bottle of whiskey.

We buried my grannie the next day, and I returned to Atlanta. About a week later, I read a story in the Atlanta Journal and Constitution about Miss Lorie being arrested by the new sheriff for illegally selling liquor. Ironically, the story pointed out that Miss Lorie had donated more money to charity than any local business since WWII.

After my 2006 interview, I started driving back to Atlanta. I had not gotten more than fifteen minutes down the road when I received a call on my cellphone from a local Tennessee area code. I was giddy with anticipation, so I was delighted to hear the voice of the mayor who told me he and the city council unanimously voted, and they wanted me to be their chief of police.

I accepted the job, and by September, I was getting settled in my new office. With my new salary added to my Georgia pension, I got used to the idea of double dipping even before my first paycheck arrived. I was also elated that I was living in a town that called meals breakfast, dinner and supper. *Ha, what did Pam know? I was right after all*, I thought.

One afternoon the patrol captain strolled in and announced that he was the person responsible for my getting the job. He said on the afternoon of my interview, he shared my *Miss Lorie* adventure with some of the younger aldermen, and that is why they offered me the job. Apparently Miss Lorie was personally known, loved, and frequently visited by many people in town, including those aldermen. I seriously doubt my adventure had anything to do with the job offer, but it was a story that circulated around town for the next five years.

It was difficult living and working three and a half hours from Pam, but I settled down in a little rental house and began nesting. By October, I was well into my new job and had new experiences daily. I started speaking on a local circuit telling the various civic groups my vision for the police department. It wasn't long before I couldn't walk downtown without being recognized. People smiled, waved, and stopped to share greetings. Except for being separated from Pam, life was good.

One afternoon I was working in my office and thought it was about 3:00 p.m. As I looked out the window, I realized it was dark. I wondered if there had been an eclipse of the sun or if my clock, cellphone, and watch were all ganging up to play a trick on me. Time had gone so quickly that afternoon that I didn't realize it was actually 4:30 p.m. Clearly I had not wrapped my fingers around the fact my new town, in the Central time zone, was very close to the Eastern time zone which made darkness come an hour earlier than I was accustomed.

## Like An Old Western Movie

Once when Pam came up for a visit, we were leaving a department store, and we spotted what I would describe as a living replica from the Old West. A very tall man wearing a dark green uniform shirt, matching pants, and matching cowboy-style hat walked past us in the parking lot. He had a large Fu Manchu mustache and wore a huge shiny badge, dark sunglasses, and the longest revolver I had ever seen. His gun belt hung so low it looked like the handle on his revolver was near his knee. It wasn't until the following day, when I described him to my patrol captain, that I learned he was a constable from another county.

Constables in Tennessee were elected by the people in the county where they lived. They were sworn and bonded peace officers with full powers of arrest. Tennessee constables didn't have to meet minimum standards, pass polygraph tests, physicals, or psychological or back ground checks. They just had to get elected.

I believe the position was left over from days gone by when the sheriff had to rely on a posse of citizens to get the job done. I am not certain why anyone wanted that job because it didn't come with a salary, and the constable had to buy all equipment including gun, uniform, and police car. The State of Tennessee required police officers to undergo 400 hours of training at the police academy before being allowed to police alone. My department then required new officers to undergo another 400 hours of training with a field training officer before they were allowed to police alone. The thing that concerned me the most about constables was the state only required them to have forty hours of training by the end of their first year. Because of the lack of required qualifications for constables, some counties in Tennessee did away with the position.

## What The Heck Was That?

Late one night one of my officers was involved in a pursuit. The following day I reviewed the officer's on-board video tape of his pursuit of a small blue car. A couple of minutes into the video I saw a pickup truck with a blue light in the dash whiz past the police car. It looked as if the driver was trying to run the blue car off the road. I turned to the supervisor sitting next to me and said, "What the heck was that?" When he told me it was a constable, I was flabbergasted. That type of fool-hardy cowboy-style driving was abolished many years earlier even in small town police departments. It was a wonder the Keystone Kop hadn't caused someone to get killed. I later had words with him, but he had the legal authority, and there wasn't much I could do.

## The Badge of Discontent

Pam was still living in Atlanta trying to sell our house, and the distance between us was becoming difficult. We hadn't anticipated being apart very long, but one month would turn into three. The distance between us, however, would soon prove to be a light issue because my darkest days were yet to come.

One morning I picked up the local newspaper, and on the front page, top of the fold, the headline read "Badge of Discontent." Twelve of my officers bypassed the grievance process and took a gripe directly to the media. At an earlier department meeting, I informed all employees that we were going to change from twelve-hour shifts to eight-hour shifts. During the meeting, I told the officers that I had conducted some research and learned that seventeen percent of our crime, and only twelve percent of our calls for police service were occurring after midnight, yet we were scheduling fifty percent of our department resources to those hours. I heard a few moans, but one young police officer raised his hand and informed me that my plan would interfere with his golf. Ostensibly, he meant the twelve-hour shift was better suited for him because each week he had a day to himself. He didn't have to take care of the children or spend time handling chores for his wife. No one else uttered a word. I thought the plan might not be the most popular plan I had created, but I assumed the complaint was pretty much a dead issue.

I had made inroads with local civic groups and citizens and speaking to folks while walking downtown was fun. Up to this point my rural town of about 15,000 people had been Shangri-La, but the newspaper story made me wish I could return to age five.

Two days after the "Badge of Discontent," the newspaper ran a sequel to the story. It made me feel lower than the sole of a boot walking through pig slop. The only good thing about both stories was the newspaper gave me equal billing. My department had rebelled, but there was a positive note: I was receiving a lot of positive support from the community. Pam was in Georgia, the days were too short, and I was all alone. It was becoming a bad memory that was supposed to be a good memory. It was certainly a low point in my career that I couldn't imagine would one day be trumped by excellence.

## The Stranger

We finally had a buyer for our Georgia home which meant Pam and I would soon be reunited. We suspected something fishy was going on with our buyers, but we really didn't know for certain we were dealing with crooks. We were pleased the buyers agreed to our asking price because it included a handsome profit over what we paid to build the house just four years earlier. Our real estate agent and mortgage banker also suspected we were selling to crooks, but no one had proof. The man who came to see the house was not the man who came to the closing. About a month after closing the buyer took a $150,000 second mortgage but never paid a penny on either loan. Thankfully for us, our funds were securely deposited in our bank account. Unfortunately for the bank, their funds were stolen.

With great anticipation of Pam joining me in Tennessee, I went to the local grocery store for supplies. About three aisles into my shopping, I sensed someone was watching me. My picture had been published in the local newspaper several times, and I realized that I could easily be recognized as the new police chief. As a career police officer, I was fully aware of the dangers of the job. I slowly rounded an endcap, and as I approached the next aisle, I saw what I thought was an older woman quickly glance around the other end of the aisle, and then quickly retreat. Taking solace that I had my service weapon under my dress coat, I finished shopping that aisle and started to the next. Suddenly and without warning a frail voice stated, "Are you Charlie Sewell?" I turned to face a spitting image of my mother who died thirteen years earlier. "I am your second cousin", the woman said. "I am Doris Lee, and I am your mother's first cousin. We played together all the time when we were children." Doris Lee told me she always wanted to be named Jo Doris like my mother. We had a really nice conversation, and I really enjoyed looking at the face of this sweet woman. In my short five years as police chief, Doris Lee attended many of the police department functions that my department hosted, and she was a great supporter.

## Together Again

Pam arrived and I wasted no time in trying to help her acclimate to her new area. All of our belongings were in a moving truck waiting to be unloaded as soon as we could take ownership of a house. For a month, we used a cardboard box as our entertainment center in front of two folding beach chairs, and my laptop computer worked as a television. For meals, we moved the beach chairs to a five foot plastic folding table that doubled as our office desk. We had a washer and dryer, a double bed, and one chest of drawers, so what else could we want? We were together.

We drove around town, and I showed Pam the recently completed downtown beautification project with brick pavers, ornamental street lights, plants and more. The rolling hills were beautiful, and the county had around 500 lovely tree farms. The area was simply charming.

There was one thing about the area, however, that we found less than charming. It seemed like every time we got in a car, especially if we were going for a long ride, we smelled skunk. Skunks tended to like the edge of forests, corners of brushy fields, fence rows, open grass fields, rock out-crops and agricultural fields, and in our area there wasn't any shortage of these places. The little mammals with small head and short legs could spray their scents up to fifteen feet, and the odor could be smelled a mile away. During the five years we lived in Tennessee, either one of us could claim to have smelled more skunk than both of us combined during our entire lives. It got so common, that we would nearly declare that we got used to the odor.

Pam asked me to show her how to get to Publix, Target, Belk's, and Dillard's. I laughed and told her I could show her how to get to J.C. Penny's and BI-LO, but the other stores were an hour and a half away. I knew she was in for a huge paradigm shift, but as the years went by, she took everything in stride. We loved our little town, we loved each other, and we loved life.

## They Loved Me

When I first became a police officer, I realized more women flirted with me. It was a nice feeling, but putting things in perspective, I knew it was probably because of my police uniform. The women in this town, however, were different. Their affection was noticeable, and since I didn't wear a police uniform, I wondered if it could be my red hair. Pam and I were having a conversation, and I shared with her that all the women in town loved me. She said, "Oh, tell me more." I told her every time I stopped in a convenience store, gas station, grocery store, etc., the women called me darling or honey. She smiled and said, "I wouldn't attach too much meaning to it, Charlie. It's their culture, and it happens to me too."

## The Caricature

I received a telephone call from a reporter from the local newspaper who heard about my unique Christmas tree. All of our belongings were still in the moving van, and I wanted the holiday season to be festive, so I picked up a few cheap Christmas decorations at a local department store and decorated a five-foot step ladder. The reporter wanted to come by the house I was renting to see the ladder and I agreed. Pam was out shopping, so I left work and met the reporter at the rental house, and she snapped a couple of pictures with her little point and shoot camera.

The next evening on the way home, I stopped and picked up a newspaper. I was elated when I saw my picture standing next to the ladder on the front page of the paper, but I was upset when I saw that I had been caricatured on the third page with a quote saying "Good grief, Charlie Brown." I thought they were making fun of me. "It's funny," Pam said, pointing out that few people get caricatured and especially in a good way. Looking at it with her point of view, I realized they were laughing with me.

## Busted

We started a *Business Watch* program where we placed a small yellow sticker on the front door of every business in town. Each sticker had a unique number along with the image of the police department uniform shoulder patch. The police dispatch center agreed to maintain a list of those numbers that correlated the contact information for each key holder. If a police officer found a business unsecured during closing hours, the officer could radio in the business number and ask the radio operator to notify a key holder. That way everyone with a police monitor wouldn't know the name of the business that was unsecure.

Implementing the program took a concerted effort by the police officers because we visited every business to collect the information, and we placed a sticker on each door. After all businesses received stickers, the patrol captain came to my office. He wanted me to take a ride with him so he could show me something. We took the ride, and he pulled into the parking lot of a business and pointed out the business watch sticker on its front door. He told me the officer who placed the sticker there was our officer who was working out his two week notice to take another job. When I looked, I could see the sticker displayed the number one, and when I looked up I saw the business was the local donut shop.

We had a good laugh, but we would get to laugh again. On the officer's last day at work, I called him to my office for a customary exit interview. Laughing silently, I told him I knew who placed the number one sticker on the donut shop.

About ten months later the same officer decided he wasn't happy in his new job, so he applied for an opening in my department. We contacted him and scheduled an interview with me, the patrol captain, and three other officers. When he came into the conference room and sat down for the interview, I slid my eyeglasses down my nose, looked over the top of the frame, and said, "You placed the number one business watch sticker on the donut shop, and now you want me to give you a job?" The room was silent as he was trying to think of something to say. Moments later the five of us busted out laughing. He got the job.

## Chapter 36

## Out of The Desert

A conference sponsored by the International Association of Chiefs of Police in San Diego CA, turned out to be much better than I expected. The training was world class, and I could select classes that were germane to my department. We were invited to fine dinners each evening, and Pam and I felt like we were in luxury on steroids. Our view of the Navy ships and the bay from our thirtieth floor hotel room was spectacular.

After the conference was over, I took a few days of vacation, and we rented a car to explore the area. After driving through Torey Pines and a great night at Del Mar Beach, we headed east to see what we could see. Riding in a new rental car, we were enjoying a beautiful day until we weren't. We noticed a sign that read *Caution, roadway not county maintained, drive at your own risk.* The hillside remained pretty, but the view ahead didn't prepare us for what we were about to encounter. We topped a slight hill and our next view was 5000 feet down. The guard rail wasn't comforting; there was very little land on the other side. We were in the outside lane and in places there was no guard rail at all. For Pam, it was like looking straight down 5000 feet. The view would have been spectacular if my stomach hadn't climbed above my eyes. With both my feet on the brakes, and both of Pam's feet on her imaginary brakes, we barely drove fifteen miles per hour.

11/13/2008

About a mile down the mountain our brakes began to smoke, and the smell permeated the car. I had no choice but to stop, I was fortunate to quickly find the only right side pull-off on that stretch of road. There was a rock wall that was perhaps ten feet tall, and there was just enough dirt in front of the rock wall for us to pull off the road. When the brakes were cool and our nerves somewhat readjusted, I inched the car back onto the roadway for a slow ride down to the Ansa Borrego Desert.

My first stop was a ranger station to find out how the heck I could get back to San Diego without driving up the mountain. The ranger told me a lot of people have the same problem, and I could rent a helicopter to take me back. I thought that was a stupid idea because I had a rental car, plus flying in a helicopter might be worse than driving. It was a great relief when he said I could drive a little out of my way to the east along the Salton Sea and take I-8 back to San Diego.

On our way home the next day traveling on I-8, we saw United States Border Patrol Agents dragging a section of chained link fence behind their large SUV across a dirt field. Pam and I debated what the agents were doing. We had observed ground crews for major league baseball teams drag infields to make them smooth and attractive, so we wondered if they were clearing the field for some type of ball game. The remainder of our trip was great. During our flight back home, Pam told me she realized the agents were dragging the dirt field because it was contiguous to Mexico, and a smooth field would be easier for them to notice the footprints of people who walked across the border.

It was embarrassing that the teacher had to explain it to the cop. I should have known what the agents were doing because I had often been alerted to after-hours vehicle traffic in places like a cemetery by using a stick to draw a line across the dirt road entrance. When a car drove across the line, it left telltale tire tracks.

## Baby Backs

Uncle Mo and Aunt Dot were coming to visit, so I bought six slabs of baby back ribs to put on the smoker. After removing the membrane from each slab, I carefully coated them with a home-made dry rub. I put them in the smoker around 8:00 a.m., and they were cooking at a constant 225° when my company arrived at 11:00 a.m. Uncle Mo helped me take the ribs off the smoker, and we wrapped each one in two layers of aluminum foil. Back on the smoker for three more hours and my fall-off-the-bone masterpieces were ready precisely at 2:00 p.m. We had already eaten lunch, so I packed a couple of slabs for Uncle Mo and Aunt Dot to take home.

A couple of days later I got a telephone call from Uncle Mo. We chatted for a few minutes, then I got around to asking him how they enjoyed the ribs. He said, "Charlie, they were real good, but they were just a little hot." My mind fast-tracked as I tried to comprehend what he was saying. Thinking

Charlie Sewell

back on the morning that I prepared the ribs, I recalled thinking that the color of the dry rub looked a little more red than usual. Faster than I could say amen, I realized that I had used 100% cayenne pepper instead of dry rub. When I told Uncle Mo about my mistake, he told me he shared the ribs with his neighbors. Amazingly enough, they still considered him a friend.

# The Emerald Isle

In August of 2009, we landed in Dublin, Ireland, got off the airplane and headed to baggage pickup area to get our luggage. We brought a mossy, gray-green suitcase and a black suitcase. Pam packed half of her clothing in each of the suitcases and I did the same. It wasn't a premonition, but we theorized that if one suitcase got lost both of us would still have clothes. Before we left home, we tied a wide red ribbon with gold edges to the handle of both suitcases so we could easily distinguish our suitcases from all the others on the baggage carousel. The green suitcase came to the carousel quickly, but when the carousel stopped turning our black suitcase wasn't there. The last suitcase on the carousel was black and it looked a lot like ours except the ribbon on the handle had a wide gold ribbon with red edges instead of the other way around. We reported our situation to airline authorities, and they told us not to worry because they would locate our missing luggage and bring it to our hotel.

We headed straight to the car rental compound, and even with the missing suitcase we were excited about being with our friends Bob and Kathy Welborn for ten days. Bob had one foot in a walking cast, and he had ordered an automatic transmission rental car for our excursion. Bob completed the paperwork, got the keys to the car, and we loaded our luggage. I was walking around to get in the back seat when Bob tossed me the car keys. He and Kathy had previously driven on the left side of the road, but I was as green as the grass in Kentucky.

I didn't hit anything, and I didn't run anyone off the road that day, so I guess my Irish driving debut was a success. I will say that driving from the right side of the car on the left side of the road felt very awkward. We had a great time touring around Dublin most of the day and got to our hotel in time to freshen up before dinner. It was a rather strange feeling when we walked to our room. We passed a dumpster with a sticker on the side that said "NO BOMB PLEASE." When we got inside our room, there as promised was our missing suitcase.

A couple of days later, we stayed in a B&B owned by a couple who had two young daughters. We had been out in the rain all day, and luckily, I had a waterproof Northface jacket and rain hat. Both sides of my hat had a small strip of Velcro that would hold the brim in place when folded up. That evening I was still wearing my rain hat when we walked in the B&B and greeted the family. We all giggled when we heard the youngest daughter say, "Mom, one of the Americans has on a Stetson."

Days later we were staying in a B&B on the Irish Sea. The inn keeper asked me to move our car because a young couple who was trying to leave didn't have room to get out. The parking lot was no bigger than my living room, and six cars were tightly packed. I walked to the parking lot with the car keys and jumped into the car. The young couple was waiting in their car and had their windows rolled down so they could say thank you. I was a little befuddled because I couldn't find the key hole, and a millisecond later I realized the steering wheel was missing. It was a deer in the headlights moment when I realized I was in the passenger seat. I looked over at the now grinning young couple who were just feet away and said, "Dumb American," then hurried around to the right side driver's seat and moved the car.

On one day's excursion, I spotted a building with a sign that indicated it was a police station. Wanting to see if I could swap police shoulder patches with a member of the Ireland's National Police, I decided to stop. The grounds were surrounded by an eight-foot chain link fence with concertina wire on top. There was a single-locked gate and a push-button, and I assumed it was for a buzzer. I pushed the button expecting to see a police officer walk out the front door. When no one arrived, I pushed the button again. Being a police officer myself, I assumed everyone inside must be busy with an investigation or taking reports from other people. I paced, kicked rocks, scratched my head and thumped the shoulder patch that I held in my hand. About five minutes later, I spotted a small sign on the right corner of the property, but it was too far away for me to read. I walked over to the sign and read, *Open Thursday's from 3:00 p.m. to 5:00 p.m.* At that point, I wasn't exactly sure what the building was. The sign clearly indicated it was a police station, but I was having my doubts. Turning my head from side to side, I wondered if I was about to see a videographer approaching me laughing and saying I was going to be on America's Funnies Videos.

As our vacation continued, I continued to share some of the driving. Driving on the left side of the road from the right side of the car took unbroken concentration. I only pulled out in heavy traffic onto the wrong side of the road once, and it took me only a second to know why the other three occupants of the car were screaming. With only a few frayed nerves, we finished our trip with sanity intact.

On our flight home, we landed in Nashville during a rather severe thunderstorm. After we reached the gate, the flight attendant announced that we should remain seated and not take off our seatbelts. She told us the FAA was going to board the airplane for an inspection, and the airlines would be fined if any passenger wasn't wearing a seatbelt. By this time I was beginning to think our government had gone wild.

About two minutes after the airplane stopped, the exit door opened, and a military police officer (MP) followed by a Nashville Police Officer came walking swiftly down the aisle. They stopped about two rows behind us, and I heard the MP say, "Stand up." Less than a minute later, the MP led a young man out in handcuffs. The flight attendant once again came over the public address system, but this time she apologized for telling a little white lie. She told us the MP needed to arrest a military deserter, and it would be easier for him to come aboard if passengers weren't getting off the airplane. Everyone erupted in applause.

It was late, and we hadn't had dinner, so on our drive home we stopped at a fast food restaurant. Pam stayed in the car, and I ran in to pick up something to eat. I ordered a Big Belly Burger <u>without</u> cheese for myself. Then I ordered a Dainty Double Cheeseburger for Pam. The clerk asked me if I wanted cheese on it. Stunned at the response to my request for a double cheeseburger, I wondered if I had miscommunicated, so I repeated my request for a double cheeseburger but with an elongated, louder, and more slurred enunciation of the word CHEESE. I just didn't know how to reply when he asked me again if I wanted cheese on it. Fortunately, our order came out correct. Communicating between human beings may be the most difficult thing people do.

## Chip Off The Ole Block of Wood

For a couple of years or more, I had experienced pain in my left foot about seventy-five percent of the time when I walked. I paid a visit to a well re-nowned orthopedist, and I ultimately had a Great Toe Cheilectomy which is surgery to remove bone spurs in the big toe joint. The doctor told me up front that this type of surgery wouldn't be a permanent fix, but it could possibly buy me seven or eight years before I would need a Great Toe Fusion. The stitches came out in a week or so and I healed quickly, but I still had a considerable amount of pain.

I went back to the surgeon about ten months later, and we scheduled the Great Toe Fusion. The surgeon removed the remnants of my left big toe joint and used metal screws to fasten a metal plate on the top of my big toe bones. After surgery I was instructed that I couldn't put any weight on my foot for three months. The idea was so the two bone could have adequate time to fuse into one. Crutches got old in about a day, so I rented a knee walker from the local drug store. A knee walker is like a tall skateboard with handlebars. I could put my left leg and knee on the padded seat and push with my right.

On our first outing I realized the knee walker clipped right along at a pace faster than Pam could walk. Since I was usually way in front of Pam, people didn't know that we were together. She told me many times how funny it was when she overheard people talking about the redheaded man on that funny scooter.

I had recently traded in my black 1999 MX5 Miata convertible for a beautiful black 2007 Miata MX5 GT convertible which had a six-speed transmission. I wasn't able to drive it for the three months because of the surgery. When the surgical boot came off and I was allowed to walk again, I realized that my foot now hurt one hundred percent of the time even when I was in bed. I felt like I had been butchered.

We were members of the Music City Miata Club (MCMC), and we wanted to attend an upcoming one day club driving event. The process of depressing the Miata's clutch with the arch of my foot caused the tip of my butchered toe to press into the floorboard, and that caused a significant amount of additional pain. Pam still couldn't drive a stick shift, so I cut a two-inch by two-inch block of wood and zip-tied it to the clutch. This way I could use the arch of my foot to depress the clutch and that left adequate clearance so my toes would not touch the floorboard. We were tickled when we got to drive our Miata to the day's event.

## How Close Was It?

In June of 2010, Pam and I were headed to a resort with MCMC to attend a three day regional Miata event. We were on the Pennsylvania Turnpike, and because of construction, there was a solid concrete barrier on each side of the road that blocked anyone from using the emergency lanes. Traffic was thicker than seniors at the grocery store on discount Wednesday, and I looked in my rear view mirror and saw what I thought was a large dump truck right on my rear bumper. It was so close that I couldn't see the emblem on top of the hood. I couldn't exit, I couldn't change lanes, and I knew if I made the slightest mistake the truck would smash my little Miata like soft butter under a hot knife.

Pam and I were both frightened. We knew it wouldn't do any good to call the police, and at the moment we were wishing for a rear-mounted rocket launcher. Our exit was just a few miles down the road, but we truly wondered if we would make it that far alive. I had been tailgated many times before, and I usually thought the tailgater didn't realize how close he was. This driver, on the other hand, was sadistic. When our exit was finally in sight, I turned on my turn signal. I am not exactly sure how the driver judged the gap, but the truck got closer. I turned off my turn signal thinking I would be able to make him think I wasn't turning, but in hind sight, I know he was too close to see my turn signal anyway. The exit ramp came up, and I continued straight until the last second then took advantage of the amazing handling capability of a Miata that will go where it is pointed. Pulling my steering wheel hard right, I shot out of the trucks clutches onto the ramp while blowing my horn and gracefully giving the truck driver an affectionate finger wave goodbye.

## We Are from Clayton County

Back home, Pam and I were riding through town and spotted a car with a Clayton County, Georgia, tag. Since we had moved from Clayton County three years earlier, we were excited to catch up to the car to see if we knew the occupants. It was a couple of cars ahead of us, and I wasn't sure we would catch it, but our luck held out, and it stopped for a red traffic light allowing us to pull alongside. The driver had his window down, and I could see clearly that I didn't recognize either occupant. I excitedly rolled down my window and shouted, "We are from Clayton County." The driver shouted back, "We are from Edinburgh, Scotland." Feeling rather stupid I softly said, "Welcome to our town," then I rolled up my window. Pam said, "You know the car rental kiosk at the Atlanta Airport is in Clayton County." I always wondered if the couple went back to Scotland and told the story about the weird redhead from Tennessee.

## Chapter 37

## An Everlasting Embarrassing Moments

O nce a person attains the rank of chief of police, it could be assumed that they were a wise old owl. By the time I became chief, however, some of my street skills were rusty, and it was usually better to leave the tough work to the tougher young officers. The radio operator broadcast a report of an armed robbery at a local check-cashing business. For our department, that was a signal for all officers to respond. The lookout stated the suspects were a white male and female driving a white SUV with a partial tag number 655. A minute later the radio operator gave another description and said the person driving the white SUV was a male.

A county sheriff's deputy was close to the check-cashing business and quickly radioed that he was stopping a white SUV with a partial tag number 655. I, along with other officers, headed toward the deputy sheriff. On arrival I saw an attractive white female driver of the white SUV. She was crying and shaking and appeared scared to death. I said to the deputy sheriff "Well, this obviously isn't our man, better luck next time." There wasn't any logic to support this nice-looking thirty-something-year-old woman being an armed robber. After all, I had more law enforcement experience than any officer there and probably more experience than several of them put together.

No one uttered a word, and all officers retreated to their cars as the woman drove off. About an hour later, the radio operator placed a radio broadcast that a deputy sheriff in an adjoining county had our armed robber in custody. The description of their suspect matched with the woman we had stopped earlier in the SUV-- I was dumfounded.

Previous experience taught me that the information provided by a radio operator should only be used as a clue and not always be taken as facts. I guess it had been so long since I worked the street, I completely forgot lessons learned. Had I not become involved and let the street officers do their job, I feel pretty certain they would quickly have found the gun that the woman used in the robbery and the stolen cash that was scattered on her back seat.

I realized that there were times my mind wandered, but on this occasion, it walked away completely. I had years of experience and had successfully captured many serious criminals over the years, but at this moment, it didn't matter. I felt as useless as a wet newspaper. Not a single negative word was ever said to me about it, but for eternity, I will never forget the day my brain let go when I turned loose an armed robber.

## It Was What It Was

At home, I often talked about work related politics, goofy people I encountered, personnel issues, and programs that I wanted to establish. I wasn't, however, one to talk about some of the more traumatic and dangerous situations I encountered during my career. In November 2010, I woke up one night sweating profusely, shaking, and I started seeing images that I couldn't make out. I knew I wasn't sick, and I felt like I was outside of my body. Someone must have started a movie on the wall because I began seeing bits and pieces of disturbing events of my childhood. I saw Aunt Martha Jean in her coffin and all the dead and injured at Yellow River Drag Strip. Then I started seeing a fast forward video of every single harrowing event of my career. I saw the bloody kitchen and the elderly woman who stabbed herself, and the twelve-year-old who was killed inside the cardboard box.

Then one by one, I saw all the bloody suicides, mangled bodies, gory burn victims and painful and heartbreaking bodies of too many dead children. I was depressed, I was anxious, and I was afraid. I was hopelessly trapped as the movie reel started over; then Pam shook me and made the movie stop.

It was like a nightmare of epic proportion, but different. Pam told me I was dreaming, but I didn't think that wasn't the case. I was a frequent daydreamer, and I had experienced lots of lucid dreams where the story line was always made up of real people going about unusual, unlikely or illogical things. Occasionally, my dreams captured fragments of upsetting life's events, but they were often surreal. These visions were tantamount to a lifetime of good quality high-resolution video recordings, not a dim apparition of a betrayed memory.

Pam asked me what was wrong, and I didn't know what to tell her. I didn't understand what I had just experienced, so I lay there trying to sort it out. I knew she was waiting for an answer, so I merely said, "Well, maybe I did have a dream," but I felt like it was something different. Sixty years of suppressed and conscious memory had quickly flashed before my eyes in what I thought was a matter of minutes. In those minutes I could see a pair of deep blue eyes and a long brown ponytail, and I knew it was an image that I could not cope with. I wanted to see it clearly, and at the same time I didn't. The face did not completely appear, and I was angry. I felt a strong sense of despair, anxiety, and hopelessness. There was still a dark cloud over my head, I silently wept.

## Trumped by Excellence

The badge of discontent had come and gone, and things were rocking right along in my Tennessee department. I could walk downtown, and people would come up to me and ask, "Aren't you the new chief," and I would always answer, "Yes, and they tell me I will be the new chief until I am the old chief." I joined the Tennessee Association of Chiefs of Police and started attending meetings. It wasn't long before the association president approached me to say she wanted me to be more involved. I figured she was going to ask me to be on a committee, but instead, she asked me to chair a committee.

My committee's first assignment was to create a state process of accreditation for law enforcement in Tennessee. My committee wrote the standards, my department participated in the program, and we were awarded the 1st Charter Accreditation by the association. In 2009, I was honored by the association with the Middle Tennessee Director's Award which is often referred to as the Chief of the Year Award. In 2011, my department received the Tennessee Municipal League Achievement Award for Excellence in Police Services. By the time I was ready to become the old chief and retire again, my department had made several notable accomplishments. In my opinion, it was one of the top police departments in the state.

## Dad and The Bayonet—Fifty Years Later

Dad was getting frail, but we still enjoyed a good conversation. About two years before he died, I went to his house for a visit, and I took the opportunity to ask him about the bayonet that he gave me back in 1962. The bayonet had held a mystery for me for fifty years, and I was pleasantly surprised when Dad started talking.

He shared with me that he was a cook on a small ship in the South Pacific during WWII. He became the cook after the original cook was killed by enemy shrapnel. The captain started looking for volunteers and asked the crew if anyone had any cooking experience. Thinking that a cooking job might be better than his current assignment, Dad said he raised his hand. Truth be known, the only food he likely ever prepared was a PB&J sandwich.

The ship landed on what was supposed to be a deserted island, and when they were allowed, they got off the ship to find their land legs.

Dad said he was scouting around, and from a row of bushes a young Japanese soldier charged at him, bayonet in hand, and shouting something he couldn't understand. A Military Police Officer with a rifle had gotten off the ship at the same time but walked in the opposite direction. Dad said at first he thought he was on a movie set, but as the soldier came closer he knew it was real. The young soldier lunged at him with the bayonet, and with a jerk and a jump he somehow managed to dodge the blade. As the soldier passed, Dad said he hooked him around the neck with his arm and knocked him off his feet. He said it wasn't difficult at all to quickly snatch the bayonet from the soldier's hand, but it was surreal and at a snail's pace when he dispatched him with his own weapon. Dad was starting to show a lot of senility, and I don't know if this played into his decision to talk, but he said he had never told anyone the story before. He told me that he had suppressed the frightening and horrific day all those years because he was bothered when he thought about the face of the dying soldier. He said, "Charlie, that was about sixty-six years ago, and it still hurts." His words flashed an image in my mind, but the image vanished as quickly as it arrived. It was troubling, it was the same image that I didn't want to see, but I didn't know why. I brushed it off as just feeling sorry for Dad.

Dad was confined to a nursing home for the next couple of years. Every time I went to see him, he asked me to take him home with me. That always made me feel pretty lousy, but I didn't have the ability to provide the care he needed. On one occasion, our youngest daughter, Erin, drove from her home in South Carolina to see her granddaddy. Once inside the nursing home, she was told by the front desk attendant that she was not allowed to see him. Pam and I were also on our way to Atlanta to visit Dad when Erin called me on my cellphone. She was crying, and she was heartbroken, hysterical and almost hyperventilating. She didn't understand how this could be, and the only thing she was told by the attendant was that her granddaddy's wife had made that decision.

Pam and I stopped to see an attorney in Atlanta to talk about the situation and our options. After we left, we drove to see Dad. I was told by the attendant that I would be arrested if I didn't leave the facility right then. I asked why, but I was not given a reason. I know in my heart why we were forbidden to see Dad, but that is another story.

## Chapter 38

## Second Retirement

When I retired from Tennessee in July of 2011, I was fortunate to carry with me one of the biggest successes of my career. The police department hosted a wonderful going away party, and lots of citizens and employees attended. Members of the citizen's police academy (CPA) gave me a heartfelt plaque because I not only started the CPA, but I attended and supported every class. The patrol captain, who I previously promoted to deputy chief, and would soon follow me as chief of police, presented me with three plaques. The first was a proclamation from the Tennessee Association of Chiefs of Police which read, *In recognition of your outstanding contribution and commitment to the Tennessee Association of Chiefs of Police and the profession of Law Enforcement.* The second one was a plaque from the police department for my contributions. When he made his last presentation, he chuckled when he handed me a framed picture of a badge with the inscription, *Badge of Discontent.*

I looked around the room and became a little humbled by the people who came out to tell me goodbye. I knew at that moment that regardless of all the programs I instituted or no matter how many awards we had been given, I would not have been successful without Pam's support and the support of my top two command staffers.

## Third Time's The Charm

We were happy to be back in Georgia and closer to family. I was fortunate to get a job as police chief in a Metro Atlanta police department that was about to dedicate a new state of the art police headquarters facility. Pam and I moved temporarily into a one bedroom extended stay type motel. When we started unloading the car and taking our belongings into the motel, Pam stopped me and said, "Ha, we are back in Georgia, so now we will resume having breakfast, lunch and dinner." With our three pensions and my new salary, quadruple dipping was going to be grand. Life was great until it wasn't, and all the money in the world would not help me accept what was about to come.

## The Big "C"

It might have been the longest commute I ever had to work and back, but the excitement of a new job and a new community made it short work. Pam learned that she had thyroid cancer and needed surgery. All of a sudden my excitement was undermined by trepidation.

I brought her home from surgery with a drain tube sticking out of her throat. I saw plenty of horrific sights in my life, but this was too close to home, and it was worrisome. I was still getting adjusted to my new department, arriving early each morning, and staying past dinner time most days. The motel provided a daily breakfast and what they called a snack supper Monday – Wednesday. Since Pam's surgery made cooking a temporary issue for her, we pushed the snack supper a little and made it work as a meal. The rest of the week I cooked if I got home in time; if not, I brought take-out from a nice restaurant. The drain tube was removed in a few days, and Pam's recovery progressed well. Thankfully, somebody besides me was looking after her.

## Our New Home

After an exhausting search for the perfect home, we settled on a short-sale, even though the price was a little over what we wanted to pay. It was a six bedroom, four bath, two-story with a finished basement, and certainly the largest house we ever owned. We didn't need anything that large, but we couldn't find anything else with the amenities we wanted. The day we closed on the house, and after we took possession of the keys, we went to take another look. The previous owners had already moved, and the empty house now revealed problems that we couldn't see when it was occupied. We hired an inspector before closing, but he missed things as well. When the sofa was removed from the living room, we could see the original color of the carpet. The master closet had a California closet system which we thought was a big plus. When we saw it for the first time it held a lot of clothing, and now it was bare. I noticed a black smudge on one of the floor boards. As I attempted to rub it off, my finger broke through the wood. A quick call to the seller revealed that termites had been previously located in two other spots and successfully treated, but no repairs were made. Before we moved in, we had the termite damage repaired, and all the carpet on the main floor ripped up and replaced with beautiful hardwood floors. The house was only 10 years old, yet I wondered what else might go wrong.

We left an environment where a half day round trip was necessary to shop at a Publix. Now we could drive to a Publix in about five minutes and two more grocery stores within fifteen minutes. Places like Belk, Costco, Target, and Dillard's were a half-day round trip before, whereas our new home made these places a short hop. What we missed about Tennessee was the ability to leave home in our Miata and be in the beautiful rolling hills and country side in a matter of minutes.

## It Finally Sold

We received bids to rent, ridiculously low offers to buy, and an insane request to use it as a hotel room, and our house in Tennessee seemed like it would never sell. Eighteen months of paying two mortgages, two property taxes, two insurance policies and upkeep of two homes took a big bite out of our wallet and our nerves. I was ready to sell my first born child, shave my head, and walk barefoot across red hot coals if I could unload it.

Finally, we had a buyer, and our Tennessee home sold for a small loss, but we were still ahead of the curve because of what we netted selling the previous house. There wasn't any more overnight trips to the house in Tennessee, no more camping on the floor, no more landscaping with inadequate tools, and no more two-home related stress. It was going to be a tough paradigm shift, but I got used to the idea when the buyers picked up the ink pen to sign the sales contract.

## Possum Posse

In January of 2012, Pam and I joined the Peachtree Miata Club (PMC) in Atlanta and quickly bonded with many of the more than 160 members. We learned that a few members owned Bushtec motorcycle trailers that they pulled behind their Miata. The trailer owners called their trailers possums, and they created an informal club within PMC called the Possum Posse. I asked some of the founding PMC members how the Possum Posse got started, and I learned it happened years earlier by happenstance.

Two members of PMC, Ernie and Betty, were also members of the Central Alabama Miata Society. They bought the first Bushtec trailer followed by a PMC couple named Ron and Patty. Ron and Patty were on an afternoon top-down ride and stopped at the ranger station at Amicalola State Park for a break. While they were there, Patty purchased a stuffed Opossum because she thought it was cute. At lunch time on subsequent club rides, Ron would frequently hold the little Opossum by the tail and yell "Road Kill."

Years later, Ron and Patty were with other PMC members, Steve and Jan, scouting for a Bushtec trailer near Monteagle, Tennessee. They stopped on the side of the road for a short break and noticed a lazy Opossum lying in the roadway waiting to get run over. Soon, a motorcycle pulling a Bushtec trailer approached, and Ron was sure the motorcycle would not be able to avoid the Opossum. He reacted by tossing his stuffed

Opossum into the air to warn the oncoming cyclist. The warning was too late, and both the little critter and the stuffed animal became entangled in the trailer's axel.

Jan said to Patty, "You know Patty, that poor little Opossum needed a group of friends to watch his back." Patty replied, "I know Jan, we are fortunate that we have our own little posse of hommies to watch out for each other." The idea festered, other members bought trailers, and the Possum Posse was born. Today, the Peachtree Miata Club has nearly 100 Miata MX5s and nineteen Bushtec trailers.

## The Flats

A best buddy named Phil Brewer, from MCMC, knew that I was interested in a Bushtec trailer, and called me one day saying he found a used one for a really great price. With my blessings he bought the trailer and had it stripped and painted black to match my Miata. He also replaced the tubes and tires. In the spring of 2013, Pam and I met Phil and his wife Betty Ann in Scottsboro, Alabama, to pick up the trailer. After some lunch and visiting, I pulled my prize possum back to Georgia.

In May of that year, Pam and I were going to meet Phil and Betty Ann in Florence, Alabama, to caravan to Eureka Springs, Arkansas, for a regional Miata event. We made it as far as Muscle Shoals, Alabama, and had a flat tire on the trailer. Bushtec trailers didn't come with a spare tire, but we were fortunate that Phil had the forethought to buy a spare after he bought the trailer. We stopped in a shopping center parking lot to change the tire, but we had to unload the trailer to get to the spare. After I removed the single nut that held the wheel in place, I lifted the side of the trailer (No jack), and Pam swapped the flat tire for the spare tie. We reloaded the trailer and were off to meet Phil and Betty Ann who were nearing Florence.

We only made one mile when the tire on the other side of the trailer went flat. I pulled into another shopping center and was tickled to see a tire store. I was not tickled when the salesman told me they didn't have a way to patch the tube in my flat tire, so I walked back to the car to tell Pam the bad news. She reminded me that I had a twelve volt air pump, and if we pumped up the tire we might be able to drive farther and look for a tire shop that could patch a tube. The pump's electric cord that plugged into the accessory outlet wasn't long enough to allow the pump to reach the tire, so I disconnected the trailer and pulled it alongside the Miata. I successfully pumped up the tire, reconnected the trailer, and we headed down the road. Almost a mile later the same tire went flat. Pulling to the side of the road, I disconnected the trailer, pulled it alongside the Miata and pumped up the tire again. After reconnecting the trailer we resumed our journey and again traveled only one mile before the tire went flat. We repeated the process two more times, made two more miles, and still couldn't locate a tire store that could help.

We had already reached the manic stage and were certainly approaching the frantic and panic stage. I called Phil, told him our dilemma, and he and Betty Ann quickly came to our rescue. He told me about a mom and pop type tire store he passed a half mile or so back, and he felt like they could patch my tube. We completed the disconnect/reconnect process once again, and with the tire inflated we drove to the tire store.

It was a relief when the attendant told me he could patch the tube. When it was our turn, the attendant quickly detached the trailer, jacked it up, removed the wheel and tire and took it along with the other flat tire inside. He came back a few minutes later and told me the reason that both tires had gone flat was because the tubes were too big for the tires, and the excess rubber got pinched by the wheel.

When Phil bought the tubes and tires, he was not aware that the company sent him the wrong size tubes. It was hard to comprehend how the trailer had been pulled almost 500 miles before the tires went flat. There is never a good time for a flat tire, but it sure would have been easier if it happened when I first brought it home.

The attendant said we would need two new tubes, so we borrowed his phone book and started making calls. We called a motorcycle shop in a nearby Florence, and the clerk said they only had two tubes of the size I needed in stock. We reached the conclusion that these were the only two tubes of that size within 100 miles of our location, so Phil rushed me in his Miata to pick them up. We hurried back, and the attendant quickly installed the tubes on both flat tires then lowered the jack. By the time I got the trailer reconnected, the right tire deflated quickly, and so did I. Leaving the trailer on the side of the road wasn't an option because I didn't have a way to transport all the luggage inside. The cargo area of the trailer was at least twice the size of the Miata's trunk, and both were fully packed.

The attendant apologized then jacked the trailer up and removed the flat tire. He discovered that he had pinched the new tube with his tire mounting tool when he put the tire on the wheel. It only took about fifteen minutes to get the tube patched. We then put our possum to a trot and headed on to Arkansas.

# The Call

About two months later I received a telephone call from Dad's wife. She said if I wanted to see my father, I should come now. Pam and I immediately headed to the nursing home. When we arrived, we expected the worse, so Pam stayed in the car. I found Dad lying motionless on his back. I had heard the term about seeing death in someone's eyes, and at that moment I understood. I spoke to Dad, but he didn't answer; he didn't move. I told him that I loved him, and I waited for his reply that never came. He was breathing, but I knew in my heart, for all intents and purposes, my father had already gone to be with my mother. His blue eyes were sunk back into their sockets.

I was on an emotional zip line, and I was going down fast. In my sixty-two years I had looked into my dad's eyes countless times, they always spoke to me, but I wasn't always sure I knew their exact message. I looked into his eyes one last time, and I suddenly saw what I had not admitted to seeing my entire life. "I taught you ethics, I taught you honesty, and I taught you how to be a man." His message was clear. Deep in my heart and my mind, even though I didn't always accept it, I had always understood his message. I sobbed for my sadness, and I reveled because as hard as it had been with Dad since my mother died, I was still proud of my dad. There was no reason for me to stay longer and cry more, so I said my final goodbye.

In a daze, I walked toward my car with my mind overwhelmed with many fond memories of life's lessons that my dad taught me. During our drive home, I told Pam about my experience. She had always been my cheerleader, she had always propped me up, and today was no different. She asked me to tell her about some of his lessons, and as I was reciting things like ethics, honesty, and hard work, I remembered something else. I wasn't allowed to win the cake at the cake walk, and I remembered being mistreated by my teacher Mrs. Riley, and I remembered the two whippings I got for causing the little girl to bump her nose on the water fountain. I realized that my career of not playing favorites wasn't a trait that I developed on my own, but one that I learned from Dad. I told Pam that I had come to terms with my life with my dad, and I hoped that now, the dark cloud hanging over my head would be finally go away.

The next morning, July 5, 2012, I got the official phone call. My dad, half of the duo who taught me to be me, had passed. He was eighty-five. Sadly and sinfully, neither of my siblings, or my daughters, were allowed to see him the last year of his life.

About a month after Dad's funeral, his widow called me to say she had some of his personal effects that she wanted me to have. Pam and I drove to her house for a short visit. She gave me the flag that draped Dad's coffin, a manila envelope with some papers, and nothing more. The envelope, the bayonet, and a few military medals Dad gave me years earlier, were all the keepsakes of his that I had.

A few months later, my step-mother called me again to ask if I had a copy of my mother's death certificate. She told me she needed it so that she could collect Dad's military retirement. I told her I did not have a copy.

Nearly four years later, when I was looking for pictures for this book, I stumbled across the same manila envelope, and I opened it for the first time. Inside, I found Dad's Navy discharge papers that clearly indicated that he joined the Navy one day before his eighteenth birthday. I was also surprised to find Mom's death certificate.

## It Was Time

One Friday morning I was running a little behind schedule on my way to speak to a group of lawyers at the local senior bar association. As I reached the end of my driveway, I noticed most people on my street had their trash cans on the curb. I put my car in park and went to the back yard to get my trash can. As I was placing it on the curb, a county police officer drove up and stopped to say hello. We were having a nice conversation, and after a few minutes he told me he enjoyed my newspaper column about looking out for your neighbors. That reminded me that I had promised my neighbor across the street, who was out of town, that I would get his newspapers off his driveway. I said goodbye to the officer and headed toward my neighbor's house.

I picked up the neighbor's newspaper and placed it on his front porch. As I turned to leave I noticed that his neighbor next door, who was also out of town, had forgotten to put his trash can on the curb. Being a good neighbor, I went into his back yard to get his trash can. His dog ran up to me, and I reached down and petted him several times.

I started again toward the curb with the trash can, and as I approached his back yard gate, I slipped on some leaves and hit my head on the gate post. When I got up, I reached for my head wondering how badly I was hurt. I said to myself, *I wonder if I need a lawyer*. It was at that point that I remembered that I was running behind schedule for my speaking engagement with the group of lawyers.

I only had a slight scratch on my forehead, and the knees of my pants were only slightly dirty, so I got back in my car and drove to my speaking engagement. When I started talking to the senior lawyers, I shared with them my story about getting distracted on my way in that morning. After I finished the story there was a momentary silence, and then the group of about twenty lawyers erupted in laughter.

## Chapter 39

## A Fun Career

I had my share of being spit on, beat up, missing my children's various performances and missing most family holidays. I got tired of hearing some of the people I arrested say things like, "I guess you are happy because you are taking milk away from my baby." I would usually respond with Oh, "I didn't realize your cigarettes, beer and tattoos were free." In spite of it all, I looked forward to going to work every single day, and other than surgery, I can count on both hands the number of sick days I used in my career.

When I started in law enforcement, my only goal was to go to work and be able to come back the next day. College was not on my radar and neither was becoming a police chief. I had no realistic goals and no plans for the future. I just wanted to be "good-time Charlie." In the beginning it was anyone's guess how my career would turn out. Unlike the immature visions of a five-year-old, the vision and encouragement of others helped me to see my career exceed my wildest expectations.

My career remained challenging, exciting and very rewarding until one day it wasn't fun anymore. When I decided to retire for the third and final time, the hate for police officers in America was at an all-time high. It wasn't 1955 anymore, and respect for authority was at an all-time low.

When I retired, a police officer was being killed every fifty-three hours in our country, and I had become weary of attending the funerals of fellow police officers who were killed simply because they wore a police uniform. After 911, people would offer to buy lunch for police officers, or at least pat them on the back and say thank you similar to the way we treat our soldiers today. But the further we got from 911, the more people forgot that police officers die every day in the protection of their communities. I gave a lifetime to law enforcement, but way too many police officers gave their life.

## Farewell

I was ready to start a new chapter in my life, but I wasn't exactly sure what the new chapter was supposed to look like. I had forty-two years of memorabilia that I had to downsize before I took it home. I loaded up boxes and boxes of knickknacks, plaques, pictures, trophies, awards, certificates and diplomas that I knew most would never be unboxed. I gave away most of my collection of foreign police hats, my shoulder patch collection, and a host of coffee cups and other trinkets. After my lifetime of moving from town to town and changing from department to department, I had not learned the art of graceful departure. Saying goodbye wasn't coming easy, but then again it never had. Wrapping my fingers around the word "Final" when I spoke of final retirement would prove to be a challenge. It was farewell to a way of life. I learned many things during my career about how to properly treat people. Probably the most valuable lesson I learned, I learned from my mother, which was to police from my heart.

After being a public servant for two-thirds of my life, I was lost in retirement. There were no alarm clocks, no night time meetings, no angry citizens and no uniforms to iron. My cellphone stopped ringing, and it would stay charged for days. Gone were the phone calls in the middle of the night, and the anguish and the stress. Final retirement had not come easy, and it took about three months for me to learn who I was, and what I found out was that I was Charlie.

I believe I achieved my purpose by mentoring elementary school students and young police officers. I raised two wonderful daughters who make me very happy. Holding doors open for other people is a purpose just like picking up a lunch tab for a soldier. My purpose was to share good as much as I possibly could, and set the example by walking an ethical and honest path. I am very thankful and fortunate that Pam held my hand and walked with me every single inch along that route. I now know that my purpose hasn't changed, and I will continue to cherish life, to love, and occasionally sleep between naps. Life is indeed good.

# It Came During The Night

One of the impetuses for writing this book came early in 2016. I woke up in the middle of the night in a cold sweat, I was shaking, and once again I started seeing images that I couldn't make out. I was anxious and angry, but I didn't know why. I knew I wasn't sick, and I felt like I was outside of my body. I thought the same movie that I saw in 2010 was showing on the wall again, but this time I was seeing a clearer image of something that I wish I had not seen many years earlier.

I began to remember what I actually saw in the back seat of the car that I first thought was a convertible back in 1962. For fifty-three years I had repressed what I didn't want to see, what I didn't want to believe, and what hurt me so badly.

When I was twelve, I nudged my way through the crowd to get close enough to the car. I saw a little girl's body with her head hanging upside down on the side of her shoulder. There was blood all over her blouse and in her long brown ponytail. I did not recognize her, but I was close enough to see that her eye lids were not fully closed. I looked directly into her eyes. They were deep blue eyes. I couldn't stop looking at them. I was captured in the moment, I was traumatized by what I was seeing, yet I started walking toward her. She looked so sad, and she was alone in the back seat of the car. I was afraid.

A man grabbed my arm, jerked me back, and yelled, "Get out of here." As I started walking back past the line of cars with my head hung low, I recognized the sound of Dad's footsteps on the pavement, then I looked up to see him coming to get me. We got back in the car, turned it around and left for home without going fishing. I didn't say a word the entire way home. Even the sound of Dad and his buddy talking in the front seat sounded like they were miles away. What I had just observed was deeply disturbing, and I was trying my best to shut down the image, but it would not go away. I struggled through the evening and into the night, to understand, to sleep, and to forget.

As soon as I walked into school the following morning I learned that the sad little girl with the brown ponytail was my classmate, Carolyn Massey. I immediately repressed the image of what I had observed the day before.

I must have thrashed around or made some noise because Pam was awake. She asked me what was wrong. At first, I couldn't answer. She asked again and I told her what I had remembered. Then I remembered the story my dad told me about dispatching the Japanese soldier, and about how he suppressed the image of the young soldier's face for nearly sixty-six years. Dad had been able to share with me his horrid experience, and I wanted badly to talk to him just once more. We had a bond, a shared experience. I wanted to tell him I understood. I wanted to tell him what I didn't tell him when he told me his story. I wanted to tell him it is okay. I also wanted to tell him about Carolyn Massey.

I thought about the day that I found the bayonet, the day my granddaddy told me it belonged to my dad. That was the same day Dad told me that he brought it home from the war. It was a Sunday. Then I realized it was the day before I saw the decapitated small body of Carolyn Massey.

During my teenage years and law enforcement career, a lot of the dead people I saw had their eyes partially open. Each time there was something surreal about what I was seeing, but I could never put my finger on it. From the moment I woke up in the cold sweat, I realized that I had been seeing Carolyn's eyes. Not once did I consciously think about her. I remembered seeing the man who was decapitated when the parachute snatched him at the Yellow River Drag Strip. For nearly five decades, I had not remembered that I had seen that type of carnage before. It was a solemn moment thinking about how hard it had been to handle the death of my classmate in the sixth grade. Then I realized how hard it had been to handle all the deaths that I encountered in my life. It was never easy, but I kept on marching because life just had a way of happening.

# Epilogue

*G*rowing up and into my twenties I did some really risky things, but the thought of my own death never occurred to me. It was a life defining moment sometime between age thirty and forty when I recognized the distinct possibility of self-mortality. I changed my ways, but I didn't want to change my career, so the dangers of being a police officer were tossed at me day after day.

When I was twenty, I was driving south on Interstate 95 near Jacksonville, Florida, and I was stopped for speeding by a state trooper. As I was receiving a deserved traffic citation, a northbound driver shouted the word "pig" and extended a one-finger hand gesture out of his car window as he passed. My tension of being stopped by a police officer was now topped by an adrenaline rush expecting the officer to erupt in boiling anger.

Surely his neck veins would swell and his eyes would bulge at any moment. His lack of reaction to the insult, however, prompted me to ask "Aren't you going to do anything about that?" He replied, "What, and prove him right?" The trooper's words are as poignant today as they were when I first heard them many years ago.

The insult offered by the other driver was probably just one of several "rewards" that trooper received for doing his job that day. When I was a patrol officer I never expected to ask a motorist to sign a traffic citation and hear, "Thank you officer, can I have another?"

I always treated people just like I would treat my own mother until they forced me to treat them otherwise. Even when a person would bring it on himself/herself, hurting anyone put a hole in my heart. I learned that I could run through the sewers of life and not come out smelling rotten. I knew I could pursue fiends without becoming one. My badge of authority would simply have been scrap-metal without compassion and consideration for others. It was a badge of authority, but the most meaningful thing to me was wearing it over my heart, because real policing comes from the heart.

Being a police officer was more than a job, it was a way of life, and I never left home for work without knowing it could be my last time. My memory is lined with every incident where I wondered if it would be my last. What I don't know is the number of times I faced death without realizing I was in jeopardy. Doing the math, it is likely that of the thousands of people I came in contact with as a police officer, at least one, if not more, backed out of their bad intentions at the last second. Was the elderly woman sitting on a gun pissed at the world because of her failing health, and then pissed at me because her car was vandalized? Had the polite young man I stopped for speeding just robbed a store, or did I walk right past the murderer hiding underneath a car? Was it my fate, good police work, or divine intervention that guided me through my career? I would like to take some credit, but the thing I know for sure is that He always patrolled with me.

I encountered many natural deaths and fatalities, and they came too often. There were babies, toddlers, teenagers and adults of all ages. Trying to comfort families of tragedy was always awkward and troubling at best. Each death was different, each one was hard, and each one confiscated a little part of my heart. I don't remember a lot of the days, but I do remember a lot of the incidents. Just like the death of Carolyn Massey, I may have other repressed memories. I do, however, have suppressed memories of awful events that I consciously choose not to remember.

Today, police officers all over our nation are being slaughtered like they are ducks in a shooting gallery. A small group of our population is even chanting death to police officers, death to the very people they call for help, and death to the very people who run to their aid when they run from danger. The tail is wagging the dog. There will always be people who hate the police, but the public outcry of hating the police seems to be cyclical, and I believe this current trend will eventually run its course. In the meantime, I pray for those who take care of us, and I wish that I had something to offer to protect them. America will be great again, I just hope it happens in my lifetime, God Bless America.

During the first part of my career, our society's values were different and often questionable. Law enforcement operated on a different set of standards, not always noble. I rose above it, and ultimately brought about change that was healthy. It took most of my life to come face to face with who I am, and it turned that out I like myself. I traded the name Charlie for the name Fox, and Fox for the title of chief, and chief for the title of columnist, and I guess if you have read this book, you can call me an author, but I'd rather you call me Charlie.

Like me on Facebook: I'd rather you call me Charlie

E-mail idratheryoucallmecharlie@gmail.com